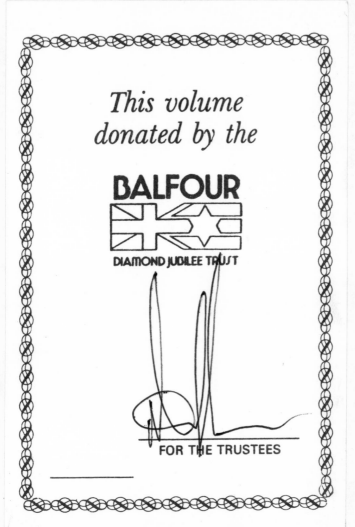

The Emissary

The Emissary

—•—

A Life of Enzo Sereni

RUTH BONDY

Translated from the Hebrew by Shlomo Katz
with an Afterword by Golda Meir

An Atlantic Monthly Press Book
Little, Brown and Company · Boston · Torono

The Emissary has been slightly abridged from the Hebrew original.

The author and publishers wish to express their gratitude to the Honorable
Mrs. Golda Meir for her generosity in providing the Afterword for this
edition.

LIBRARY OF CONGRESS CATALOGING IN PUBLICATION DATA

Bondy, Ruth.
  The emissary.

  Slightly abridged translation of ha-Shaliaḥ.
  Includes bibliographical references and index.
  1. Sereni, Enzo, 1905–1944. 2. Zionists—Italy—
Biography. 3. Givat Brenner, Israel—Biography.
I. Title.
DS151.S4B6613 1977   956.94′001′0924 [B]   77-6754
ISBN 0-316-10130-3

ATLANTIC–LITTLE, BROWN BOOKS
ARE PUBLISHED BY
LITTLE, BROWN AND COMPANY
IN ASSOCIATION WITH
THE ATLANTIC MONTHLY PRESS

Designed by Susan Windheim

*Published simultaneously in Canada
by Little, Brown & Company (Canada) Limited*

PRINTED IN THE UNITED STATES OF AMERICA

Contents

Introduction

Time raises havoc with memory. But whoever knew Enzo Sereni, even briefly, is not likely to have forgotten him. His friends
smile when they talk about him as if a certain essence of his
nearness still remains in the air. For others in Israel who did
not know him, it is the last chapter in Enzo's life that fixed his
image, a direct continuation of his way in life, and consonant
with his views and convictions and character.

In his early youth, he dreamed of writing the model novel
that would reflect his generation, the story of his Roman family
against the stormy background of the period between the two
world wars. But he never had the time to do this, for life itself
preempted all his energies. He did not write his great novel —
he lived it stormily. His life was a work of art; the writing of it
was left to others.

The urge to participate in events and not be a mere observer
was an integral part of Enzo Sereni's *weltanschauung*, and he
demanded of himself and of others a readiness to testify with
deeds to their convictions, to change the world and not only to
interpret it. It was his belief that convictions must be expressed
in deeds that led this son of the Italian court physician, and a
doctor of philosophy with an assured future in the world of
science in his own right, to become, at the age of twenty-two, the
first Halutz from Italy to pioneer in Eretz Israel. It was this

belief, too, that caused him, at the age of thirty-nine, to parachute behind the German lines in an attempt to rescue whatever could still be saved from the remnant of Italian Jewry and to contribute his share to the struggle of the Italian people for its freedom.

This double mission reflected the two equally powerful components of Sereni's personality: he was a Jew and an Italian. He made his home in Eretz Israel but remained attached to the Italian landscape. He belonged to the post-assimilation generation, and his return to Jewishness was an act of voluntary choice. A voice within him compelled him to go to Eretz Israel, but part of his heart remained in Italy, to which he kept returning like a migratory bird. Though he knew the Bible and Hebrew literature, he was raised on Italian literature. He was fluent in Hebrew and was zealous on its behalf, but Italian remained his inner language.

On the face of it there was nothing in Enzo's childhood and youth to turn him toward Zionism, and when at the age of seventeen he made that turn, he did so not out of ideological conviction but rather as a consequence of a kind of revelation. His goal in life did not change — only the road to it. His involvement with Socialist Zionism was part of the search for the complete life, for justice to the Jewish people and the entire human race. In the social landscape of Eretz Israel — the land of Israel — made up of pioneers from eastern and central Europe, Enzo Sereni was unique. There was no one like him either before or after, and, though he gained admiration and love, to some extent he remained isolated. He was different, exotic, Italian, rebellious, too much the individualist. During the bloody Arab riots he remained a pacifist, and he advocated cooperation between Jewish and Arab workers while the struggle was on for the employment of Jewish labor. Though keenly political, he at first refused to join a political party, and even after he joined Mapai — Labor party of the land of Israel — he retained his ideological independence, especially as regards relations between the Zionist movement and the Arab national movement.

Sereni's restlessness, adventurousness, and lust for life did not allow him to complete any of his enterprises. His missions to Germany, the United States, Egypt, and Iraq were terminated before their natural culmination, ostensibly as a consequence of objective circumstances, but to no small degree because of his impatience and his being alternately torn between the longing for the quiet life of the man of thought and the urge to activism and to facing new challenges. The story of his life even after he settled in Eretz Israel reads like a traveler's timetable. For all his devotion to his home kibbutz, which he regarded as a stronghold of the Serenis and the prototype of his vision for humanity, he never stayed in it long. He'd go away and come back, longing for faraway places when he was in the kibbutz and powerfully drawn to it when he was away.

The entire Jewish community in Rome was convinced that the three Sereni brothers were destined for great things; even before they had decided about their way in life, people used to discuss the future achievements of the Sereni brothers, the wonderful deeds they would accomplish with their combined forces. It was therefore a critical time for Enzo when he remained alone of the three. Enrico Sereni, the oldest, most restrained, and calmest of the trio, died accidentally of gas poisoning. Emilio, the youngest, who in his early youth embraced Zionism and even studied agriculture in preparation to follow in Enzo's footsteps, was converted to Marxism and became a central figure in the Italian Communist party. Enzo and Emilio tried in vain to convince one another of the correctness of their own views. At times it seemed that throughout his mature years, far away from his brother, Enzo was engaged in a wordless dialogue with him. One reason for his stubborn insistence on going to northern Italy in the spring of 1944, when it was still under German occupation though the war was nearing its end, was the desire to search for Emilio, who had been captured by the Fascists. It seems that this final mission of his was also a preparatory step for the meeting with his brother after the war. How would he face Emilio, who had been active in the underground throughout the years of the Nazi occupation, in constant danger of his life, while he, Enzo, spent those years in the relative safety and peace of Eretz Israel, where World War II only contributed to eco-

nomic affluence? But the most powerful drive behind this last
mission, at such a late hour, was his awareness of the Jewish
tragedy and his refusal to stand by passively.

Even before Hitler came to power Enzo sensed the great
danger facing the Jews of Germany and urged them to leave the
country; as World War II neared he became increasingly certain
that it would bring destruction to much of European Jewry.
Long before the policy of organized extermination started, he
was aware of the approaching end, and his chief aim throughout
the war years was to reach the Jews of Europe, to warn them, to
raise the alarm, and to lead in the rescue work. But Nazi-occu-
pied Europe could only be reached with the aid of the British,
who were in no hurry to utilize Jewish volunteers for fear of
antagonizing the Arabs. When, after many efforts and strata-
gems, he finally succeeded in the spring of 1944 in reaching
Europe, it was to a large extent too late. Those Italian Jews who
had not succeeded in finding a hiding place had already been
shipped off to the extermination camps, and half of Italy had
already been liberated. Logically there was no longer any reason
for a man nearing forty, a father of three children, and without
any experience as a parachutist, to undertake a mission to Nazi-
occupied northern Italy. But Enzo did so, contrary to the wishes
of his wife, his friends, and his superiors, because he regarded
such a mission as a personal duty stronger than reason. Analyz-
ing Sereni's personality on the basis of biographical facts, Erich
Fromm concluded that he was driven by a death urge. But I
doubt that, though aware of the dangers that faced him and
accepting the possibility of his death, he sought martyrdom. I
believe that deep in his heart he hoped that his luck and his
daring would stand him in good stead, that he would approach
the abyss without suffering harm, that the soil of Italy would
not betray him, that Providence would guard him and he would
return alive.

Nowadays, when rabbis are welcome guests in secular kibbutzim, and part of the younger generation seeks a way back to
traditional Judaism, Sereni's faith appears less surprising. But
back in the thirties, it was the age of Socialist rebellion against
old traditions and abandonment of all bonds with religion, and

within the framework of the kibbutz Enzo Sereni was an exception; he fasted and attended religious services on the Day of Atonement and sought to establish bridges to tradition. He not only believed in a Higher Power but publicly talked about his faith.

It was this many-colored aspect of his character that enabled Sereni to impress all those who knew him, each in accordance with his individual tastes. For he was a Socialist and a believing Jew, a man of politics and a philosopher, a dedicated emissary and a sober and skeptical person, an educator, and a man capable of enjoying all the pleasures of life. He exerted a magnetic influence on people and at the same time could be self-enclosed and silent about the secrets of his being. He contained a great abundance and generously bestowed it on others, sometimes in order to surprise and impress, for, like a true Roman he loved drama and the dramatic entrance. His clock was faster than those of others; he ate faster, he read faster, he understood more quickly, he acted faster, at times putting action before calm consideration. He was a man endowed with many sparks but with one permanent flame. And when he faced the highest test at Dachau, he revealed his full inner strength and stability. In this place of hunger, torment, and horror, he was a guide, a brother, and a support. In Dachau, where the very image of humanity had been erased, he held out hope and consolation. This was the last testimony of his love for mankind, and few who were with him there survived to tell about it.

RUTH BONDY
Ramat Chen, 1976

The Emissary

1

The House on
Cavour Street

The big house on Cavour Street had been intended as a family estate, a fortress of the Sereni dynasty for generations. When this five-story residence was built in the nineties of the past century, Rome was in the first stages of its growth as the capital of the united Italian kingdom, and the Jews of Rome still felt keenly the sweet taste of the new freedom and equality which the soldiers of Victor Emmanuel II bestowed upon them when they conquered the city from the pope. This house was the first residence of the Serenis outside the walls of the ancient ghetto on the banks of the Tiber; it was a symbol of their new status — solid, spacious, with raised reliefs around the windows that were protected by brown wooden shutters, and with reliefs resembling pillars at its three entrances. It was a bourgeois house, solid like the other houses on Cavour Street, neither towering over them nor humbly lower than they. It was a house built to last.

The opening of the gates of the ghetto in 1870, and the end of the pope's secular rule, were regarded by some of the five thousand Jews of Rome as a command to put a certain distance between themselves and the site of their past humiliations, as an excuse for severing all bonds with their former way of life, to live like Italians among Italians. Others found it difficult to abandon all at once the warmth of life in a closed community, the nearness of coreligionists, the sense of belonging, and found residences in a reassuring proximity to the old Jewish Quarter. Only the area of the Roman Forum separated the Serenis' house at 340 Cavour Street from the ghetto. A few minutes' walk and they were back on native ground, where were born all the sons of Moshe Reuven Sereni, a rabbi and merchant in the ghetto who died in 1881 at the age of seventy and was one of the last to be buried in the ancient Jewish cemetery at the foot of Aventino Hill.

All Italians, and Italian Jews in particular, regarded the family as a fortress and shield against the unfriendly outside world. The family was the basis of their existence and the center of their life — assurance against all troubles. Two, three, and even four generations, uncles and cousins, lived together, worked together, and brought up their children as a group. Even during the generation before the liberation — and before that no one remembered — the Sereni brothers conducted their business jointly. First they traded in cloth, and when the time of unrestricted opportunities arrived in Rome, they also tried their hand in real estate. The lot on Cavour Street was the last of their holdings after the first flush of their splurge in this direction and was the joint inheritance of the Sereni clan.

Enzo Sereni's father Samuele was the youngest in his family. When his brother Angelo, a lawyer, married the young and beautiful Ermalinda Pontecorvo — the daughter of a neighboring Roman Jewish family comparable in its intellectual distinction and ancient traditions to the Serenis — Samuele went to live with them on the fourth floor of the house on Cavour Street. When his turn came to marry, it was natural that the choice should fall on Ermalinda's sister, Alfonsa Pontecorvo. She was not nearly as attractive as Ermalinda, and she was generously proportioned, but she was also intelligent, educated, diligent, competent in all matters pertaining to household management, and had a strong character. In short, she was a young woman who would make a good wife. As was customary at that time, the marriages of the two Sereni brothers to the two Pontecorvo sisters were the results of arranged matches but had the consent and approval of all parties. At that time too, no son of a respectable Jewish family would consider proposing marriage to a young woman before he was sure that he could support her comfortably, and it was thus that Samuele was thirty years old and a doctor when he married Alfonsa Pontecorvo, who was nine years his junior. They settled at 340 Cavour Street, on the same floor with Angelo and Ermalinda. Each couple had a separate apartment, but there was a connecting door between them.

Here, on the fourth floor of the house on Cavour Street, were born the five Sereni children: Enrico, the oldest, at the turn of the century; Emilio, Mimo, the youngest, in 1907; between them Valia, who died in infancy; Leah, born in 1903; and Enzo, born on April 17, 1905. Within a short time the entire clan became aware that three geniuses were growing here. Leah, the only girl, was not reckoned among the geniuses, first because she was a girl, and second, because she was her mother's daughter and soon realized that woman's role consisted in guarding the family nest for the men and the future generations.

Samuele was much loved. The children called him Lilio, Zio, or the diminutive, Ziolio. Wearing gold-rimmed glasses and sporting a trim pointed beard, he was shorter and thinner than his wife, and kindly and gay. Everyone enjoyed his company during the brief moments when they had an opportunity to do so, for Dr. Sereni was a very busy man. He did not have a clinic at home and visited his patients, mostly on foot, striding energetically and coatless even in winter and always in a hurry. The Queen Mother, the widow of King Umberto, who was assassinated by an anarchist in 1900, devoted much of her time to welfare activities and was acquainted with Dr. Sereni, having met him in the hospital for consumptives, which was under her patronage. As a result of her intercession, he was appointed court physician — not the personal physician of King Victor Emmanuel III, who knew him well, however, but physician to the Quirinal Palace and its employees, who were numerous.

Dr. Sereni's clinic was located in a wing of the palace, a low brown-and-yellow building that occupied the summit of the Quirinal, one of the seven hills of ancient Rome, and that had served as the summer home of the popes before it became the royal palace after the annexation of Rome to the United Italian

Kingdom. In addition to his private practice, his work in the royal clinic, and in a hospital, Samuele Sereni was also an instructor at the University of Rome where he lectured on histology. Always on the go, professionally and by nature, he was continually rushing his family — hurry or we'll be late.

Contrary to certain other distinguished Italian Jewish families — who could trace their line through many generations — the Serenis' knowledge of their genealogy extended back only to the eighteenth century, even though it was known that the family had been living in Rome for many centuries, possibly from the very beginning of Jewish settlement on the banks of the Tiber before the destruction of the Second Temple. It was this awareness that "we have been here since before Christianity began" that accounted for the pride of the Roman Jews and that stood them in good stead during times of oppression and humiliation. The feeling of *civis Romanus sum* was as deeply ingrained in them as their Jewishness, and sometimes even more so. Because the family name Sereni, unlike Sacerdote or Buonoventura or other names common among Italian Jews, has no Hebraic root, the Serenis toyed with the notion that, like certain Roman noble clans, they were represented in the ancient burial grounds along the Via Appia, a notion based on the discovery of the tomb of a liberated slave named Serenus. Another belief held by the Sereni clan was that they were descended from one of the ancient patrician families of the early empire who were converted to Judaism as a reaction to paganism and the dissolute life of the rulers.

But though the origin of the Serenis is shrouded in mystery, one thing is certain — that they were living in Rome at the time of the large influx into Italy of Jewish exiles from Spain at the end of the fifteenth century. Like all solidly established communities, which throughout history have worried lest their status be undermined by the new immigrants, the Jews of Rome met the exiles from Spain with mixed feelings, and even appealed to the Holy See not to permit the newcomers to settle in Rome. This petition was also signed by a Sereni, as Enzo used to tell in later years with unconcealed glee.

The differentiation of the Jews of Rome according to their origins did not become blurred in the course of time. As late as the twentieth century they still prayed in groups apart, following different orders of service — Roman style, which derived directly from the style of prayer in ancient Judea prior to the destruction of the Temple, as well as special prayer arrangements deriving from Sicily, Portugal, and Germany — in five crowded chapels located in a single building, until Angelo Sereni built the new central synagogue. This was located on the banks of the river Tiber, on a plot that had been cleared of the ruins of old houses in the Jewish Quarter. Nearby was the church of Santa Maria del Pietà, which appealed in a Hebrew inscription to "the rebellious people who follow in evil ways" to come and find shelter under her wings.

Angelo Sereni, by profession a lawyer, was president of the Jewish community of Rome from 1896 and served in this post for thirty-one years, followed by another five years as honorary president. When the synagogue he built was completed in 1904, it stood solid, like the Jewish bourgeoisie that built it, and King Victor Emmanuel III honored its opening with his presence. Angelo also held numerous other posts of honor in Jewish and Italian life, but he was especially proud of being named administrative consultant to the Monti di Pietà of Rome. These were the loan associations established by the Franciscan order in Italy toward the end of the fifteenth century to undermine the activities of Jewish money lenders and caused the latter much trouble. After numerous transformations the Monti di Pietà became truly charitable loan societies that served the poor without regard to religion or race.

Uncle Angelo was the one to greet all prominent Jewish visitors to Rome, and Aunt Ermalinda, beautiful, elegant, a lover of music and holding humanistic views, was the first lady of the community — Regina Madre, as the younger generation called her. In their apartment on Cavour Street there was a large salon that was used for the entertainment of visitors and for festive family occasions. The apartment, on the fourth floor, was served by an elevator while the Samuele Sereni apartment on the same floor had to be reached on foot. (The Sereni children were strictly forbidden to use the elevator.) From the balcony, one had a magnificent view of the domes of Rome, its roofs and its

towers. Directly ahead was the Palatine Hill, home of the
Roman emperors, of whose palaces there now remained only
reddish ruins covered with vegetation. On one side of the house,
in the direction of the Piazza Venezia, were the remains of the
ancient Roman marketplaces, the pillar of Trajan crowned with
a statue of St. Peter, symbolizing the triumph of Christianity
over paganism, and the ruins of the Forum of Augustus. Behind
the house, on the upward slope of Cavour Street, stood the palace of the Borgias; and in front, the street sloped down to the
Coliseum and the Arch of Titus, testifying to the defeat of the
Jewish people; no Roman Jew, believer or free thinker, would
pass under this arch — some for fear of bad luck, others out of
national pride.

Enzo recalled little from his early years, "only that I was wild,
and no one except mother could curb me." But his mother, a
powerful influence upon him, noted with pride the early manifestations of his brightness: how he was discovered in some
corner uttering a flow of disconnected words, and when asked to
explain the meaning of this, declared that, like Demosthenes, he
was practicing to be an orator. She especially delighted in telling
how, when he was nine years old, she took him to a lecture of the
Minister of Agriculture of that time, at the end of which he
approached the speaker, shook hands with him, and declared
enthusiastically, "You have guessed my ideas exactly."

Enzo entered directly into the second grade of the municipal
elementary school on October 3, 1911. A photograph of that
class is still preserved: the children, wearing black smocks, bent
over open books on ancient desks scratched with the testimony of
innumerable former bored classes, and presided over by a corpu-
lent teacher wearing his hair pompadour-style, in the fashion of
that day. Enzo did well in his studies but did not attach much
importance to this accomplishment; at the age of eleven, in his
diary, he dismissed it as worthless. "Only at age seven does
intellectual development commence. My first love is proof of
this. This was a certain swarthy Maria whom I met in 1912 in
Civitanova, and it was the purest love of them all. The second
was Adriana Piacentini, in 1913, blond and blue-eyed, who con-

quered me totally. This too passed, and in the winter of 1913 I fell in love with Silvana Ascarelli, my cousin."

Alfonsa herself would escort her children to school, meet them when classes were over, and take them for walks. Jewish mothers still harbored vague memories of the terror of forced conversion of Jewish children, and old women of the Jewish Quarter were careful not to pass by the open door of a church while escorting a child lest it be kidnapped. More than forty years had passed since the Mortara case aroused all Europe, but Jews still talked about it. A Christian servant-woman in Bologna had performed some kind of symbolic baptism on her one-year-old charge, Edgaro Mortara, the son of her Jewish employer, when she thought his life was in danger. Six years later she told her father confessor what she had done, and he called it to the attention of the higher church authorities, whereupon the child was forcibly taken from his parents and brought to Rome to be brought up as a Christian. Thousands of Jews had been forcibly converted to Christianity during the dark period between the Inquisition and the emancipation, but the Mortara case was especially remembered because it had occurred at a time when most of Europe and a large part of Italy already enjoyed a liberal regime. A number of prominent personages, ranging from Moses Montefiore to Napoleon III, intervened with the pope on behalf of Mortara, but to no avail. Edgaro Mortara was raised in the bosom of the church, and later, when he was free to decide for himself, he no longer wished to return to the faith of his fathers. This case was often talked about in the Pontecorvo household, and the younger generation still preserved the legend of a delegation of three Jews of Rome, including a member of the Pontecorvo family, who went to intercede with the pope. When they returned, they would not say a word of what had happened to them at the Vatican, but a short time later all three died in quick succession.

Whether there was something unnatural about these deaths, or the tale merely reflected a shadow of old terror, the memory of these forced conversions was in any case deeply engraved in the hearts of the Italian Jews. The Casa di Catecumeni, the shelter for new converts established by the founder of the Jesuit order, where most Jews were held against their will — and which, ironically, was maintained by revenue from a forced levy on the Jewish community — still stood between the Jewish Quarter and the Capitol. Many years later a Palestinian student in Italy asked Alfonsa Sereni how she differed from other Italians, since she lived like them, did not observe any of the traditional Jewish customs, did not know Hebrew, and was not a Zionist. She replied: "Why, there are still people in the ghetto who remember the terror of the Casa di Catecumeni."

Eastern European Jews might have regarded the Sereni family as assimilated, but compared with most other Italian Jews they were highly traditional. That which the Catholic church did not succeed in attaining by means of pressure in the course of centuries was achieved by a liberal regime in two generations. The Jews of Italy became so estranged from their religion that only a pale shadow of it remained. A mixture of a vague sense of belonging and family solidarity was accompanied by the abandonment of distinctive customs that had become outdated. Moshe Reuven Sereni, who had been a rabbi, did provide his offspring, in addition to a higher education — the ambition of most Jews since they had attained equal rights — with a modicum of knowledge of Judaism and its tradition. Samuele and Angelo could read Hebrew and boasted no little of this rare accomplishment, even though they could not understand what they read, and it was they who endowed the house on Cavour Street with its traditional flavor. The Pontecorvo girls had been raised in a much more secular fashion.

The Sabbath was a regular working day in the Sereni home, differing from other weekdays only in that the women did not on this day either sew or crochet. The Jewish holidays were observed in their season. On Hanukkah candles would be lit; on Passover two festive seder meals were served, usually in the apartment of Aunt Ermalinda, in the presence of the entire family and invited guests. Purim was not observed as a festive occasion because it was the memorial day for Grandfather Sereni, and the holiday was distinguished only by distribution of sweets to the children. But on the Day of Atonement the adult Serenis fasted and the children joined them in the fast at an early age, not because it was expected of them, but to demonstrate that they were growing up. On the eve of the Day of Atonement the entire family would go to visit its dead, first to the old cemetery at the foot of the Aventino (which was removed in the automobile age; only a row of cypresses, some flower beds, and a memorial tablet mark the spot) and then to the new cemetery at the end of Via Tiburtina. This pilgrimage was staged on foot, pebbles were placed on the ancestral graves, and days gone by were recalled.

But though the Serenis differed somewhat from the bulk of Italian Jewry in their relative observance of Jewish traditions, they shared with all the others the sense of complete identity with the homeland. The Serenis were Italian to the core, attached to Italy's culture, customs, landscape, language, and foods, zealous for its independence and consciously patriotic. The Jewish community had been active in the Risorgimento, realizing that the freedom of a united Italy would also mean freedom for them. They were among the most loyal supporters of Mazzini, who led the Italian people to its freedom. During the days of his exile in London, he had received support from the local Jewish community. At the time of his death in 1872, when he was persecuted in his own homeland, he found refuge under an assumed Jewish name in the home of his Jewish friend Pelegrino Rosselli in Pisa. Jews fought in the army of King Victor Emmanuel II against the Russians, the Austrians, the French, and the forces of the pope, and the number of their officers in the regular army was above their proportion in the population. In some Jewish families, especially in northern Italy, professional military service became a tradition, and from one of these came General Giuseppe Ottolenghi, royal advisor and minister of war.

The Sereni children talked much about their plans for the time when they would grow up, and found it hard to decide between literary, political, and scientific careers. For all roads were open to them in the new, united Italy, the most tolerant country in Europe. Italy waited for the Sereni brothers with open arms. All they had to do was to study and aspire, and the road to the summit was theirs.

2

Too Young
to Be a Hero

Enzo finished the fourth and last grade of the elementary school in June 1911. In October, when he was nine and a half years old, he entered the Visconti Gymnasium. This was a new status and a new stage of growing closer to his older brother, Enrico, with whom he jealously competed, and who treated him with paternal affection. This period in Enzo's life coincided with a time of general political turmoil. All of Europe was engaged in a brutal competition and Italy guarded its neutrality, partly out of a policy of "sacred selfishness," since the country still maintained a bond, albeit a weak one, with the Triple Alliance. At the same time the country had a treaty of friendship with France and felt deep sympathy for England, which had supported the young kingdom during its initial difficulties. Once the war of 1914 had begun, interventionist sentiment gained ground; it was urged that Italy enter the war on the side of England, France, and Russia. Motivations varied. Some, indulging in vague mysticism, believed in the purifying power of war. Others hoped for brilliant victories to erase the shame of Adowa, when Italian forces had been routed by Ethiopia in 1896. War, they felt, would strengthen Italy's position as an imperialist power. Republicans and radicals in the country believed that, to fight alongside France would hasten the hoped-for end of the monarchist regime.

Gabriele D'Annunzio, poet-hero of that period, prophet of sensual romanticism and the creed of aestheticism, whose regal way of life, with its race horses, hounds, gaudy palaces, and dramatic love affairs, excited the world no less than his writing, returned to Italy after five years of conspicuous exile in France (where he had fled to escape his creditors) to encourage his people to join the war. He was given an enthusiastic reception when he orated from the balcony of the Regina Hotel, "Italy has ceased to be a museum or family pension and has become a living nation." Enzo, who at the outbreak of the war declared himself a supporter of Germany, was swept away by the tide, and, shortly after Italy joined the conflict, he became a supporter of the war, though he was not particularly impressed by the Allies. "I always hated the English and always will," he declared.

As the first war enthusiasm wore off, hoarding and speculation increased. The Sereni family did not resort to the black market as a matter of principle and because of strong opposition to it by Leah, who was a great believer in law and order and preferred to stand long hours in line for meat and other products when these were rationed. The numerous uncles, who knew the healthy appetites of the younger Serenis, saw to it that there was enough bread, and the rest of the diet was supplemented by roasted chestnuts.

Time finally took its toll from Alfonsa's father, Pelegrino Pontecorvo, who hated the thought of getting old, preserved the sparkle of youth in his eyes till he was seventy-six, and was a devoted participant in all the joys and sorrows of his numerous grandchildren. He died on October 23, 1916, after a heart attack. For a moment it seemed to Enzo that everything died with him, and for years afterward, in his diaries as well as in his first story, "Good Children," a description of life in the house on Cavour Street, he kept referring to the good, understanding grandfather. Enrico, too, who that fall entered the medical school of the University of Rome, expressed in his diary his deep grief at the passing of this man whom he loved for "his constancy, conscience, sense of justice, patriarchal simplicity, and

unbounded love for freedom and justice." After an interval of
three generations, the family would still point to some unusual
sign of intelligence or strong will in one of the grandchildren as
"coming from Pelegrino."

After the death of old Pontecorvo, Enzo, encouraged by his
mother and following the example of Enrico, began keeping a
diary. Alfonsa wished to provide an additional channel for her
sons' excess energy. She wanted also to be able to follow their
inmost thoughts. For his diary Enzo selected a notebook bearing
the portrait of Vittorio Alfieri, a poet and tragedian of the
eighteenth century with a tendency toward melancholy, whose
motto "I wanted, I always wanted, I wanted with all my might,"
seemed to him to express his own feelings. He, too, wanted with
all his might, but he did not yet know what it was he wanted. In
his foreword to his diary he described himself as "1.35 meters
tall,* not fat, swarthy, black-eyed, hair almost fair, with a tendency to melancholy, a bit romantic, kind, generous, a Socialist
but also loves girls." (The "but" was based on the notion that
"socialism," however it was understood at the time, and "love of
girls" were somehow contradictory.)

Alfonsa used to look into her sons' diaries, but after the war
broke out Enrico asked her not to do so any more since he was
no longer the same "trustworthy and genuine human being." But
Enzo could not suppress his curiosity, and after much lying in
wait, found an opportunity to get to the drawer where Enrico
kept his diaries and poems. He not only read them — he also
passed judgment on them. "In some places Enrico's diary is
worthless; in others there is something of value; and here and
there it is quite valuable." As for the poems, he characterized
two odes as "nonsense," and the translations from Latin, except
for the first ode of Horace, he thought unimpressive.

Sexual lust troubled Enzo deeply now and he struggled with
it as best he could, crying out. "Oh this filthy lust! I am a pig!"
It was such a distortion of the elevated vision of pure love he felt
toward the girls who casually crossed his path, such as the beau-
teous Sara Lampson to whom he dedicated a love poem after
seeing her momentarily, in the company of a British officer, at

* 1.35 meters is roughly 4 feet 5⅛ inches.

the opening of an exhibit of war photographs to which Uncle
Angelo took him and Enrico. The death reflected in these photographs he sensed as something very close during those days of
bloody battles, and he was moved, at the ripe age of twelve, to
make out his will.

In October 1917, when the situation at the front became
grave, Enrico enlisted in the artillery at the age of seventeen and
left Enzo, who had been competing with him for priority, far
behind. It was a time of crisis for the country, both at the front
and in the rear. Desperation seized the people because of the
endless slaughter (Italy lost 600,000 soldiers in World War
I), and under the influence of the Socialists, who had opposed
entry into the capitalist war from the very start, serious riots
broke out in the north, which were suppressed with great cruelty
by the Orlando government. The Germans and Austrians tried
to cut off the Italian armies and this led to the terrible defeat at
Caporetto, which became a symbol of humiliation and helplessness. "At this tragic moment," Enzo wrote, "when no one knows
what will happen, I feel that Italy needs our help, that we are all
in its debt. Long live Italy!" He grieved that he was too young to
fight and could only help the women with their work for the
wounded; this feeling tormented him throughout the war.
"When will there be another war? When will I be able to return
home bearing decorations and scars of wounds? Or, if it must be
so, not return at all? The trouble is that I am young, too young."

Enrico, it is true, spent most of his war service in training and
in officers' school. But in October 1918, he did get to the front
and participated in the final great attack on the Austrians near
the Piave River — and was regarded as a hero by the entire
family.

Enzo had no trouble with his high school studies, winning the
approbation of his teachers, though not always of his classmates,
whom he grouped in his diary as admirers, neutrals, nihilists,
and supporters of his two chief opponents — the one opposing
him out of "envy," the other "out of anti-Semitism and super-
ficiality."

This is the only time that anti-Semitism is mentioned in

Enzo's diary in connection with school. There were few Jewish students and they were lost in the vast majority of Catholics. Affections and hostilities were the result of personal traits, not of religious affiliation. Indeed, there was little to distinguish the two groups either in appearance or in style of life, except perhaps for the three additional holidays that Jewish students enjoyed as a consequence of their religion. When Enzo described opposition to himself as stemming from anti-Semitism, it was because of his intense sensitivity on this subject. Jews just then were experiencing great excitement as a result of England's promise to support a Jewish national home in Palestine, and Enzo responded keenly to the echoes of this event that penetrated the house on Cavour Street. In May 1917, his uncle, Angelo Sereni, escorted Nahum Sokolow, who had come to Rome on behalf of the Zionist movement, on his visit to Premier Paolo Boselli. Italy, with a direct interest in the Holy Land by reason of its imperialist aims overseas and as a Catholic power, decided in June 1917 to send a minute force to the front in the Middle East, which participated in the attack on Gaza. This would assure her of equal rights with England and France in the shaping of the regime that was to arise in Palestine after the expected breakup of the Turkish Empire. With the publication of the Balfour Declaration on November 2, 1917, which the Italians interpreted as a British attempt to dominate Palestine, a Zionist mission headed by Chaim Weizmann set out for the Holy Land. The Zionists of Italy consented to add two delegates of their own to the mission, which consisted of representatives from Great Britain and the United States, hoping in this manner to win Italian support for the Jewish national home; but it was rather their function to look after Italy's interests than to help Zionism.

Enzo's preparations for his Bar Mitzvah coincided with this time of heightened Zionist activity in Rome. His talks with Angelo Sacerdoti, chief rabbi of Rome, awakened within him speculations about the common grounds of the various faiths, the titans and the tower of Babel, Jubal and Apollo, Tubal-Cain and Vulcan. For a time he abandoned the great Roman and Italian authors in whose footsteps he hoped to follow, and devoted some of his literary efforts to Jewish themes.

First he wrote a poem about the exile who had lost his homeland:

Do not despair. The day will come and you will see again
The liberated hills of Zion, the Temple rebuilt,
And a free man you will sing to your native air
The song of the exile longing for his homeland.

Then followed speculations in prose. "Of all the great expressions of modern culture, the finest is the one which declares that every people should live in its own land and gather its sons under one flag. Has this been done? No. Trieste and Trentino are still under the enemy yoke. Transylvania and Poland are still subjugated. And one people to whom civilization is so much indebted is dispersed, persecuted, and oppressed. This is the Jewish People."

The Bar Mitzvah was celebrated modestly at home in Aunt Ermalinda's living room on account of the war. Enrico was in the army and Dr. Sereni had been drafted as a medical officer. On March 29, 1918, Enzo participated in the services in the new synagogue on Balbo Street in the presence of a full congregation. He was excited, his eyes shone more than usual, and his cheeks were uncommonly flushed. Later it was discovered that he had the measles. In his diary he noted that everything went over smoothly, "only in the last prayer did I mumble a little." The crisis of puberty had formally set in.

There began for Enzo a period of feverish writing. A heroic poem on the theme of Garibaldi; a novel named *The Duty;* a novella, *Three Sisters;* a comedy, *Desire;* and a plan for a play "about a blinded soldier who marries a beautiful woman whom he had known before the war; she is unfaithful to him and he commits suicide." His subjects were always huge and elevated — love, treason, heroic death. Since in these compositions he not only tested his literary abilities but also sought to express his ideas, readers' opinions were just as important to him as the writing itself, and he submitted his manuscripts, fresh out of the oven, to editorial offices of literary journals, to publishing houses, and to men of letters, secretly and without his parents'

18

knowledge. For the contest sponsored by the Writer's Union, he planned to dramatize the story in verse, *Shadow of the Past*. Under the pen name Paolo Romano he prepared for publication selected poems, *Songs of Darkness and of Light*, which included such titles as "Alone," "God," "Love and Life," "Separation," and "Chopin."

The process of growing up pressed heavily on him with its sense of total aloneness: pointless quarrels with members of the family; disgust with deeds performed secretly and entirely contrary to the visions of higher purity which he demanded from the heroes of his writings, such as swiping cookies from pastry shops without paying for them; worry over "low" dreams, weariness of the struggle against lust, "that oppressive thing called flesh"; and also pain over unrequited love and feelings of inferiority because he did not know how to behave in the company of girls, either showing off or being too shrinking. Study and reading seemed to provide the sole remedy, but even after indulging in this therapy he still felt "confused before the glance of a woman." Writing provided no support. The great etymological dictionary, in which he planned to provide for the ignorant corresponding words in Italian, German, Spanish, Portuguese, English, Latin, Greek, and Hebrew, was still in the stage of chapter headings. "Nothing that I have done is complete. Most of the poems are abrupt and poorly constructed. The prose, too, is incomplete. Whatever I did still awaited maturity." And death seemed to lurk in the background. "These may be the last words I am writing. I had thought that I would die an old man among books. Now I think that I will die young on the barricades." And there were moments when suicide seemed to be the only way out.

The sorrows of growing up, along with the Italian trait of looking at life through an aesthetic veil and regarding life itself as a form of art, added to the Jewish veneration of the written word, together combined into an intoxicating brew. The Sereni home was filled with books. First there was the family library and Dr. Sereni's scientific collection. Then Enrico's books, and then Enzo's. From the age of eight they each received an allowance for buying used books in good condition and were acquainted with all the used book store owners throughout Rome. Generally, they were not censored in their reading tastes on account of age. Alfonsa only objected to her children reading the adventure stories of Salegari, a popular author of that time, because she considered them vulgar and badly written. Enrico objected when Enzo showed a marked predilection for reading matter dealing with sex, which naturally did not deter him from it, and he frankly avowed his "great pleasure in reading the crude pornography of Petronius's *Satyricon*."

Shortly after school opened in October 1918, all studies were suspended in honor of the great event: the Austro-German front collapsed and Italian forces quickly occupied Trieste, Trentino, and northern Dalmatia. On November 11 came the armistice, which ended the greatest war till that time. Even though Italy was on the conquering side, the Versailles peace conference in February 1919 deeply disappointed her. Woodrow Wilson supported the new state of Yugoslavia and its demands for an outlet on the Adriatic Sea in Fiume. True, the secret London agreements of 1915 had not specifically promised Fiume to the Italians, but it was assumed that Fiume would go to Hungary rather than to a new Slavic state that could become an emeny of Italy. In addition to this bitterness against a world that refused to take into account Italy's natural right to Fiume, which had an Italian population and in a popular referendum expressed its wish to join Italy, there were tremendous problems in returning the country to a peacetime economy, and the disillusionment of the workers and peasants who had expected better living conditions after the war. The masses of demobilized soldiers were not given that enthusiastic welcome of which they had dreamed during their suffering in the Alps and Carst mountains, and became unemployed strangers in their own homes. This disillusionment was taken advantage of by Benito Mussolini, the son of a blacksmith, a teacher, journalist, and effective orator, who had been expelled from the Socialist party in 1914 for his advocacy of Italy's entry into the war. Now, in 1919, he organized, together with the writer Marinetti, the Fasci di Combatimento, a group with a clear program, partly Socialist and partly nationalist, which attracted anarchists and conservatives, artists and businessmen, religious believers and an assortment of embittered people, unemployed veterans, patriots who wished to return to Italy the glory of Rome, and youngsters who had not served in the war but were attracted by militarism, its symbols, and the salute with upraised arm in the manner of ancient Rome.

Gabriele D'Annunzio, who returned from the war a national hero after having fought in three armies, dropping leaflets from a plane over Vienna, losing an eye in an accident, and collecting numerous decorations, expressed the wishes of many when he organized a movement of opposition to the defeatism of the government establishment on the question of the Adriatic. On May 6, 1919, he addressed the people of Rome from the Capitoline Hill, the symbol of sovereignty ever since the founding of the city, and among his excited audience was Enzo, who succeeded in squeezing his way to the poet and exchanging a few words with him. He also was granted a personal meeting with D'Annunzio on the following day in the lavish Regina Hotel. Greatly excited, Enzo appeared at the appointed time before the bald, short poet who inscribed two of his volumes, which Enzo had brought with him, he spoke to him graciously, and invited him to come a second time. Either the sincere enthusiasm of the boy, or his quick grasp and familiarity with literature (Enzo knew many of the poems and entire scenes from D'Annunzio's plays by heart), caught D'Annunzio's attention, for he singled him out from the many thousands of admirers who sought his presence. Several times during his three-week stay in Rome he received Enzo, and gave him an autographed copy of a speech of his that had been published illegally. His son allowed the boy to read one of his father's speeches from the original manuscript.

D'Annunzio was, at that time, the prophet of the Fascists, the first to introduce dialogue between speaker and audience, to talk about "purging political opponents with castor oil," and to preach the cult of nationalism. Under the influence of his meetings with him, Enzo joined the Fasci Italiani di Combatimento. Triumphantly he brought his membership card home but, as might have been expected, Alfonsa was not enthusiastic and explained to him that a boy of fourteen was too young to make such an important decision as joining a political party. She per-

suaded him to give her his membership card and begged him not
to participate in any political activity until he reached sixteen; if
he then still felt that he wanted to follow in the path he had now
chosen, he would be free to do so. She knew that two years were
a long time, especially so in the case of Enzo.

From D'Annunzio and excitement over nationalist romanticism Enzo passed to the next logical stage and, in the spirit of
that time, became enchanted, like many other young people,
with the Futurists and their seductive appeal to abandon the past,
to liberate oneself from the bonds of conventional values, and to
adopt pure activism. He spent June 20 in the company of ultra-
revolutionary Futurists, made friends with Enrico Rocca, editor
of *Roma Futurista*, and participated in a demonstration honor-
ing an Italian patriot who fell in Fiume. He regarded it all as a
glorious day: "A crowd of about two hundred young people,
including me, went to the Corso and the carabinieri chased us.
We found the Corso blocked by files of police and we turned
aside and ran toward the parliament, but the square was jammed
with soldiers. As we approached there was a blare of trumpets,
the carabinieri drew their swords, and the crowd broke and fled
to a nearby square. Someone shouted 'Down with Italy.' (A
rumor passed around that it was a street railway employee, but
when I saw him he was half-naked and one couldn't tell.) The
crowd ran toward him. The police didn't interfere, but the
streetcars stopped and the conductors pulled him into one of the
cars. I believe that this was the first day of the Italian revolution."

June 20, 1919, did not turn out to be the first day of the
Italian revolution, as Enzo thought, but only another step in the
direction of the revolution of which everyone talked — left-wing
workers and right-wing activists, hopefully; the bourgeoisie,
with deep misgivings. The Bolshevik triumph in Russia deci-
sively affected the mood of the Socialists, some of whom now
substituted the hope for a dictatorship of the proletariat for their
former reformist plans. Greater numbers than expected flocked
to the ranks of the Socialists and the trade unions. But Italy,
unlike the Soviets, lacked organized cells that could serve as the
bearers of revolution, and most Socialist leaders decided to wait

for the crumbling of the bourgeois regime and the revolution that would come by itself, in accordance with the teachings of historical determinism. Meanwhile, the general dissatisfaction because of economic conditions was sharpened by Italy's defeat at Versailles. Prime Minister Orlando was compelled to resign and his place was taken by Nitti, a moderate who genuinely believed in the persuasive power of reason and logic. Enzo was skeptical: "I do not believe that Nitti will succeed in forming a government without a representative from the Fasci." When two days later Nitti did succeed in forming a government, the four-teen-year-old activist characterized it as "black, so as not to call it something worse than that."

During this period Enzo wrote a composition titled "My Struggle," but judging by his diaries his thoughts were preoccu-pied with a much more important subject than the struggle for Fiume — that of his loves, three of which occupied the center of his attention. His mother's authority was still strong, but he already resented the reins, and his rebelliousness against the limitations imposed by the family found expression in a mani-festo which he composed in honor of Tomaso Campanella, a utopian philosopher of the sixteenth century.

This manifesto repudiated the Socialist establishment as well as pacifism, Nitti's biased government as well as the oligarchy of republicans and monarchists, the shapeless mob as well as the Fascist supermen. Against these Enzo asserted the teaching of the Campanellists, whose first principle was the abolition of the family, which had ceased to be an area of peace, as it had been in ancient times, and compelled young people to fight their hard battles within the home. The family, which suffers from every disadvantage and has not a single advantage, has become an anachronism since it suppresses the youngest and best forces. Can it perhaps be viewed as a means of providing the necessary increase of the human race? But for that purpose free love would suffice. The offspring of such free love could be the wards of the state from the day of their birth until the completion of their education, and their separation from their parents would liberate the latter from the need to accumulate wealth, the main element of exploiting capital, since the urge to accumulate also leads to the will to dominate.

Under a Campanellist regime, Enzo argued, everyone would have to work according to prescribed quotas. Those who wanted to could work beyond such quotas, but refusal to work would incur severe penalties. Invalids, the aged, and children would be deprived of the right to vote. While older people might be allowed to serve as legislators, the executives who would head the government would be few and very young. "But even as we conduct our struggle," he concluded, "we are pursued as by a nightmare by the doubt about the usefulness of life. If mankind is destined to be divided into tyrants and oppressed forever, is it not our duty to destroy it? We could answer this question in the affirmative, without any doubts, were we to believe that justice will never light up the world. But since we firmly believe in the near triumph of justice and equality, we have to reject this possibility, for it is a shattering vision. . . . But should we lose our faith, we will not hesitate to join the ranks of the destroyers."

Enzo pleaded with his mother to have him transferred for the last three years from the Visconti school, which he had attended since 1914, to the Terrenzo Mamiani Gymnasium. Whether his mother had influenced him in this direction or the wishes of both happened to coincide in this instance is not clear. It was known in the Sereni family that Alfonsa had for some time considered transferring him to another school because she was displeased with the special treatment he enjoyed at Visconti: the high grades he received with but little effort, the freedom he was given to do his lessons as he pleased, the frequent praise that teachers lavished on him in his presence. Concerned lest this overabundance of praise would put notions into his head and affect his character, she preferred the Mamiani Gymnasium, which had a reputation as a severe and strict school.

Thus it came about that on October 20, 1919, he appeared together with his mother at the Mamiani school. He was wearing glasses for the first time. In the ancient schoolyard they were met by Ada Ascarelli, a distant relative on both sides of the family, who occasionally came to play with the other children in the house on Cavour Street and went with them on the family Sunday outings. Short of stature, sweet-moon-faced, with large brown eyes and a long black braid, Ada was assigned to the same class as Enzo.

3

Ada

Enzo's highly developed sense of criticism more than once re-
stored him to solid ground before he was swept away by the
tides of his enthusiasm for various causes, and he brought it into
play in his appraisal of the very young man whom he knew
best — himself. Examining himself with the eyes of a stranger
he wrote in the third person: "I don't think there exists another
person as paradoxical as Enzo Sereni. Sometimes he uses para-
dox as a weapon against his opponents, other times merely to
play with them. Judging by the skeptical smile always on his face
one might conclude that it indicates contempt, but I have seldom
found anyone among the young people who so easily becomes
enthused and is less capable of satire. He often commits blun-
ders, but these are aesthetic. His critical sense is highly developed. He will seldom find anything to approve in his opponents,
and he has to be in a special mood (which occurs more frequently now that he has read St. Francis) to admit that his
opponent has merit of any kind. But should someone attack his
opponent, he will leap to his defense (perhaps out of a desire to
appear contradictory)." The four untouchables of the author of
the above self-portrait still remained D'Annunzio, Futurism,
Tomaso Campanella, and classical literature with Virgil in the
lead. But the appearance of St. Francis, the lover of all living

things, on the arena of Enzo's spiritual struggles foretold the rise of a new ideal — Christianity.

"I don't know why," he wrote, "but Sereni always leaves me with a sense of emptiness. In all his appearances there is a disproportion between the man and his ideas, between the ideas and his actions. Shaken by the persistent hammering of his words, which seem to be addressed to a political rally, I feel a void, as if he had uprooted all the weeds that grew in his garden but failed to grow anything else.

"I don't know why he is not liked. Ask most of his close friends and they will say that they can't stand him. Only a few, who know him very well, will say that he is charming. As far as I am concerned Enzo goes through four stages. First impression — charming. Second impression — standoffish. Third impression — repulsive. Fourth impression — a dear friend. One must practice a lot of patience to reach the fourth stage.

"Sereni is bashful. You won't notice it at first glance, but only after you consider his attitude toward his flames. Sereni, Enzo Sereni the daring, never knows how to tell a girl that he likes her. And all out of shyness. Unbelievable."

He exaggerated a bit about people's negative attitudes toward him. It was difficult to argue with him for few could withstand the power of his reasoning. He was as demanding of others as much as of himself. Some feared him, some were drawn toward him, and still others admired him. At Mamiani he acquired a new circle of friends, but on his fifteenth birthday on April 17, 1920, he noted in his diary, "I am alone! Alone!"

When he returned to Rome after the summer vacation new hopes arose: Maria Teresa, Clara Julia, Ada. His sense of inferiority about his short stature — five feet three inches, never more — subsided, and at the large dining table at home he now boasted that he was popular with the girls.

The "crowd" frequently went to concerts at the Augustio, a circular structure that had once been a mausoleum over the graves of Tiberius and Caligula and was transformed during the nineteenth century into a concert hall and a meeting place for young Romans during those far-off days before the age of the movies. Students could buy the cheapest tickets for two lirettas which provided them with seats way up under the ceiling, but it was necessary to stand in line for hours to be among the early birds at the ticket window. This long waiting line provided the young people with an excellent opportunity to argue about everything under the sun, as well as exchange gossip about who was in love with whom, since when, and so on. There was no dearth of information. It was impossible to keep secrets. Boys and girls did not, in those days, pair off except under the guise of walking to and from school, and most attempts to get close to one another took place in the midst of a larger company, in class, at lectures, concerts, visits in each other's homes, during hikes, choosing adjoining seats, handshakes at parting, a furtive touch, and especially in little remarks sandwiched in between big talk. Even among progressive students it was not customary for a girl from a decent bourgeois home to spend time with a young man unchaperoned, and most certainly not in the evening. The doors were locked and the keys were in the pockets of the parents. Any instance of a return home at a late hour was at once known in the entire neighborhood. It was therefore natural that the entire group should be well informed about all romantic doings, especially regarding Enzo, who was incapable of concealing his feelings. Even Maria Teresa, she of "the glorious hair" who had enchanted him for a while and who had declared that he was a saintly and calm person, had noticed that Enzo seemed soft on Ada — after he had loudly announced that she had changed for the better — and that Ada seemed to be soft on him.

At first Enzo vouchsafed to her only a question mark in his diary: "Flirt with Ada?" She, too, seemed to have doubts. Coming out of school where Enzo awaited her in the rain because she had no umbrella, she suddenly said to him: "I've heard some nice things about you. They say that last year you were in love with Emma Machi and that she is the heroine of your novel." But Enzo refused to confess his sin. A short time later the question mark in his diary gave way to exclamation points: "Ada! Ada! Ada! Oh God, if only it were true!" He sighed and switched to long trousers permanently.

On December 28, 1920, Grandma Giuditha Pontecorvo died

of cancer in the home of her daughter after months of suffering. Enzo did not go to school because of the family mourning, but he found an opportunity to write his first letter to Ada. She became closer to him from day to day. At the beginning of the new year he wrote: "Ada more than ever. We have been together such a long time. Today, when she and Paolo Milano and I left the lecture, he asked her: 'Tell me the truth, when the two of you go home together, don't you get bored sometimes?' She denied it and said: 'A year or so ago he sometimes revolted me with that hat and coat of his.'" In fact, Enzo was never particular in matters of dress, either under the influence of Mama Alfonsa, who paid no attention to her own exterior and wore shapeless clothes, or because he was always in a hurry and never had time to tie his shoelaces or straighten his socks. Ada was his exact opposite, always neat, always restrained, and attractive even in the black apron which was the school uniform.

One of Ada's grandmothers was a Sereni, but the two families had little in common. Ada's father, Ettore Ascarelli, was descended from a family of exiles from Spain, one of whose offspring was Deborah Ascarelli, an Italian poet of the sixteenth century. Ettore was a successful businessman and his children grew up in a home where nothing was lacking. In her parents' house Ada had a separate little apartment boasting even a private bathroom, a rarity in those days, and she was so used to having money available that she never carried any on her person. Ettore Ascarelli, a lover of history and owner of a large library, was an atheist, in accordance with the finest tradition of the new Italy, and so far as he was concerned, the Jewish question had been settled when they were granted civil rights in 1870. But he knew the Bible and at family meals he would tell the children stories about the patriarchs, much to the displeasure of his wife who inquired acidly whether she would always have to eat in the company of these biblical ancients. She was indifferent to religion, Jewish or any other, but whenever on summer trips the family came to some chapel dedicated to one of the miracle-working saints of whom there are so many in Italy, she too would light a candle, reasoning that if it did no good, the loss was only the cost of a candle, and if it should be of benefit, was not the acquisition of a friend in heaven worth a candle?

Ettore Ascarelli died in 1919 when Ada was fourteen. His loss left her with a sense of void and a longing for someone to be close to, for there was not much sympathy between Ada and her mother, a beautiful and elegant woman who loved money and material comforts and did not conceal her ambition to marry off her attractive daughter to some well-to-do businessman who would provide her with the good things in life. After the death of the father, the Ascarelli family for a time moved to their grandparents' house which was near Cavour Street and this provided the young pair with an opportunity for frequent walks together, Enzo escorting Ada to her door, and then she accompanying him to his, thus back and forth until there was no longer any avoiding the return home.

The entire crowd went to visit the Vatican and Enzo talked to Ada about pilgrimages, trying to impress. He sat beside her at the theater. Together with Leah, Silvana, and a small group of friends he took her to visit churches and talked to her about God. And then he escorted her home, and she walked back with him to his house, and then back again. She declared she would like to believe in God but did not know how. He suggested she read the New Testament. She declared she needed a spiritual guide. He noted in his diary: "Does this mean she is looking for love? She said she needed someone who would penetrate her soul and direct her: 'Do this. Do that.' Would God this were I."

It was not by accident that he gave her the New Testament. To win Ada meant also to win her to his convictions. By 1921 he was already far from his enthusiasms for D'Annunzio and the activists and was attracted by the charm of Christianity. To some extent he was no doubt influenced by the mood prevalent among some of the younger intellectual circles in Italy. The generation that during the war lost its illusions about the sanctity of native land and international peace was looking for a new anchor. Some found it in the promise of the Socialist future, others sought it in Christianity. This was a kind of reaction to the older anticlerical generation and its war against the church

in the name of freedom. The return to religion found expression
in the writings of Giovanni Papini, then one of the most widely
read authors in Europe, who turned away from the destructive
views of the Futurists and pointed to the religious truth in the
life of Jesus. But the trend of religious revival centered mostly
about Professor Ernesto Buonaiuti, a Catholic priest whose advanced views brought him into frequent conflict with the Catholic establishment. During the papacy of Pius X, an extreme
conservative who repressed all movements of rejuvenation
within the church, Buonaiuti was unfrocked. He did not bow to
this decree, however, since he did not want to fight the church
from the outside, but rather to oppose the petrified tradition of
the establishment with a vision of early Christianity in its pris-
tine simplicity.

When Benedict XV, a man more liberal than his predecessor,
was elected to the papacy in 1914, Professor Buonaiuti was
again permitted to lecture at the Collegio Romano, the Vatican
University, and he exerted an immense influence on the younger
generation. His lectures on the history of early Christianity at
the Collegio Romano as well as at the University of Rome attracted large numbers of college and high school students, Jews
as well as Catholics, for life in the shadow of Christianity left its
mark on the Jews of Rome. Women entering a synagogue kissed
their finger tips in a gesture resembling Christians crossing
themselves; Jesus was referred to as "the relative"; and changing
trends in Christianity were reflected in the thinking of Jewish
intellectuals.

The Mamiani Gymnasium was very close to the University of
Rome and Enzo and his friends would rush to hear Buonaiuti's
lectures as soon as their classes were dismissed. The lecture
ended, a crowd of admirers would surround the professor, who
was dressed in his clerical habit, and shower him with questions,
demand explanations, and argue with him. A group of closer
intimates would go for walks with him, visit him in his peasant
cottage, and spend Sundays with him. Enzo, who was invariably
overcome with missionary zeal whenever he embraced a new
idea, now read the New Testament in Greek and interpreted it to

his Catholic fellow students, and during his summer vacation he debated religious problems with the local priest.

Summer brought a bitter disappointment. Enzo was never especially well-behaved in class, and a teacher could gain his cooperation only if he appealed to reason instead of relying on authority. Since he excelled in the humanities, and the teachers knew how to appreciate a gifted student, he allowed himself liberties. His conflicts centered on the teachers of the natural sciences, which interested him little. The math teacher, who was known for his timidity, found a smoking inkwell on his desk and was met by outcries from the class: "Professor! Watch out! It will explode!" Or he would find a dangling wire and be warned that it was live, and, whether Enzo had a hand in these childish tricks or not, he would never seek to avoid a share in the collective responsibility. To overcome classroom boredom, he and other rebels would clandestinely read books more to their taste while they were connected by strings which one of them would pull at the sign of approaching danger. To get even with the teacher of Greek and Latin, who particularly interfered with their reading, they would resort to spasms of loud coughing whenever he stared too intently down the neckline of some girl student. But not everyone would acquiesce to the superiority of Sereni, and the chemistry instructor, of whom Enzo was openly contemptuous, had his revenge.

It was customary to let outstanding students skip the eighth grade and enroll in a university upon the completion of the seventh, if their grades were up to a certain level and on condition that they take qualifying tests in the fall. Enzo had assumed that he would enroll in a university at age sixteen, like his brother Enrico, and that even if the chemistry instructor were inclined to give him a low grade, the other teachers would prevail upon him not to detain the budding genius. But when at the end of the semester the grades were posted, he found that his grade in chemistry was seven, one point below the minimum, final and subject to no revision. It was a bitter moment for Enzo, who did not know how to take defeat.

During the vacation he recovered somewhat from the disap-

pointment. He took long hikes in the mountains, and missed
Ada. "I believe that Ada will be mine. Ada! Ada! I need her."
What would she look like when they returned to Rome? Their
first meeting after vacation was not promising. It was his way to
be rough, the more tremulous he felt inside, and he tried to
arrange a meeting with her at the home of a friend by means of
a humorously threatening, unsigned letter. To no avail. Even an
anonymous telephone call failed to bring her. When she finally
came in the company of a girl friend she was standoffish and
ironical, despite such pleasantries on Enzo's part as: "Why did
you come? Who invited you?" But a couple of days put an end to
this childish game. Enzo had matured. On September 10, 1921,
he wrote in his diary: "Incipit Vita Nova. From now on a new
life, a new diary. A new attitude to Ada." And at this point, as in
a Victorian play, the curtain goes down on the first kiss. There
was no longer any need to write of love in a diary since it existed
in reality, real, earthly. And gradually there was no need for a
diary altogether. Reality supplanted the written word.

There was something puritanical about the Serenis, perhaps
due to the influence of Mama Alfonsa. The three brothers drew
back from sexual lust. Emilio, Mimo, was dreadfully bashful.
For Enrico, the most restrained of the three, as for many of his
generation, the war served as a first love, leading to a painful
disillusionment, and he clung to the idea of equality between the
sexes as it was understood also by the youth movements of Germany at that time — that both the man and the woman should
preserve their virginity till their marriage, an idea that was
contrary to prevailing custom in Italy that permitted to the man
what it prohibited to the woman — gaining sexual experience.
Enzo, the most sensual of the three, was in this regard a true son
of Italy. When one of the girls in his class held up a copy of
Petronius's *Satyricon* which she had taken from the school library, Enzo, who had so much enjoyed its "crude pornography"
forcefully took the book out of her hands with the argument that
it was not "suitable reading matter for a girl her age."

4

Dreaming of a Better World

Enrico decided not to follow in his father's footsteps but instead to devote himself to research. In the summer of 1921 he took a trip to Germany and Austria, and while in Vienna, following the custom of the Serenis, he visited libraries and bookstores. In a bookstore that specialized in Judaica, his attention was caught by a poster announcing the meeting of the first post-war Zionist Congress in Carlsbad in Czechoslovakia. "As long as I am in this vicinity, I have decided to visit the Congress," he announced in a postcard home. "What do you think? It may be interesting. Maybe I'll return a saintly penitent."

Instead of visiting for a couple of days as he had planned, Enrico stayed for the duration of the Congress. He was attracted by the lively hubbub and the lack of self-consciousness among Jews which he witnessed for the first time. "He did not return a penitent, someone who had had a revelation, nor even as a Zionist, merely filled with a sense of reverence and admiration. But for me, and not for me only, this visit — more correctly this faded penciled scribble on a postcard of August 1921 — symbolized the beginning of a new life." Thus Enzo wrote ten years later, at the Zionist Congress of 1931, when his thoughts harkened back to his brother.

The story of Enrico's faded postcard sounds poetic, but it does not reveal the whole truth. Even a less intellectual person than

Enzo would not have become a Zionist overnight because of an accidental visit of his brother to an exotic show called a Jewish congress. There was here a dim spark going back to the days of his Bar Mitzvah and the Balfour Declaration; also the natural curiosity to understand what went on about him when during holidays he sat next to his father in the synagogue. There was the desire to understand the faith from which sprang the early Christianity of love and equality that Buonaiuti described. And above all, there was a sharp turn at the line beyond which there is no turning back, a conclusion based on a general reassessment that he, as a Jew, could not attain within Christianity that wholeness which he sought. In addition to these explanations of the turn that came at the very extreme edge of assimilation, there is also a "Salvation Army type of story" of how Enzo beheld the great light overnight.

In the autumn of 1921, Dr. Israel Reichert, a graduate of the school of natural sciences of the University of Berlin, spent some time in Italy in preparation for the establishment of an experimental agricultural station in Palestine. During his studies in Berlin, Reichert had also served as a Zionist emissary and established a Zionist pioneering youth organization which he named Hapoel Hatzair, after the parent Labor Zionist organization in Palestine. This organization stressed national revival instead of class struggle. Like most east European Jews, Reichert was enchanted by the aristocratic ways of the Italian Jews, and decided to spread the message of Labor Zionism, which advocated the redemption of the people by means of physical labor and the establishment of a society based on equality and justice. In Florence, then the center of the Zionist movement in Italy, Reichert's fiery address made a deep impression. The local Zionists, including the Russian-born Moshe Beilinson, asked him to meet with a few gifted young people who were drifting away from Judaism, the most prominent of them Carlo and Nello Roselli and Enzo Sereni.

Zionism at that time meant giving individual attention to each precious prospective convert. Reichert therefore journeyed to Rome with Moshe Beilinson, who had left Russia after he became disillusioned with bolshevism and would live in Italy prior to settling in Palestine. Together they went to the Collegio Romano where Enzo attended Buonaiuti's lectures. Beilinson had met Enzo before in Uncle Angelo Sereni's house. They now waited until the end of the lecture, and when Enzo finally detached himself from the crowd arguing with the lecturer, Beilinson introduced him to Reichert and discreetly left them alone. Still under the effect of the lecture, which dealt with the prophet Hosea and his concept of a God of justice, Enzo described to Reichert the vision of a new world without oppressors and oppressed, and how only the religion of love could bring it about. An expert propagandist, Reichert knew how to adapt himself to the trend of thoughts of those he tried to persuade. He now proceeded to talk about the teachings of the prophets, the wisdom of the Aggadists, the compassion of Hasidism for all sufferers, the uniqueness of Judaism, and the will to realize the ultimate ideal: establishing a new society in Eretz Israel, purified of all the imperfections that had gradually infected Judaism in the centuries of the dispersion — the Diaspora.

The conversation which began in the yard of the Collegio Romano continued through the night as Enzo and Reichert walked through the streets of Rome. Reichert turned from the past to the present and talked about the immigration of Jewish idealists to Palestine, the idea of pioneering, and the redemptive value of physical labor, of collective life without exploitation. (He did not go into the less pleasant details such as unemployment and struggle with the employing landowners.) By the time dawn rose over the bell towers of Rome, it was Enzo who was speaking about Eretz Israel, and he expressed his wish to commence the creation of a pioneering movement in Italy at once, for time was pressing.

The neutral name Avoda — Labor — was chosen for the new organization. Two days later a first meeting was held at the Sereni home on Cavour Street in the presence of the three founders — Reichert, Beilinson, and Enzo Sereni. A number of young people, mostly of the Sereni clan and their friends, attended, and also Dante Lattes, chairman of the Zionist Committee in Rome, a fine journalist and a man of broad education. Reichert opened the meeting, then Enzo spoke with much heat

about the great tasks that faced Zionist youth in Italy, and the
need to introduce a change in the life of Italian Jews if they were
to survive. The organization was formally established with Enzo
as secretary. He was then not quite seventeen and had no previous Zionist training or organizational experience.

The Avoda group formulated a program whose aim was "the
revival of the Jewish people in the Land of Israel on the basis of
a free Hebrew society without exploiters and victims." With this
aim in view every member was called upon to: (1) Regard
himself as a pioneer of this revival. (2) Acquire the basic elements of living Hebrew culture, such as Hebrew language,
literature, and so forth. (3) Prepare himself for settlement in
Palestine. (4) Establish for himself a productive life while still
in the Diaspora. (5) Act to the best of his ability among the
masses in the Diaspora to win them for Hebrew culture and
constructive life.

The program was basically like that of numerous other such
groups that briefly flared up and faded throughout Europe at
this time. It took the enthusiasm of an Enzo Sereni to try to
transform the program into reality among Italian Jews, and with
that sense of dedication that was a Sereni family trait, he was
totally in earnest about it.

Before the establishment of this Avoda group — and also, it
must be said, afterward — Zionism was peripheral to Jewish
life in Italy; its burdens were shouldered by a handful of faithful. Altogether there were only some forty-odd thousand Jews in
Italy in 1922. The number of Zionists among them was minute,
and the number of those devoted to Labor Zionism was micro-
scopic. It is true that when Dr. Chaim Weizmann came on a
political visit to Italy in 1921, he was received by the king, who
spoke highly of Theodor Herzl whose portrait stood on his desk.
But Cardinal Gaspari, the Vatican's secretary for foreign affairs,
was chiefly interested in the fate of the holy places, and remained unimpressed even after Weizmann described to him the
work of Jewish settlement in Eretz Israel and the projected
establishments of higher education. "It is not the settlements that
frighten me," he said to Weizmann, "but your university. That's
what I am afraid of."

Like most eastern European Jews, Weizmann, too, was impressed by the dignified and respected position of Italian Jews and found it hard to understand why they, who did not suffer from any discrimination, who enjoyed the status of respected citizens and held influential positions in the political and cultural life of the country, would turn their eyes to Zion.

But even though their eyes were turned to Zion, their feet were firmly planted on the soil of Italy. Prior to the organization of the Avoda group, not a single Italian Zionist carried his convictions to their logical conclusion and immigrated to Palestine. With all their reverence for Herzl and Weizmann and their longing for Zion, Italian Zionists were convinced that Eretz Israel was destined for the poor persecuted Jews of eastern Europe, and that their own duty consisted in helping these unfortunates materially and spiritually.

Enrico, according to his own diagnosis, was the bearer of the Zionist germ, which he brought from his visit at the Carlsbad Congress, but himself remained immune to it. Though he attended the meetings of the Avoda group, it was only as a bystander who came to learn but not to identify. Mimo, on the other hand, who was then only fifteen, was captivated, and since his character was less mercurial than Enzo's, he became the most fanatical Zionist of them all. Enzo knew his younger brother thoroughly. When they once visited at the home of his classmate Enriquetta Valenziani, and her mother showed particular affection for Mimo, Enzo warned her: "Watch out, Signora Valenziani. He is capable of bringing us all to the guillotine."

Ada Ascarelli, too, underwent an intensive course in Zionism in the course of her wanderings with Enzo through the narrow alleys of Rome, and especially on their clandestine walks on the Aventino Hill among the ancient cloisters where time seemed to have stopped. But she did not participate in any organized Zionist activity. In fact her mother had strictly forbidden her to do so out of a healthy maternal foreboding that dreamers like the Serenis threatened her plans for a secure future for her daughter. Since Enzo and Ada were the only Jews in their class (and despite their overall assimilation their Jewishness contributed

not a little to their friendship) there was no point in seeking
converts to Zionism there. Still, it was impossible for Enzo not
to initiate them into the new ideological world he had discovered, and some Catholics in the class also underwent Zionist
indoctrination.

The Avoda group did not want to become a restricted little
circle of intellectuals and decided to extend its activities among
high school students and especially among the children of
Rome's ghetto. The Jewish bourgeoisie looked upon the ghetto
with disdain and apprehension. They had no sympathy with the
feeling that motivated thousands of Jews to prefer living among
their own in the ghetto's dim alleys, in crowded houses and
amid the turmoil of sidewalk markets where children played
among the pushcarts, even though the entire city was open to
them. The ghetto children, sophisticated, wise in the ways of
the city, remote from the idealism that animated the members
of Avoda, weren't interested in Zionist activity and preferred
cigarettes, movies, and boxing. But Enzo didn't give up. Two
groups of about thirty children, according to the highest esti-
mate, would be taken by him once a week for hikes, games,
and calisthenics and were also taught Hebrew and the history of Zionism. Like all youth movements they lacked leaders and means, and Enzo pointed an accusing finger at the
wealthy Jews who did not realize that "the shame of the moral
and physical conditions prevailing in the ghetto is also their
shame." In Florence, where a second Avoda group was established, there was no ghetto, and its members debated whether to
rent a piece of land to cultivate during their free time, or to
engage in handicrafts, as was suggested by Enzo Bonaventura, a
psychologist. (Twenty-five years later Professor Bonaventura
was one of the Hebrew University staff who were killed in Jerusalem as their convoy was ambushed on its way to Mount
Scopus.)

When in July 1922, six months after the founding of Avoda,
Enzo had to summarize the achievements of the group, he had to
admit that only a small step forward had been taken, but compared with other Zionist activity in Italy, there was room for

satisfaction. His report concluded with words of thanks to Moshe Beilinson who had been an energetic guide and did not tolerate weakness. In him Enzo found a new teacher. Beilinson, who was then thirty-two years old, had been brought up on Russian culture and was estranged from Judaism. He had been active in the Russian revolutions of 1905 and 1917, but later became disillusioned by bolshevism. He left his native land and substituted Socialist Zionism for the faith of his youth. He introduced the Serenis to the world of Socialist thought. (Forty years later, when Emilio Sereni was a Communist deputy in the Italian Parliament, he declared that Moshe Beilinson had exerted the most powerful influence on his life.) Despite their deep roots in the culture of ancient Rome and modern Italy — or perhaps because of it — most young Jews of Rome were quite provincial and lived in a closed world, whereas Beilinson had lived in Russia, Germany, and Switzerland, and since 1918 in Italy, where he gave up the practice of medicine for writing and translating. He was a man of broad European culture, and realized that Italy was only a segment, and not the most important segment at that, of turbulent Europe. The friendship between him and Enzo was based on personal contrasts. Enzo was impulsive, made friends easily, and talked incessantly; Beilinson was taciturn, self-centered, sober, shunned crowds, and never spoke before first chewing on his cigar or his mustache. Beilinson felt responsible for his young charge whom he introduced to Socialist Zionism, and this sense of responsibility persisted till his dying day.

But Enzo's ideological leap nevertheless took place against an Italian background. He wrote: "The indication of the degeneration of the Jews is their constant debate whether to continue as Jews, and yet one has never seen an Italian questioning whether he wished to remain Italian. It was in his nature. Judaism too must regain this naturalness. Italian Jews do not have to renounce their Italianness for the sake of their Jewishness, but neither must a good Italian citizen renounce his Hebrew culture. What Jewish values have the people of Israel contributed to Italian life through sons scattered in this wonderful land? It is our task to infuse new thought into the Italian world. . . . Where is the historian of Hasidism or of the Essenes who would inform the Italian world of these two religious trends that are unknown here? We must give the world something of our own, something befitting the people of the Bible and the Talmud.

"For the sake of a better understanding of Jewish reality, I think it is desirable that we observe also the practical commandments of Judaism, and if not observe them, then at least feel their vitality, refreshing charm, and be aware that they are not identical with those unfortunate manifestations we see about ourselves which are the traits of a dying generation, and that they contain values of great importance also for modern man."

From the standpoint of its attitude toward religion, Zionism in Italy differed from that in eastern Europe, where the urge for national revival paralleled the rebellion against the restraints of an outlived religious tradition. Here the reaction was exactly opposite that of eastern Europe, and the urge for national revival brought about a return to Jewish tradition, which the older generation had abandoned. The spokesman of the return to Judaism was Alfonso Pacifici, the son of a rich merchant of Florence, whose interest in Judaism was aroused when he was a high school senior in the course of his debates with his professor of philosophy on the traits identifying a nation. Pacifici developed the idea of integral Judaism that is neither religion nor nationality, neither race nor tradition, but embraces all aspects of life. He demanded from those returning to Judaism that, one by one, they reclaim observance of the religious commandments, without seeking explanations or justifications for them, for only through such observance would they attain complete faith. In contrast to the Zionists of Herzl's generation, he demanded of all his friends that they learn Hebrew, for Zion's sake, and also because in his opinion translation distorts the meaning of the Bible. Convinced that in the small Italian community quality had to take the place of quantity, he advocated his ideas in the course of personal encounters throughout the country, a form of advocacy in which he was highly successful. He also visited the Sereni home, and was served a more or less kosher dinner — that is, Alfonsa bought kosher meat in the ghetto and did not serve dairy dishes with it.

Here he made two disciples. Enzo and Mimo gradually became observant Jews. From an orthodox standpoint their observance was a shaky thing indeed, but from the standpoint of friends and relatives, it was astounding. They covered their heads during meals and in public places. They demanded a kosher kitchen at home, which meant avoiding pork or adding parmesan cheese to pasta with meat. They attended synagogue and did not travel on Saturday. Enzo even tried the nearly impossible task of finding a rational basis for religion. When, in the course of an argument, he was asked how he could reconcile return to religious tradition and attendance at synagogue with the anticlerical views of Croce which he prized so highly, he replied that he regarded faith and return to tradition as a necessary stabilizing factor in the building of the new Jewish state which was about to arise.

5

Not All Italians
Are Fascists

Italy was becoming aware of Mussolini. The Fascist movement, which became a political party in 1921, gained strength as a result of the mounting unemployment, the collapse of the central banks, and the inflation. Fascist assault units engaged in bloody clashes with the Socialists, and helped break the strikes of agricultural and industrial workers in northern Italy, which had virtually paralyzed the economy of the country. After the general elections in the autumn of 1921, they entered Parliament with thirty-five members under Mussolini's leadership.

Pope Benedict XV, who was openly suspicious of the Fascists and supported the Christian Democrats, died early in February 1922. And when the cardinals gathered in the Sistine Chapel to elect his successor, Enzo and Ada were in the crowd in Saint Peter's Square waiting for the plume of smoke that would announce the election of a new pope. The new pope, Cardinal Rotti, called himself Pius XI, and by the choice of name informed the world that he would follow a conservative line. Indeed, his election marked a radical change in Vatican policy. A scion of a conservative aristocratic family, the new pope opposed the Christian Democrats with their trade unions, and even when he still served as cardinal in Milan, the first stronghold of fascism, he had realized that here was a new force that might rule Italy some day. And Mussolini, who began his career as an outspoken anticlerical, hinted to Pius XI that he would protect the rights of the Holy See.

As chaos mounted in the Italian economy, there was increasing talk about the only alternative that could restore order — a military dictatorship. The storm troops of the Fascist party were organized by Italo Balbo on a military basis with the aim of seizing power and succeeded in gaining control of most urban and rural centers in the north with strong-arm methods of suppression. They were opposed by a labor movement that was exhausted and split by the establishment of the Italian Communist party in January 1921. Many regarded the Fascist entry into the government and the framework of law as the only way to prevent the collapse of the state, but Mussolini was no longer interested in being a partner in a coalition, and assumed that all power could now fall into his hands if only he knew how to take advantage of the appropriate opportunity.

In July 1922, Enzo completed his high school studies and chose to pursue the study of philosophy, in accordance with his natural bent, and without any connection with the needs of Zionist pioneering. Ada would have preferred to study chemistry, but since the natural science building was remote from the humanities campus, she decided to take up literature. These studies, and the walks together to and from school, provided a fine opportunity for tête-à-tête conversations without unwanted company.

On the day they went to register at the university, they found the bridges blocked by troops and barbed wire. Rome was preparing for a struggle against the Fascists who had concentrated their forces at the approaches to the city in preparation for the march on Rome. Rumor had it that a full seventy thousand Fascists were ready for action; actually there were no more than about twenty thousand, most of them without regular military training, and the garrison of Rome, which numbered twelve thousand, could have easily overcome them had it been given a chance. But the isolated king, who had no illusions regarding the fickleness of the masses, drew back at the threat of civil war and refused to sign the necessary emergency decree demanded by the prime minister who, in turn, had no alternative but to resign. The head of the Fascist party, who had preferred to remain in Milan, safely near the Swiss border, just in case, during the preparations for the march on Rome, was called to the palace to form a new government.

On October 28, 1922, the Fascist units entered Rome without meeting any opposition. The next day Mussolini arrived from the north in a sleeping car. Dressed in a borrowed frock coat and a black shirt, he reported to the king, and, in addition to the premiership, he also took the portfolios of foreign and internal affairs. Five other Fascists received cabinet posts. Many Italians sighed with relief; some looked to Mussolini to save the country from bolshevism; others regarded him as a strong man who would restore order. Those who had no confidence in him consoled themselves with the thought that he would not last more than a few months. Few understood the full significance of Fascist rule during its first days in power as well as seventeen-year-old Enzo, who wrote, "As of yesterday we have entered fateful days. Fascism is on the rampage. It's a horror. I went out this morning, and also in the afternoon, and I saw the destruction of the offices of *La Epoca*. Disgusting, is all one can say. But the reaction will be terrible."

The following day Enzo witnessed the encounter between Socialists and Fascists in the San Lorenzo workers' quarter. "Fascists everywhere," he wrote, "stopping pedestrians, searching, armed with pistols and rifles. When I reached the railroad bridge where the Fascists were concentrated I pretended to look for a relative who was one of their members. They were courteous. Then they left the bridge and returned to town, all the while firing through windows. I was shaken. But Democracy won't die. Long live Democracy."

The Jews did not regard Mussolini as an anti-Semite despite some articles he had written in 1919 condemning the domination of Jewish wealth in the world. Some Jews were among the founders of the Fascist movement, and prior to the march on Rome there were as many as seven hundred Jewish members in the Fascist ranks. The chief rabbi of Genoa congratulated Mussolini on his triumph and received a cordial reply. Jews were to be found in all the Italian parties from left to right, and those who opposed fascism did so as Italians, not as Jews.

Even prior to his rise to power Mussolini had struck an anti-Zionist note which was particularly directed against the ostensible dual loyalty of the Italian Zionists. The Zionist Organization, which was sensitive to the moods prevailing in the Fascist movement, sent Vladimir Jabotinsky to Rome in 1922 in an attempt to clarify matters. He established contact with some leading Fascists, but did not succeed in getting to see Mussolini. Continuing this attempt to gain Mussolini's ear, a delegation of three, consisting of Dante Lattes, the director of the Zionist office in Rome, Moshe Beilinson, and the chief rabbi of Rome, Sacerdoti, appeared before him early in 1923. Mussolini frankly declared his opposition to the Zionist movement, which, in his opinion, was a tool in the hands of British imperialism and aroused Arab anger. The delegation, on its part, argued that Italian Jews would always remain loyal to their native land and could help establish relations with the Levant through the Jewish communities living there. Mussolini then changed his tone. "This I can understand. . . . When Weizmann visits Italy I will be glad to meet him."

When Weizmann did come to Italy toward the end of April, he was received by Mussolini in the duce's office, an immensely long room almost devoid of furniture where the visitor had to walk a long way before reaching Mussolini's desk. In those good old days it was still possible to jest. "You know, Dr. Weizmann," Mussolini said, "that not all Jews are Zionists." To which the president of the World Zionist Organization replied, "Nor are all Italians Fascists." When the conversation turned to the British, Mussolini maintained that they were using Zionism as a ball in a power game, and he added, "You know that we could build your state *en toute pièce*, from the bottom up," to which Weizmann responded, "And I also remember that it was the Romans who destroyed it *en toute pièce*."

(Weizmann left the meeting under the impression that Mussolini was not basically opposed to Zionism and that his suspicion and hostility were directed against the British.)

In August 1923, Enzo went to Carlsbad to attend the thirteenth Zionist Congress. He wanted to become personally acquainted with the Jewish people and its parliament and was
present at the opening of the Congress. At 8:30 P.M. Weizmann
entered the hall and was greeted with a prolonged ovation. After
reading a greeting from President Masaryk of Czechoslovakia,
and messages from other government officials, he addressed the
Congress in Hebrew and expressed the hope that the Arabs, who
owned huge areas outside Palestine, would recognize the world's
growing sympathy for the revival of the Jewish people. Enzo
was ecstatic. Though he understood Hebrew and Yiddish — the
two chief languages at the Congress — only with difficulty, he
was excited by his contact with living Jewry. Naive as only an
eighteen-year-old can be, everything appeared to him in the light
of perfect truth. Weizmann, he felt, was one of the foremost
figures, if not the foremost, of eastern European Jewry since
emancipation. And here was Weizmann announcing the partial
opening of the Hebrew University of 1924; and following him
Ussischkin reported on what was being done in Palestine — a
vegetable oil factory had been opened, 73,000 dunam of land
bought in the Valley of Jezreel, the *moshav* of Nahalal and the
kibbutzim Ein Harod and Tel Yoseph established, a labor bank
set up, the Nordau quarter built in Tel Aviv to provide housing.
The Congress sessions went on for thirteen days and each lasted
to the small hours of the morning. Enzo enjoyed it all. "Everything here is interesting," he wrote. "Day before yesterday I met
Martin Buber. Deep impression. A man of stature, and
friendly. This morning I again met with Beilinson and we
worked out the principles for nonpartisan Zionist ideological
activity — education of the masses, especially in eastern
Europe."

A year after Mussolini's rise to power there was calm in Italy.
The strikes ended, the financial situation of the country im-
proved noticeably, and to many it seemed that despite fascism
with its storm troopers, violence, and raised arm salutes, a firm
hand was preferable to the chaos that had reigned before. Enzo
agreed that "the victor is strong, not a fool, and his triumph is

firmly established," but in his heart grew a sense of disgust and aversion, which he regarded as the best proof of his firm Jewishness. The departure from the past was not easy. He read the catechism of the Council of Trent and *Catholic Morality* of Manzoni, and with every moment he felt his growing distance from them, and the pain of distance. "I feel the new man being born within me, both because of my constant and close contact with Jews as well as because of my departure from the old world. The hour requires that I dedicate all my strength to the Jewish people without digressions and diversions." His choice had been made — not without pain.

And having made his choice, he extended it all along the line. If it were to be Zionism, then it must be pioneering; and if pioneering, then it meant immigration to the land of Israel, together with Ada. Ada knew that they would get married some day after Enzo had finished his studies and become independent, and she was reconciled to both Zionism and immigration to Palestine, but she drew the line in religious matters: they were not to have a kosher home, nor religious upbringing of children. Self-sacrifice had its limits, even for a young woman who had been brought up according to the Italian tradition that a woman must follow in the footsteps of the man, make his hopes her own, his faith hers, and his wishes her own.

Mussolini unwittingly provided a substantial reenforcement to Zionism in Italy. In order to win worldwide sympathy for the Fascist regime, he opened Italian universities to foreign students, granting them free tuition as well as reduced transportation rates. These unusual privileges were at once taken advantage of by young Jews from Poland, Hungary, Rumania, and Russia who could not pursue their studies at home either because of the *numerus clausus* or for lack of means. A large group of students also came from Palestine where there were no facilities for higher education at that time. They studied in Rome, Naples, Florence, and Padua, and established contact with local Zionists: with Beilinson whose writings were known to them from the Hebrew labor press; with Dante Lattes of the Zionist press; with Pacifici and Professor Cassuto in Florence; and with the Serenis of Cavour Street. Since most of them had no means, they sought sources of income, mainly through teaching Hebrew. Beilinson studied Hebrew with Emanuel Ben Dor, who came from Jerusalem to study archaeology. Enzo and Mimo were tutored by Emanuel's brother Raphael, who came to study architecture. But while Beilinson had to struggle with the Hebrew language stubbornly and at cost of much anguish, the language yielded to the Serenis without undue difficulty, and within a year they could speak and write it fluently. They had always been fluent and articulate in their native tongue and now were so also in Hebrew.

The students from Palestine could not understand the eternal debates among local Zionists as to what is a Jew and who is one, and were impatient with the interminable philosophical discussions on the essence of Judaism. So far as they were concerned all problems concerning the nature of Judaism had been solved long ago. On the other hand, coming as they did from a remote province which had no art museums or concert halls or theaters worthy of the name, and altogether lacking in aesthetic training, they keenly felt their ignorance compared with the Italian Jewish students who knew so much, and especially compared with the Serenis. Enzo appointed himself their guide and teacher and showed them the wonders of Rome. He took them to museums and on tours, he showed them the statue of Aphrodite emerging from the sea, the frescoes of Lippi, and places beloved by him. He explained and taught and recited entire cantos from the *Divine Comedy*, waxing enthusiastic together with his charges.

A popular meeting place of the Palestinian students was in the house of Xenia Pamphilova, a slim Russian woman with a crown of braids on her head, who, together with her husband Leib Silberberg and other Socialist revolutionaries, had fought for the overthrow of czarism, and fled from Russia after her husband was hanged for a terrorist act before the revolution of 1905. In the course of her wanderings, Xenia passed through Siberia, Finland, Belgium, and France, until she arrived in Italy together with her young daughter in 1917, and earned her living by writing for emigré journals and operating a boarding house for Russian refugees and foreign students. Moshe Beilinson was her friend and boarder, like her bound by memories of the revolution to Russian culture and longing for a lost world. Thus it happened that Xenia and her daughter became acquainted with the Sereni family. She sought for some meaning in the cruel death of her husband, who had only seen his daughter once, and concluded that it was a punishment for his having abandoned the faith of his ancestors. She decided to transform her daughter, who was a bit Russian and a bit Italian, partly Christian and partly Jewish, into a full Jewess. Enzo and Mimo took her, a slight, delicate, and fragile girl, to the Zionist meetings and she studied Hebrew together with the rest.

Mimo, who was nothing if not thorough, took another step toward Zion and decided to study agriculture. The widespread Sereni family, which accepted the Zionist fever of its two sons with relative calm, and even reconciled itself to the invasion of orthodoxy and the constant stream of Zionists that visited the house — among them not a few charlatans — became concerned. One Zionist son is all very well, but two, one of whom was stubbornly determined to study agriculture, a useless occupation for Italian middle-class people, taxed the tolerance that normally prevailed on Cavour Street. Particularly concerned were Dr. Sereni and Uncle Angelo, a true and long-time Zionist, but within the bounds of common sense, who loved Zion from afar without ever treading on its soil even for a brief visit. Father Sereni appealed to his oldest son, now Dr. Enrico Sereni, a specialist in physiology doing research work in London, to influence Mimo, who was then visiting him, to abandon Zionism. But, in the Pontecorvo tradition, Enrico answered: "I am in agreement with Mother who feels that it is impossible to change the system of freedom that was always practiced toward us. Naturally, every system of upbringing has its faults, but you can't abandon it suddenly to avoid its shortcomings. I think that exerting pressure on Mimo will only lead to estrangement."

Mimo pursued his chosen path in Naples and every weekend returned home to Rome. Though there were numerous Palestinian students and some revolutionists from Russia in Naples, he chose to room with a pious Catholic friend who saw to it that Mimo followed all the commandments of the Jewish faith. His orthodoxy went so far that once, on a train from Naples to

Rome, when he realized that the sun was setting and the Sabbath was about to begin, he left the train at a small town stop in the middle of the journey and spent the day there without informing his worried parents, since use of the telephone is forbidden on the Sabbath. Early in his student years he wrote an article on the problems and possibilities of Jewish agriculture in Palestine. He devoted his main attention to the question whether settlement in Palestine was possible without displacing the Arab inhabitants. Yes, one might fight for Jewish labor, he concluded, but one must also look for new approaches in agriculture and industry and the investment of money and effort in order not to displace people who had lived in the country for generations.

6

Following the Call

During the first year of Mussolini's rule, anti-Fascism was restricted to a handful of people of tender conscience, but the murder of Matteoti revealed the true face of the regime to many. Giacomo Matteoti, a scion of an aristocratic family from the north and a leader of the reformist Socialists who had dedicated his strength, wealth, and finally his life to the poor, was seized on June 10, 1924, at the door of his home, beaten, forced into a car, and taken to an unknown destination. His kidnapping was a direct consequence of the general election of April of that year, in which the Fascists received little more than half the votes, despite a modification of the election law and a campaign of pressure and violence. Mussolini hesitated whether to depend on the moderates in his party who had ties with the army and the royal house or to back the extremist elements who demanded severe measures against the opposition. In May Matteoti, who had been a Socialist representative in Parliament since 1919, delivered an impassionaed speech in which he demanded that the representatives of the majority who had been elected by the use of force, pressure, and money should be disqualified. The Fascists then decided to resort to stern measures, using a special group organized for terrorist purposes.

Following the public outcry against Matteoti's abduction, Mussolini promised to conduct an investigation and severely

punish the guilty. In August the broken body of Matteoti was
found on the outskirts of Rome, and for a while it seemed as if
this would spell the end of the Fascist regime. The opposition
left Parliament and organized a protest movement, on the Aventino, named after the hill where the ancient Roman rebels who
opposed the ruling patricians had gathered before they left the
city. The public was deeply shaken and Cesare Rossi, a leader of
the Fascist party whom Mussolini had chosen as a scapegoat in
the affair, began to reveal secrets in an attempt to save his skin.
When it was no longer possible to hush up the murder, a symbolic trial of those directly involved in the crime was staged. The
opposition limited itself to passive criticism and Mussolini prepared the ground for totalitarian rule.

Anti-Fascist groups that until now had functioned more or
less openly in the guise of cultural and political study groups
went underground. Fascist hoodlums smashed furniture and
burned documents in opposition centers. Surveillance of the
press was strengthened. Assaults on known anti-Fascist professors increased in number. Still, no anti-Semitism was apparent. It is true that when Jewish Socialists were abused, their
Jewish descent would sometimes be referred to contemptuously,
and in attacks on Freemasons the word Jew would at times be
added, but in doing so the Fascists only followed the old tradition of the Catholic church. On the other hand, the Fascist party
was still open to Jews, and between 1924 and 1928 nearly nine
hundred Jews joined it and a few even attained prominence in it.
Mussolini himself declared in an interview in 1924 with Angelo
Sacerdoti, chief rabbi of Rome, that "anti-Semitism is a malig-
nant growth which cannot arise in Italy."

Politically conscious young Jews had three alternatives: joining the Fascists, joining the extreme left in the belief that only a
radical solution could change the regime, or turning to Zionism
and to the Jewish tradition as outlets that were above the murky
tide. The search for such an outlet was best expressed at a
Jewish youth conference held for three days in November 1924
at Leghorn.

Nello Roselli was the chief spokesman of those who regarded
themselves as Italian above all. A scion of an ancient Florentine

family, refined and aristocratic in manner, he brought cheering tidings to the two hundred participants of the conference — unlike the other speakers, he promised to speak briefly. As a Jew who was neither a Sabbath observer nor a Zionist, who did not know Hebrew, was indifferent to tradition, and for whom Judaism was not a central issue but merely touched certain aspects of his life, he regarded his Jewishness as something hard to define, a kind of sense of responsibility to a specific community, a faith that regards other religions as forms of paganism. In his opinion* it was "precisely their Judaism that compelled Italian Jews to be more Italian than the Italians themselves."

Enzo, who was on the stage, his hands in constant motion, took up the challenge. He did not deny that Italian Jews were also Italian. Didn't they sit in an Italian hall speaking Italian? Weren't Italian poets and thinkers close to their hearts? "But the tone is Jewish, and the special way we stress our lives. How then could Nello Roselli divide himself into fragments, pasting a label 'Jewish' on one and labeling another 'Italian,' acting as a Jew on some occasions and as an Italian on others, while actually he will always remain but one, and therefore always a Jew." Here was an Italian version of the eternal argument going on in assimilating Jewish communities in the Diaspora, an argument that has not yet been concluded — and both Enzo and Nello were right, for it is impossible for the Diaspora Jew to keep his loyalty whole or undivided.

This was not the only confrontation at this conference, which was marked by much excitement and personal confessions and repentances, and also with a sense of elation at its conclusion. First generation Zionists, who regarded political Zionism as primarily intended for others, clashed with the second generation as represented by Pacifici for whom it was a personal matter. And here came Enzo, one of this generation, who was no longer satisfied with the moral commitments of Zionism, religious observance, and knowledge of Hebrew, who was repelled by fruitless discussions, demanded a radical departure along the lines of proletarianization, and made this demand to well-intentioned, middle-class people whose parents had done everything in their power to get away from the peddling and trade-in-rags of the ghetto. "Palestine does not need Jewish capitalists and managers," he declared, "but farmers and laborers, otherwise we will be driven out of Eretz Israel just as we were expelled from Spain and Poland. . . . An autonomous Hebrew culture is conceivable in Palestine only on the basis of a normal economy. We go to Palestine to live as free Jews, with all the joys and sorrows that this implies. In the terrible process of this transition we will no doubt have to suffer physical and spiritual losses, but we go there with the full realization that this sacrifice is unavoidable. . . . We pray that He who makes us pay for the sins of our fathers will show mercy to our children for the sake of what we do."

Ideologically there was nothing especially new in this speech, which derived from the thoughts of Borochov, Gordon, and Pacifici. But it struck a new note characteristic of Enzo — determination to transform words into deeds, and a conviction that one must act in accordance with one's principles. His public declaration: "I am going to Palestine," did not electrify the audience, and only one young man from Ferrara, Nino Hirsch, came up to Enzo at the end of his speech and told him, "I am going with you." He kept his word — ten years later. To underscore the irony of the situation, it was not proud and convinced pioneers who were the first to emigrate from Italy to Palestine, but a ghetto family, Spanioletto. Following a murder in which a member of this family was implicated, the entire family decided to flee the country, and because of the insistence of their daughter, Clara, who had belonged to the Avoda group that Enzo sponsored, the parents and their four children went to Palestine where they settled in Tel Aviv. At that time Beilinson too went to Palestine and became an agricultural laborer in Petach Tikvah.

At a large conference of Jewish students in Italy, held on the campus of the University of Florence during Passover of 1925, Enzo delivered a fiery oration against dual allegiance. His progress in Zionist polemics was demonstrated by his savage attack on the members of the Bund, an anti-Zionist organization to which some of the students from eastern Europe belonged. The Palestinian Jewish students, who could not stand the Italian

Jews because of their superpatriotism, nor the east European ones because of their Diaspora mentality, were ecstatic over Enzo's fluent Hebrew and his Zionist ardor and regarded him almost as one of themselves. He was elected president of the organization of Jewish students in Italy.

Enzo was outgoing, always ready to put his arm around people, to slap them on the back, to make each feel that he was the best friend. Ada, on the other hand, to the extent that she could mingle in Zionist circles — and there were many conflicts over this at home — was reserved and kept her distance. But there were times when passion was stronger than the great taboos of Italian society and the well-known puritanism of the Serenis in matters pertaining to sex; the permissive atmosphere among the Palestinians and their willingness to put their rented rooms — if only they had a separate entrance — at the disposal of the couple, helped matters. But their sexual relations were kept a deep secret from family and friends.

If Enzo continued his anti-Fascist activity, he did so in complete secrecy. Indeed, it was becoming increasingly difficult to combine Zionist with anti-Fascist activity without endangering the Zionist movement, which still enjoyed legal status even if not the sympathy of the authorities.

Yet despite his opposition to the Fascist regime and his enthusiasm for Zionism, it never occurred to Enzo to go to Palestine without first fulfilling his civic duty of serving the compulsory term of one year in the Italian army. A son of an old Roman family, he regarded this as a matter of honor. And possessing higher education, he was spared the more unpleasant aspects of the service and spent most of his time in Rome or its environs. In the army he first came in contact with the masses of ordinary Italian soldiers; he grew to love them and to value their readiness to make sacrifices for their native land. He passed with distinction an infantry officers' training school, and was commended for "unusual intelligence, discipline, and tactical talents." But even in army uniform made of heavy cloth, in riding breeches and leggings, Second Lieutenant Sereni still looked like Enzo — sloppy.

It was a pale and bewildered officer who came early in 1926

to Rivka Ashbel, one of the Palestinian students in Rome, to seek advice. The problem — Ada was pregnant. Only one familiar with conditions in Italy could understand the dimensions of the catastrophe. Here were a student of literature, daughter of a well-to-do, middle-class family, and a young man who still could not support a family. There were Ada's mother, who had opposed the friendship with Enzo all along, and the Sereni family with its respected status in the Jewish community and its moral principles. And above all, there were the plans for the move to Palestine, which the new situation made problematical. In the Palestine of that day no one was shocked if one of the Jewish pioneering girls appeared visibly pregnant before the rabbi for the wedding ceremony, or if a girl in this condition sent a friend to substitute for her at the wedding ceremony, or even if they skipped the rabbinical blessing altogether. Rivka Ashbel naturally advised Enzo not to get excited and to reveal the truth to his mother.

Alfonsa Sereni had just undergone surgery: the first member of the family to be informed was Enrico, in whom the news aroused a wellspring of emotions toward his brother. "It is true," he wrote, "that only now do I realize how much I loved him, this brother, more than one loves a brother — with almost paternal love. . . . It is possible that Enzo and Mimo will not be happy, but it is certain that they can only blame themselves for their suffering and congratulate themselves for the joys that come to them. All those who knew us always thought that we had a weakness for sentimentality, and this tendency might have been strengthened by the firm upbringing we received that did not allow emotional outpourings and we therefore sought outlets outside; Enzo and Mimo sought it in love, and I in the craving for love. I was therefore very close to him yesterday. Friend, brother. The new situation affects us both. Knowingly or not we both tend to be zealots. Let us say this word even if it sounds wrong."

After the first sense of shock, Alfonsa remained true to herself. Enzo was her son, it was she who had trained him to independence, and at stake was her grandchild about to be born.

She extended her protection also to Ada, who went to live in the house on Cavour Street. The marriage was registered without any accompanying ceremony, and the only snapshot of that time can be regarded as depicting the true situation. In this snapshot Enzo stands with lowered eyes, Ada in a shapeless skirt, an expression of bewilderment in her eyes, like that of a child who had been wronged. Enrico stands behind his mother; the tightly closed mouths of both speak of a firm decision to take full responsibility before the entire world. Not a single smile on any face, and the only flower was on the dress of Signora Ascarelli, who sat rigid and whose expression said clearly: "I knew it all along." It was a scandal that all Italian Jewry talked about. People of the older generation blamed the free ways of the young and Zionism, with its revolutionary ideas. Younger people reacted partly with admiration and partly with surprise, as if saying, "Well, it's fine to hold advanced ideas, but is it necessary to enact them in one's private life?"

When the child, a girl whom they named Chana, was born in July 1926, the sorrows of the unexpected pregnancy were forgotten. In the first family picture after the infant was born, Mama Alfonsa holds her in her arms, Enzo beams, and Ada, true to her rebellious spirit, had cut her long braid and appears with a short and daring haircut. According to plan, Enzo, Ada, and the baby were to leave for Palestine in a short time to join a kibbutz. They were to remain there for a year and a half or two until Mimo would arrive, having completed research in the writings of Marx and Lenin for his dissertation on cooperative economy. But at this point both Sereni parents intervened: if Enzo wanted to go to a primitive and backward country, very well, let him go, but they would not allow their grandchild to be taken to a land where, as everybody knew, malaria and all kinds of other diseases proliferated. It was therefore decided that Enzo and Ada should go by themselves to examine the situation, and send for their daughter only after the necessary arrangements had been made. The chief opponent of Enzo's emigration was Uncle Angelo, who tried to persuade his beloved nephew with the logical argument that there weren't many like him in Italian Jewry and that he was therefore needed in Italy more than in Zion. But Enzo was already beyond persuasion and would listen only to the call of Eretz Israel.

It was not the lure of adventure that beckoned him. "Those who seek adventure," he wrote, "should go to Africa to hunt lions, or to America to cut down the jungles. And those who seek honor should go to the great capitals of the world. Nor is there any ground to expect idyllic peace. Life in Palestine is hard, and one of these days there will be bloody clashes. But in Eretz Israel we want to shape a new kind of human cooperation, a form of life that implies not only new social and political arrangements but a new brotherhood between people, like that which found its first expression in the kibbutz."

In February 1927, the Serenis bade farewell to all their friends. In preparation for the new life Enzo adopted the Hebrew name Chaim, like that of the president of the Zionist Organization, and Mimo chose the name Uriel, out of reverence for Uriel Acosta, the rebellious philosopher and anathematized heretic who was persecuted for his views until his death.

Before their departure the Serenis arranged a modest farewell party for members of the family, friends from the university, and people from the Palestinian colony. They drank a little wine, extended best wishes, and went their way. On February 7, the family escorted Enzo and Ada to the train from Rome to Naples, and despite the smiles, the backslapping, and the handshakes it was a difficult moment for all. The next day they sailed on the *Italia* from Naples to Alexandria. A large group of Palestinians and pioneers sailed on that ship. They sang Hebrew songs and danced the hora on the deck despite the stormy winter sea, but the Serenis did not join them — Ada, because it was not in her nature, and Enzo, who did love to sing even though he was often flat, could not participate because he suffered from seasickness and spent most of the time on the way to the promised land horizontal.

After a brief stay in Egypt, sightseeing in Cairo and the inevitable tour of the pyramids, they took a night train on the line Kantara-Beirut, on which the women, with faces covered, sat in separate cars. At dawn the train passed the groves of tall

palms at El Arish and a while later it stopped at Ramleh where
the Serenis had to change to the Jerusalem-Jaffa line. It was a
typical oriental scene: tremendous confusion, deafening noise,
the passengers, mostly Arab, running, shoving, shouting, boarding the cars, coming out again, loading bundles and unloading
others, and the employees of the station, proud of their important office, blowing their whistles endlessly. Half an hour later,
when the train began moving in the direction of Jaffa, Ada and
Enzo noticed among the reddish dunes the green orange groves
and the white houses of the Jewish settlements. At nine o'clock
in the morning, on February 17, 1927, they reached their goal.

7

A Special Kind
of Pioneer

Tel Aviv was, at that time, a mere suburb pretending to be a city, with small white or gray houses of one or two stories, whose architectural style was a mixture of the requirements of modest living, the Jewish *shtetl* in eastern Europe, and the Jewish fantasies about the Orient where presumably spring is eternal. Tel Aviv's glories were the Rothschild Boulevard and the Herzliah gymnasium, which provided an urban atmosphere, but most of the narrow streets quickly petered out in sandy expanses where wooden barracks and other temporary and ugly structures popped up amid fenced-in empty lots. The charm of Tel Aviv consisted of its clear blue sky, signs in the Hebrew language, horse-drawn carriages usually driven by Arabs, plus a great variety of costumes: laborers in caps and heavy work shoes, ladies in hats and gloves and carrying handbags in imitation of big-city styles, swarthy Yemenites with their baskets of vegetables, and all kinds of merchants and peddlers who looked as if they had just left Lodz or Warsaw. From a distance Tel Aviv resembled any small Italian port city, and this strengthened Enzo's and Ada's determination to settle in a village. If they were to live in Palestine, then it must be in a rural village; if it were to be city life, then Rome was preferable.

Their first trip from the little railway station led to Moshe Beilinson, already living in Tel Aviv and, since 1925, an editor of *Davar*, the new labor daily headed by Berl Katznelson, a central figure in the labor movement in Palestine. After a bitter struggle with the mysteries of the Hebrew language, Beilinson could now write his own articles in this language without having to resort to a translator. Because of his writing and his close friendship with Berl, he belonged to the summit of the labor movement, though he remained reserved, silent, without roots in Jewish tradition, and hence an outsider. Beilinson then lived in one of the tallest buildings in the city, a house of three stories. After an excited meeting with the newcomers, he did the only thing that a man of the labor movement at that time could do when confronted with a difficult problem — he took Enzo to Berl Katznelson.

Berl was the conscience of the Jewish workers, and the Halutzim — the pioneers — flocked to him as Hasidim flock to their *rebbe*. He had already heard about the remarkable immigrant who was about to arrive — a Ph.D., a scholar, a writer, the son of Italy's court physician. The workers in Palestine, mostly from the small towns of eastern Europe, had never seen a Halutz — a pioneer — like him, and they were excited at the prospect. Berl, who was always on the lookout for new talent among the younger immigrants — the working population was very young and a man of forty like Berl was already regarded as a veteran — at once appreciated the intellectual power and education of this newcomer, sensed the sincerity of his convictions, and tried to spare him the main hardships that were the lot of the ordinary immigrant who felt forlorn in this land that consumed its dwellers, and forced them to wander from place to place in vain search for a day's work. He took an exceptional step and wrote a letter to Moshe Smilanski, a leader of the well-to-do orange growers, and begged him to employ Enzo on his orange plantation in Rehovot.

The Serenis left their belongings in the Barsky Hotel, a small, modest, homely establishment where the language used was mostly Yiddish, as in all the hotels in Tel Aviv in 1927. They took a squeaky bus to Rehovot to look over the situation, still laughing at their first experience in ordering a meal in the Holy Land. They had gone into a café and Ada ordered fish, but what the waiter brought her looked like a cutlet floating in a cold liquid. "Thank you," she had said to the waiter in German, "but I didn't order meat." The waiter was adamant, "This is fish, just as you ordered." Only then did these newcomers from Italy discover the secret of *gefilte* fish, the special delight of eastern European Jews.

The road, which was more or less paved as far as Rishon L'Zion, now dwindled away and the bus continued through deep sands, descending into ravines, then loudly chugging its way up again, a progress that astonished Ada but left the other passengers totally indifferent. The snorting bus finally came to rest in the center of Rehovot and Enzo and Ada went directly to Moshe Smilanski's house.

Erect of stature and sporting a little beard, Smilanski wore a light suit as was customary among the affluent of the land. A planter, a soldier, a politician, a writer, editor, and autocrat, he could not imagine how he could use this Italian Ph.D. in his orange grove, or in agriculture in general. But Enzo, for whom the productivity of the Jewish people, and his own in particular, was an inseparable part of his faith, insisted, and Smilanski consented to hire him as a laborer at ten *grush* a day, though the accepted wage for Jewish workers was seventeen *grush* a day. As a matter of fact, Smilanski did not need an additional laborer, and certainly not one who was a beginner with uncalloused hands. But what doesn't one do for Zion, out of respect for Berl, and to show consideration for an exceptional personality like Enzo?

This was a year of economic crisis and rampant unemployment in Palestine, which affected one-third of all day laborers. In the cities, especially, the mood was one of despair and depression. Skeletons of buildings, empty houses, stores, and lots with For Sale and For Rent signs were everywhere. The ships that left the country carried more people than those arriving.

A short time after their arrival Enzo went on a tour of the country in the company of a Belgian parliamentarian and Shlomo Zemach, one of the early pioneers who came before World War I. As they went through the Valley of Jezreel, Zemach told them of the hardships of the first pioneers who drained the swamps and begrudged themselves even the comforts provided for animals, such as permanent dwellings, but lived in tents. They passed the scattered houses of Afule, later to become the center of the Emek, and in the evening they reached Degania, mother of the kibbutzim, where everything was done in common — from work to bringing up children. Enzo was deeply impressed by the style of family living, which appeared to be calm and contented, by the happy and healthy children, by the Halutz whose skin had been bronzed by the hot sun, and who explained to the amazed Belgian that if a kibbutz showed profits at the end of the year it was a sign that it had too much land and should give part of it to other kibbutzim.

The following Saturday Enzo was in Jerusalem and saw the men in their fur hats and the women in their weird velvet dresses who streamed through the narrow alleys of the Old City to the Wailing Wall. He left his companions in order "to touch, for a moment, my people by myself, to get close to the wailing crowd praying and kissing the stones of the holy wall, all ours, barren, prophetic, tragic. . . . After my visit at the Wailing Wall I have almost completely forgotten the Emek and its heroic sons, and I am only sensitive to this past which I encountered today, that lives within me. . . ."

Once again Enzo and Ada went to Rehovot, this time for good. The porter who helped them carry their baggage from the station through the sands was not only Jewish but also spoke nine languages and was familiar with world literature and the Talmud. They had rented a room with kitchen privileges; toilet facilities were in the yard. Their landlady, an orthodox woman, was amazed at Ada's total ignorance — why, she couldn't even speak Yiddish. In connection with the preparations for Passover, she instructed Ada to make a bundle of all her cutlery and to dip it in boiling water, and she was deeply shocked when, after all the preparations had been made for the holiday, she discovered that Ada had a bottle of alcohol in her possession; Ada on her part could not understand why alcohol should not be kosher for Passover. Ada, who knew Greek, Latin, and Italian literature, could not cook; nevertheless she prepared all their meals, for an Italian beginner's meals are tastier than all the eastern European

menus provided by Rehovot where carrots were sweetened, cab-
bage was sweetened, the *gefilte* fish was sweetened, and the
borscht was sour-sweet.

And so one rainy morning Enzo showed up for work in Smilanski's orange grove, and the eyes of all the other workers —
Halutzim, Yemenites, and Arabs — were turned on him. After
a few hours of digging holes for new planting he was dripping
with sweat, his clothes were covered with dirt, and his hands
were blistered. But he persevered, driven by ambition to keep up
with the other laborers who advanced in line with a steady pace.
The overseer advised him to come next time in clothes more
suitable for an agricultural laborer, and Moshe Smilanski,
though he was a demanding employer, transferred his newly-
hired doctor of philosophy to lighter work pruning trees and
paired him off with another intellectual among his employees,
Yona Kossoy (later Kesseh) who, according to the prediction of
his employer, was also not destined to last long as a laborer.

The experienced workers showed Enzo how to handle a pruning hook and how to trim a tree and clean the trunk after pruning, and he, who applied himself to the theory and practice of
tree pruning with the same earnestness that he devoted to the
theories of Kant, shortly acquired the ways of an old-timer. It
required no effort on his part to acquire the unkempt appearance
of a farm laborer. He'd show up at work in a collarless shirt, in
dust-covered trousers held up by suspenders, muddy shoes, a
cap, and with a *turiya* (a broad-bladed, short-handled hoe for
heavy digging) on which hung a wicker basket. In the winter
the working day lasted from seven in the morning till four in the
afternoon with an hour's break for lunch. To keep his mind
occupied during the long hours of work he would recite aloud
cantos from the *Divine Comedy*, and poems by other Italian
poets. Yona Kossoy, his fellow worker, was much impressed,
especially after Enzo soon learned to recite Dante in Hebrew in
Jabotinsky's translation.

During the lunch hour the workers would settle down under a
tree and eat their lunch, usually consisting of bread and olives,
supplemented with oranges from the grove in which they
worked. Enzo, who was a master at fast eating, would finish first

and apply himself to reading *Corriere della Serra*, which he received regularly, or some book which he brought in his basket. Contrary to the custom practiced by most farmers in Rehovot who employed only Arabs, Smilanski clung to the principle of employing mixed Jewish and Arab labor to promote peaceful coexistence, and in his groves one could find eastern European Jews and Yemenites as well as Arabs and Bedouins from the vicinity. Sereni made friends with all of them, remembered personal Arab names, inquired about their way of living, visited them in their homes. At that time there was an open competition between the Arab and Jewish workers. As a matter of prestige, the latter tried to keep up with the Arabs, who were accustomed to hard physical labor, even if this made them spit blood and fall down exhausted in the evening when they returned home — as long as the national honor was upheld.

And so the Serenis had a livelihood of sorts, even though the ten *grush* a day that Enzo earned covered no more than his reading and postage expenses. The chief source of income came from Italy. And now they also had a home. They found a new place consisting of two small rooms and a kitchen, with the additional great technological advantage of an indoor shower and bathroom. This being the case, Ada left for Rome early in April to bring the child and Enzo's library, and returned in May. Visiting in Rome was like landing on another planet. There life proceeded as usual, people sat in cafés along the Corso, elegant ladies drove by in chauffeured cars, the streets were lit brightly, and the Serenis gathered daily at Aunt Ermalinda's on Cavour Street.

Rehovot of that day was an agricultural village thirty years old with a population of some two thousand, mostly people from Russia. It's true that its farmers were different from those of Petach Tikvah and the other Jewish villages that had been sponsored by Baron Rothschild — they were more independent, more Zionist, more open to the outside world, and among them were even a few men of letters and scholars. They also showed more regard for Jewish laborers; and yet with all that, Rehovot was but a remote outpost at the southern edge of Jewish settlement. Rehovot had a Peoples' House with arched windows where, on occasion, Golinkin's Hebrew Opera or some Yiddish theatrical troupe appeared. A lecture on the history of Palestine accompanied by slides was a great event, and a popular, and cheap, form of entertainment for workers was listening to speeches. The leaders of the labor movement provided such entertainment amply. They would talk for two or three hours at a time, and some, like Berl Katznelson, could hold an audience spellbound for five or six hours on end. Indeed, there were giants in those days.

Enzo would go out to work at six in the morning and return about five. He'd wash, eat, and take the child for a stroll in her carriage along the unpaved streets. In the evening he'd again go to the wooden barrack that served the workers as combination employment office, cultural center, labor council, and club. There, by the light of a kerosene lamp, the representative of the workers' council would try to distribute fairly the twenty or so jobs he had, after so much effort, secured for the next day among the one hundred who were unemployed. All about him was the noise of the crowd, arguing or just waiting and looking for moral support from their comrades. The Jewish workers of Rehovot traditionally belonged to the Hapoel Hatzair (Young Worker) party, which repudiated class struggle and stressed the creation of economic conditions in which it would be possible to establish a workers' society, and especially the return to manual labor. But some of the newcomers belonged to Ahdut Ha'avoda (Workers' Unity), a movement that aimed to unite all workers without regard to their ideological, philosophical, or religious attitudes, as long as they lived by the toil of their hands and wished to build the land on the basis of social justice. Though Ahdut Ha'avoda was not Marxist, it advocated socialism and international labor solidarity. Enzo did not belong to either of these two organizations but was considered an Ahdut Ha'avoda man, partly because in numerous practical matters he shared its views, and partly because his two closest friends, Berl and Beilinson, were spokesmen for this organization.

Enzo soon acquired status in the Rehovot Workers' Council. When the small collective group, Atid, decided to break up but refused to relinquish their communal dwelling and appealed to the Histadrut, the general federation of Jewish workers in the country, to adjudge the dispute (the Histadrut was then the highest judicial authority for the workers; who would bring a dispute before British judges? Only rich farmers, kulaks), Enzo served as chief judge, assisted by two other laborers, immigrants from Russia. With the prevailing lack of cultural events, even such an intra-group trial attracted a crowd. The barrack in which the trial was held was jammed with laborers from the entire neighborhood. The young chairman refused to put up with the turmoil that normally prevailed during hearings, which, in this instance, lasted all day Saturday. He demanded, and also obtained, complete silence. His own speech, full of pathos, earned him the respect of the audience, mostly bachelors under twenty, for whom Enzo, who was all of twenty-three years old, married, and the father of a child, was practically a middle-aged man.

All this time Ada would sit alone with the baby in the house on the outskirts, beyond which were darkness and the orange groves, and the only sounds were those of barking dogs and wailing jackals. She had no friends nor anyone to talk to during the day for not a soul in Rehovot knew Italian, only a very few knew German, and Ada herself understood Hebrew imperfectly. She had no mother to consult with — her own mother in Rome declared before Ada's and Enzo's friends that, of all the countries in the world, she hated Palestine most for having robbed her of her daughter. She had no one to console her for the hardships of life, where she had to cook on a spirit lamp, shop every day for lack of refrigeration or even ice, and wearily drag herself with a baby carriage through the sands. She felt lonely, sad, depressed, and was again pregnant.

And Enzo, too, needed friends even though he knew practically everyone in the village and everyone knew of him. He would therefore drop in on the group of Lithuanians who had set up a tent camp and a minute barrack to serve them as dining room and kitchen behind the synagogue. They were mostly children of lower-middle-class families who had undergone training in Europe and were competent workers, but since coming to the country in 1926 they had experienced unemployment, hunger, isolation, and ideological confusion. The secretariat of the kibbutz in Ein Harod sent Chaim Ben-Asher, one of its oldest members — three entire years in the country — to sustain the group of Lithuanians, to strengthen their morale, to help them join other groups like them in order to form a unit capable of settling on the land. Ben-Asher, a native of Russia and a man of broad education, was the only one capable of filling Enzo's need for intellectual dialogue. To him Enzo was a revelation: a teacher, a comrade, a dreamer who could also make plans. Together they explored the environs of Rehovot, reciting poetry which they knew by heart, arguing, and meanwhile also on the lookout for a piece of land suitable for the Lithuanians to settle on.

Enzo first thought in terms of establishing a community of Italians consisting of his friends and relatives. The plan envisaged a community of ten families, with room for additions. Ten families living as a commune, he thought, were the minimum essential to sustain the most basic necessities, such as a library, sanitary installations, medical and educational facilities — things that single workers could not aspire to. People in Italy were accustomed to such facilities on an unlimited scale and should not be denied them "so that within ten years we should not become disillusioned invalids." He visualized such a community as economically based on a dairy, an orange grove, vegetable growing, poultry raising, and fodder growing. He left the technical details for the arrival of his brother Emilio, who was an agricultural expert.

Enzo's plans shrank as it became more unlikely that the Sereni-Pontecorvo clan would come. Each of them had his own reasons, which were primarily based on their deep attachment to Italy. Most of them, like Enrico, had become active in anti-Fascist Socialist groups. Since none would come from Italy, Enzo was prepared to consider candidates for settlement who at least knew Italy and had some connections with it — Palestinians who had attended Italian universities. But even these did not hurry to join him.

Enzo scoured the country but could not find suitable candidates for his planned community. He wanted a communal group, and although he knew the dangers besetting a small commune, his experience in the country as laborer had convinced him that the life of an individual laborer leads to the subjugation of the wife and mother, and that it would be impossible to achieve anything in the country without a concentration of forces. Dr. Reichert, and his Palestinian friends, argued that it was necessary to purchase a tract of land as soon as possible because of the soaring land prices. Acquaintances suggested a tract, available at eleven pounds, to the west of Rehovot. In a letter to Mimo, Enzo described his plan for their future home in great detail. It was to have an indoor pool, a central dining room also suitable for meetings, a kitchen, seven living rooms surrounded by a veranda, a common children's room, and collective services. The main question was, would Mimo consent?

After finishing his studies in agriculture, Mimo had to serve his turn in the army, but even before he completed his service, Mimo proposed to his fiancée to hasten their marriage, and little Xenia gladly agreed. The wedding took place in a synagogue, a Jewish wedding with all the trimmings, since the bride became converted to Judaism.

But at that time Mimo was already involved with the underground Communist party, studied Russian, and his heart was no longer in the projects of his Zionist brother. But since he maintained that the crisis he was undergoing and the process of clarifying his basic principles had not yet been completed, Enzo hoped that by means of arguing with him in letters "our differences may be reconciled to the advantage of the Jewish people in Israel." Mimo promised: "I will come. Don't worry." But in long letters to Enzo he explained his rejection of philosophical idealism and Zionism, which his brother answered with letters equally long and even more philosophical.

Enzo pleaded with Mimo to examine his Marxist determinism as a scientist and philosopher, abstractly and without preconceptions in favor of the proletariat. But Mimo, in his orthodoxy, refused to listen to this appeal out of fear for the consequences. Enzo became angry. "You remind me," he wrote "of some repentant sinner who has perceived the truth and bordered it with hedges lest he give way to temptation. This is a fatal error for a man who knows that the truth requires constant reconquest, every day, every hour, and we must not, even for a moment, hedge it in against reexamination. The truth must be saved every second. The experience of fascism has convinced me of the superiority of free thought and criticism, and has uprooted within me any tendency to idealize inquisitions, be they for God's sake or for the sake of the proletariat."

The Jewish Question remained the chief bone of contention between the brothers. "It is the policy of the Third International to oppose Palestine as a solution to the Jewish Question, but now that I live here I am convinced that it can be solved only here," Enzo wrote. He opposed Jewish Communists in Russia as well as in Palestine because they rejected personal return to physical labor. And so far as their rejection of Jewish tradition was concerned, he declared: "What is the Jewish people without its history?" Of the objections to British imperialism he said: "Of course it would be better if there were no British Mandate over Palestine. But do you dare abandon one principle (Palestine) for the sake of another (struggle against British imperialism)? In any case, I can't do so. . . . Just as the Bolsheviks were justified in signing the Brest-Litovsk peace agreement with German imperialism in order not to lose everything, so is it worth while to tolerate the British Mandate, for at this time there exists no other political option outside the British that would assure the building of the country, and above all, Jewish immigration."

Enzo used to answer his brother's letters at night by the light of a kerosene lamp. After an exhausting day of work in the orange grove pruning trees, hoeing, or picking the fruit, though his brain was clear he sometimes could barely summon physical strength to write. Mimo had asked him categorically: "Are you a Socialist or a liberal?" "Both," Enzo replied. "Liberal for the sake of the freedom to criticize, to repudiate all postulates and assumptions, and for the sake of systematic skepticism, and a Socialist as a political being, but with restrictions that Marxists reject." He accepted socialism as the striving for logic and for a rational economy; he agreed that collective production was more efficient than the capitalist order, and regarded class struggle as an absolute plus, for only a deprived proletariat is interested in new social forms. In February 1928, he still hoped that Mimo would change his views about historical materialism in general and the Jewish Question in particular, because Mimo's arguments seemed to him to stem from psychological rather than ideological roots. Perhaps by the time Mimo completed his military service in October of that year, things would be clarified and "we will solve all these problems with the love that is more than fraternal that unites us, for you surely know how it pains me to write these things. I hope that time will heal this rent which almost broke our lives. . . ."

At first Enzo used to sign his letters to his brother with his adopted Hebrew name Chaim. Later this became Chaim or Enzo Sereni. The final letter was signed only Enzo Sereni. He began writing in the evening of February 6, 1928, broke off, and later added a brief announcement: "I must stop now. When I began this letter Ada was seized by labor pains. It is now 11:30. Ada gave birth to a girl."

The birth took place at home with the aid of the local midwife and everything went well. Enzo wanted to choose a name for the child that sounded attractive and also signified the brotherhood between Jews and Arabs. The name chosen was Hagar, a symbol of the relatedness between the sons of Abraham and Ishmael.

From the moment that he came to Palestine Enzo realized that Jewish-Arab relations would be one of the central problems of the country as it evolved, and he lost no time in seeking a solution to it in the area of personal relations and direct contact, convinced that bonds of friendship would arise out of Jews and Arabs knowing one another. When, in July 1927, the country experienced an earthquake that left more than one hundred people dead, he welcomed the positive aspects of the catastrophe — manifestations of mutual friendship. Jews contributed to relief funds, and the Arab inhabitants of Nablus, the center of the anti-Zionist movement, received bread from the Jewish city of Tel Aviv. "These are small things, but they might conceal the seeds of much greater ones," he wrote.

Yet with all this sympathy for the Arabs, he supported the principle of Jewish labor in the Jewish sector of the economy, convinced that it would be immoral to base Jewish settlement in the country on the labor of others. When, during the orange-picking season, a conflict broke out between the planters and the Jewish laborers in Petach Tikvah, because the former refused to hire Jewish workers even though there were one thousand unemployed in the town, Enzo's rage was directed at the planters who reaped high profits and showed no concern for the Jewish Question or Zionism, and were only motivated by their business interests and their hatred for the Jewish workers, those crazy idealists who worried about "productivization," return to the land, the need for a Jewish majority in the country, and so on. The workers set up picket lines; the planters appealed to the British authorities. Rioting ensued in which a dozen workers were injured and others were arrested.

A year had passed since the Serenis had come to Palestine and the hope for the establishment of a community of Serenis faded. Ada, especially, felt that it was beyond her strength to continue living as they did. In addition to the feeling of enslavement to her private household, there was the dissatisfaction that she and Enzo had to rely on financial assistance from their families in Italy. Enzo was capable of making many demands on her, but he did not dare demand that they join a kibbutz, as long as she did not volunteer to do so. Both of them knew what life in a kibbutz at that time meant in terms of living standards, housing, and diet. When they told Beilinson they were thinking of joining a kibbutz, he thought they were mad. His opposition to such a step stemmed from the concern that Ada, who had been brought up in a well-to-do home, would not be able to endure the conditions prevailing in a new kibbutz, and he feared that if they were to fail in this attempt, as he himself had failed, they might decide to leave not only the kibbutz but also the country.

The settlement group in Rehovot which Ada and Enzo were thinking of joining had a history that amply illustrated Beilinson's fears. Pioneers made of firmer clay than Ada, and more accustomed to physical labor than Enzo, broke under the conditions then prevailing in the country. This group of Lithuanians had been formed two years earlier; since then its members had fallen away one by one, with aching hearts but on the assumption that their situation as unattached laborers could not be worse. Only thirteen remained and it was clear that with such a meager number they could not long remain as an organized group unless they received reenforcements. To accomplish this, Hakibbutz Hameuchad (a nationwide federation of kibbutzim) combined them with a group of immigrants from Russia in nearby Nes Ziona, who also struggled to maintain their existence because further immigration from Russia was cut off and because of disappointment with conditions in the country, and with still another group from the northern Ukraine which was in a state of disarray for similar reasons. Only one thing was now lacking for this combined unit — a piece of land to settle on.

Land was then scarce for anyone who could not pay for it out of his own pocket. The policy of the Executive of the Zionist Organization was very different from the thinking of the pioneers who had felt that financial problems could somehow be overcome as long as there were visionaries devoted to the idea of establishing a collective settlement. "Efficiency," and "balanced budgets" were the slogans of the Zionist Organization, and the tendency was not to establish any new kibbutzim after an investigating commission of American experts had discovered that only one kibbutz out of all those previously established had balanced its budget.

Enzo fought against this trend toward "efficiency" with all his might, not merely because it was contrary to his character but because he was convinced that vision is more important than bookkeeping. "The moment we renounce the principle of labor as the foundation of our social structure for the sake of efficiency," he declared, "Zionism will no longer provide a solution to the Jewish Question." Formally the three principles of nationally owned land, self-labor, and the right of settlers to choose their own form of social organization in accordance with their principles were not renounced, but new kibbutz settlement was strictly limited, in part for the simple reason that the till of the Zionist Organization was empty.

At this time Ben-Asher learned that an unused tract of two hundred dunam (about 50 acres) four kilometers south of Rehovot was in the possession of the Jewish National Fund after the planned establishment of a regional tree nursery had been

abandoned for lack of funds. Enzo and he went to look over the
site in the midst of gravelly brush-covered hills, and both liked
it. A stony ridge looked out toward the sea on one side and
toward the hills of Judea on the other. This would be suitable as
an area for living quarters, and the remaining one hundred and
fifty dunam was arable land suitable for irrigation and the growing of field crops and fruit.

The Jewish National Fund agreed to set the land aside for
laborers from Rehovot, but left the decision as to its allotment to
the Settlement Department of the World Zionist Organization.
It declared that "we have had bad experience with kibbutzim
organized during the past four years in the villages. Most of
them disbanded and the investment was lost."

The group with whom Ada and Enzo associated faced a dilemma. Some were reluctant to occupy the land contrary to the
wishes of the Jewish settlement authorities; others wondered
whether their meager resources could sustain them if they were
to be denied outside support from the national funds. There
were those who dreaded the isolation of the spot and its distance
from Rehovot, and some feared that occupation of the land without approval would prejudice any chance of being assigned land
in the future. On March 24, 1928, a meeting was held, with the
participation of Enzo and a representative of Hakibbutz Hameuchad, which urged upon the doubters that they had sufficient
strength to settle this land even if it meant a struggle, and it was
decided to do so at the earliest opportunity. On the eve of Passover 1928, two dismantled barracks were loaded on wagons and
after a laborious trip they reached the goal. The freight was
unloaded and three round tents were set up, which from a distance looked like three white banners. When the entire group
came to visit their new home on the night of the Seder, all
doubts were forgotten, the dark mood lifted, and they danced a
hora and sang. Two guards were left on the spot to set up the
barracks which were to serve as barn and stable and, mainly, to
establish a presence.

A new troubling possibility arose. To the west of this spot
there stretched a fairly extensive area growing a pitiful crop of
barley that was the property of an Arab landowner from the

vicinity who, so it was said, was willing to sell it. When Enzo and Ben-Asher saw Smilanski stroll on this land in the company of foreign investors, they were disturbed, for should it fall into private hands, the last hope of escaping from the confines of a labor camp to real settlement would vanish.

Sensing the urgency of the situation, which provided an opportunity which would not occur again, Enzo turned to Joshua Hankin, a legendary figure who in his youth had vowed to dedicate his life to acquiring land in Palestine for the Jewish people and who was sixty-five years old. He learned that the Arab was willing to sell 950 dunam (about 250 acres) of his land at a price of nine pounds a dunam — 1,000 pounds down, 3,500 pounds within six months, and the balance within two years. When Hankin asked Enzo, whom he had never met before, on what basis he could depend on him to raise the money, Enzo replied: "Why, I am a father of two daughters."

On the occasion of the birth of her grandchild, Hagar, Mama Sereni came for a visit to Palestine, and following her came Professor Sereni bringing 500 pounds donated by Italian Jews, a first installment on the purchase of the land. Enzo and Ben-Asher went to visit Berl Katznelson, who gave his blessing to this mad plan that the Rehovot group — which actually meant Enzo — should undertake to raise 9,000 pounds for the purchase of the land, a sum equivalent to the income of a fair-sized kibbutz during ten years, and promised to persuade the Worker's Bank to underwrite 1,000 pounds, which the Sereni family undertook to raise from Italian Jews. Enzo took his mother to the sandy area covered with wild grass where lizards were the only living things visible, and proudly pointed out to her: "Here will be the central dining room, here the dwellings, here the farm buildings, and here the cultural center — a model collective settlement." Alfonsa understood and sympathized, just as she had understood when Enzo as a schoolboy, dreaming of a just division of wealth among the children, had collected the ten o'clock snacks the children in his class had brought from home and divided them equally between all the kids, rich and poor.

8

An Illegal Kibbutz

By the time all the necessary preparations had been made on the hill, the area had been cleared, and the stable, barn, and central barrack had been set up, there remained only thirty-five people in the group, including Enzo, Ada, and the two girls, out of the original eighty. On June 28, 1928, which was a Friday, all the members of the group who had outside employment went to work as usual so as not to lose a day's pay and only toward evening did they load their pathetically few possessions on two wagons and start the small caravan on its way. Once the tents had been set up and the wagons were unloaded, they all sat down in the provisional kitchen — Ada and the children had remained in the village for a few days — and emptied a bottle of wine in honor of the occasion; they felt, for the first time, that they had attained a certain permanence. It was a clear summer night and the stars appeared very close.

The first days were particularly difficult. Despite the hardships of the life of a hired laborer among hard-hearted landowners, a village was not something to be underestimated. It had running water and places of employment, stores, and a workers' cooperative restaurant, it provided the company of people and a sense of security. But here on the hilltop was isolation. Water was obtained through a thin pipe from some distance and it extended only part of the way. At that point tin cans

were filled and carted on donkeys. Where the pipe ended in the
middle of nowhere, a temporary laundry was set up consisting
of a tent, a table, and a washboard. One night tent, table, and
washboard vanished through the courtesy of some wandering
Bedouins.

Only a few members of the group worked nearby; the rest
had to spend two or three hours going to and from work, on the
lucky days when they had work. Whoever craved the luxury of a
shower at the end of a day's hard labor had to take the two large
tin cans and the donkey and go to the end of the pipeline, fill
them, come back, pour the water into a barrel that had been set
up over a hut made of reeds, and having filled the barrel, he
could enjoy a shower. Sanitation facilities were out in the open:
pits surrounded by a reed fence. And it was here that a few days
after pitching camp, Ada, daughter of a wealthy home, came
with her two daughters Chana and Hagar. Giving the children a
bath was a complicated project. When they contracted an eye
infection and had to be taken daily to the clinic of the Workers'
Sick Fund in Rehovot, Ada would carry one of them in her arms
some distance, then put her down on the ground, and go back to
bring the other, for it was out of the question to push a baby
carriage through the sands, and thus she would cover the entire
four kilometers.

The Serenis were the only family in the group and were assigned a kind of enclosure within one of the barracks, which also
contained the communal kitchen and dining room. The enclosure had two small rooms without floor or ceiling, only a tile
roof, and here were put up one large bed and two small ones.
The rest of the space was occupied by the belongings of other
members temporarily stored there. After these were finally removed, the larger of the two rooms now boasted a writing table
and Enzo's library, which had been brought from Italy, the wonder of all book lovers — volumes bound in old leather with gold
lettering, entire sets in Greek, Latin, and Italian, the classics,
philosophy, politics — the aroma of a remote world.

But for the time being they were squatters. The Settlement
Department of the Zionist Executive demanded of the Agricultural Center of the Histadrut, the Federation of Labor, to take

all steps to compel them to leave the land which they had occupied without permission for, "It is clear that if they do not obey our demand to get off the land, they will not receive, either now or in the future, any assistance from any Department of the Zionist Executive."

Some talked of leaving and a few actually left, full of doubts, disillusioned, and desperate. At a meeting of the group Ben-Asher analyzed the motives of some of the seven who left during the first five weeks. One left because he was new in the country. Three others he accused of hypocrisy, but the departure of the fifth he condemned as unforgivable because he had been a member of the group for two years and had dreamed together with the others of establishing a kibbutz on the land. Enzo agreed that leaving a kibbutz was sometimes tantamount to treason. In the midst of the meeting another member announced that he was leaving for ideological reasons — he no longer believed that the land of Israel would be built by unusual means. Life had demonstrated this. The idea of a people's Zionism financed by national funds conflicted with reality. The Jewish bourgeoisie had now come to life. Capitalism was expanding in the country and there was no room for collectives. The idea of the kibbutz appeared on the scene too soon and had proved to be a utopia like any other. For the past six months, he declared, he had no longer been a Zionist and his participation in the Zionist enterprise was a fraud. He rose and left.

In the fall there was little work, a dead season. Everyone waited for the rains, and meanwhile the deficit grew. But Enzo felt that the main problem was recruiting additional people for the kibbutz. With that achieved, all other problems would be resolved. Gradually he left his regular employment at Smilanski's orange groves, the dream of every hired laborer, and devoted his time to the necessary arrangements within the kibbutz, especially its nonexistent finances. The duties of kibbutz treasurer, secretary, and outside contact man were but poorly defined and at times he fulfilled all three of them, which consisted largely of but one preoccupation — obtaining means, credit, and food to remain in existence. Since the difference between starvation and feeling fed rested on bread, the most urgent economic enterprise was setting up a bakery. He obtained a loan of fifty pounds from the Workers' Bank and bought flour on credit. The oven was acquired from British military surplus and the bakery was set up in the barrack that for a time had served as stable. The winter vegetable garden began to produce. And while the members of the group worked in the groves they could feed on oranges. In this way it should be possible to survive the winter somehow.

All of Jewish Palestine depended on a regular turnover of immigrants. Each new wave of immigration announced an improvement in the economic condition of those who had come before, and it was also essential for the continued existence of the tens of kibbutzim scattered throughout the country. Newcomers were needed to strengthen settlement units that had shrunk as a result of sickness, emigration, death, and above all, as a consequence of the abandonment of the ranks of labor. When the first new pioneers from Germany arrived in October 1928, after an interval of two years when none had come, Ben-Ahser and Enzo wanted these young people who were cultured, educated, and had undergone a period of difficult training with German farmers near Hameln.

Few newcomers from Germany had been successfully integrated into the collective settlements of the pioneers who came from eastern Europe, and their vain attempts to do so had left a bitter taste with both sides. Products of German culture, they had a different conception of the nature of the Jewish renaissance (and immigrants from Germany to Palestine in the twenties came for ideological reasons only) and were imbued with ideas about leading a pure and ideal form of life. They differed from the pioneers who came from Russia and other eastern European countries who were more deeply rooted in Jewish life, more folksy, with stronger bonds to the international labor movement. Many were therefore convinced that the German pioneers were not fitted to meet the requirements of colonizing pioneering, and that it was best if they engaged in professional pursuits after the eastern immigrants had prepared the ground for them.

But Enzo's presence in the Rehovot collective was one of the chief motivations for the group of Germans in joining it. Here he was, an intellectual, a westerner, a philosopher — he would probably understand their complexities. In his first meeting with them he described to them without embellishments the economic woes of the group, but these newcomers, who had been in training two years with German farmers, working ten and twelve hours a day in snow and frost and often sleeping in stables together with the horses, or in attics, were not frightened off by the sight of torn tents, a dining room without a floor where mice ran about among the rafters and spiders crawled on the walls, and they were least of all intimidated by debts.

The collective learned to depend increasingly on Sereni's financial wizardry. He was authorized to find means to dig a well and to buy irrigation pipes. When the supply of food in the kitchen ran out completely, he was the savior at the last moment. Everyone felt confident that he would somehow take care of things. He wheeled and dealed, he borrowed wherever he could, he promised to pay and obtained extensions on loans, and whenever his Italian charm did not suffice, he was aided by the fact that Berl Katznelson was backing him — a fact that, in that day, opened doors, hearts, and cash registers.

Enzo obtained goods on credit by means of smiles, wiles, and threats, using those various forms of extortion as the situation called for. With the fat woman from the neighboring Arab village of Zarnuga who supplied the collective with eggs, he would chat and flirt and embrace her until she forgot all about payment, and when her husband later came to collect it, he would take him into the communal kitchen and offer him one of the girls in payment, since he didn't have other means at the moment. To the Arab from Ramleh who used to sell them meat for the Sabbath, a courteous and gentle person, he would declare sadly that he knew that the debt was already too high, and so they had no other choice than forgo eating meat, and the kindly meat dealer would plead with him to continue eating meat and he would wait for his payment. The Yemenite vegetable dealer from Rehovot who pleaded to be paid because he had five children to support would beat a hasty retreat when Enzo threatened to commit suicide if forced to the wall (and then, troubled by

conscience, he would find some way to pay him before others).
In the warehouses of the workers' consumer cooperative,
Hamashbir, he would firmly insist on labor solidarity.

But the very members of his kibbutz, who depended on Enzo
to get them out of their financial difficulties by means of his
daring, harbored doubts about him for the same reason — he
was not sufficiently cool and reasonable, he was too different,
Italian. Couples paired off in the kibbutz and they would steal
together into a tent — a substitute for formal marriage —
when no one was around, yet Enzo would declaim at the top of
his lungs about love and the need to set up families. The delicate
girls who had been brought up on Pushkin and Dostoevski
would wince, but would forgive him because of what they regarded as his southern temperament. They would lower their
eyes when they saw him go to the shower in his shorts, or
loosely wrapped in a towel, a symbolic garment, which did not
meantime prevent him from stopping and indulging in discussions of economic or social topics. His faithful adherents found
his mad ideas irresistible, and later could not account for what
made them follow him.

Only by the spring of 1929 did the acquisition of the one
thousand dunam become a reality and the prospect of actually
settling on the land radically changed the mood on the hill.
Plans blossomed: an orange grove, a vineyard, a dairy, poultry — what couldn't one do with one thousand dunam (about
250 acres)? Enzo thought they should start with the acquisition
of cows, to have their own milk supply, and also suggested that
they replace the horses with a tractor, for horses eat even when
they don't work. At a membership meeting on June 20, he noted
enthusiastically that the employment situation in Rehovot and
the condition of their own land now made it possible to absorb
many newcomers, perhaps even double the number of the kibbutz, which stood at sixty.

In the course of a discussion about the rights of the individual
within the kibbutz, Enzo introduced a revolutionary proposal:
that instead of the existing distribution of minor supplies to the
members, each should receive a specific sum, which he could
spend as he wished. This aroused a storm: "Does not the kibbutz

aim at real instead of merely formal equality? From everyone
according to his abilities and strength, and to everyone according to his needs? Where would this pursuit of freedom lead
to?" Enzo declared that all the talk about collective thinking and
culture was childish. The basic problem in a kibbutz was economic. Make better economic arrangements in the kibbutz and
everything else will follow. "I have not yet seen people eating
well in a kibbutz. There must be a large kitchen where every
member can receive his food within the framework of a definite
menu, according to his taste. Of course we have to bear in mind
existing circumstances and that not all needs can be fulfilled.
We must remember that we live as laborers. But within the
present budgetary allowance, say eight *grush* a day for food, the
kitchen can function autonomously and, without exceeding this
sum, provide the members with food items they like. For one can
eat poorly for a year, or two, or even ten years, but not forever."
Other members objected and said: We must remember that
when one builds a kibbutz, one cannot think of the present moment but only of the future. One must also learn to adapt to not
eating well. Consider the Jewish intellectuals in the Diaspora
who go about hungry but do not forgo theater performances.
True, someone also pointed out, this is individualism, but in a
kibbutz we create collective attitudes. If we follow Sereni, we
will have neither the kind of kitchen he recommends nor will we
build a collective society.

But Enzo insisted: We need permanent workers in the
kitchen, just as in other fields of work. The constant changes in
the kitchen personnel stem from the incorrect attitudes of the
women comrades, and the women workers' movement is to
blame for this. Why is it all right to work for years taking care
of cows or chickens or plants, but forbidden to take care of
people's needs in the kitchen? The efforts of the numerous
women comrades who have specialized in dairy work and vegetable growing do not make up for the tremendous loss caused by
the lack of well-organized kitchens in the kibbutzim.

But here Enzo touched on a most sensitive nerve of the
women's movement which, out of devotion to the ideals of world
socialism, aimed to liberate women from the chains of the

kitchen and children's room so that they could take their place
alongside the men in field and factory. "Why is it that we understand the shoemaker who comes to Palestine in order to engage
in agriculture, but refuse to understand the woman?" one woman
asked. "Even those who criticize the women would not want to
restrict themselves to kitchen work solely." Enzo understood the
hint, and when the disorganization in the kitchen continued, he
volunteered to work there and to introduce some order. Some
supported him, knowing that for a time now he had been anxious to return to physical labor, and some in the hope that he
would succeed in obtaining supplies even when there was no
money. But others objected, not against the introduction of a
man into the kitchen, but because he didn't know the first thing
about the work. The meeting finally decided against Enzo's
being assigned to the kitchen. But when one day he received a
box of genuine Italian macaroni, he informed the cook on duty
late in the evening, gave her instructions how to prepare it, then
rang the bell to wake those who were already asleep and distributed his treasure to all who showed up — it came to two strands
of macaroni per person.

It was decided — or, more correctly, Enzo decided — that he
should go to Italy to try to raise the money for the land, but just
before he left the bloody riots of 1929 broke out and changed
the entire complexion of affairs in Palestine. The immediate
cause of the outbreak centered in a dispute about the Wailing
Wall, which was the property of the Moslem Council and where
Jews had only the right to congregate to pray but were not
allowed to put up benches or a partition to separate men and
women or to blow the *shofar*, prohibitions that in the past had
led to a number of incidents. When the Revisionist organization,
Brith Trumpeldor, staged a demonstration at the Wall on the
Ninth Day of Ab, the Arabs staged a counterdemonstration the
following day and Arab Jerusalem buzzed with rumors about
Jewish plots to seize Islamic holy places. On Friday, August 23,
Arab worshipers were incited at the Mosque of Aksa to attack
the Jewish Quarter, and for the nine days that followed the
country was thrown into bloody turmoil.

This was not a spontaneous outburst, but a planned campaign

of violence that surprised the Jewish community by its scope and severity. It amounted to an attempt against its very existence, and the shock was tremendous, both because it came after eight years of relative quiet, and also because the cruelest slaughter occurred in Hebron and Safed, two ancient communities where the Jews relied on bonds with their Arab neighbors that had lasted for generations. The Arab attacks spread throughout the land. Ramat Rachel was burned to the ground. The inhabitants of Old Motza were slaughtered. Hartuv, Kfar Uriah, Be'er Tuviah, and Hulda were destroyed. And by the time the British decided to act, 108 Jews had been killed and 190 wounded.

The people of Sereni's commune were surrounded by Arab villages on three sides, and there was no opportunity to defend the place, which had not a single stone structure. On instructions from Haganah — the Jewish defense organization — the settlement was evacuated. The men went to an adjoining kibbutz where the dining room, barricaded with a window-high wall of sacks of sand, served as a security post. The women were brought to Rehovot. Ada and the two children found refuge in Smilanski's house. Enzo was in command of a defense post — a pit in an orange grove manned by six persons, three on duty and three off, one of them armed with a rifle and the rest with metal bars. Contrary to the feeling of the others in the defense post who were bitter over the Arabs' treachery, Enzo argued that the climate of hostility would change and ways would be found to come to an understanding with them. During the day some of the members would go up to the hill to work and to guard the unoccupied settlement, but at night they would return to the adjoining kibbutz where they had taken refuge.

The Arab bands did not get to the hill and two weeks later it was reoccupied by the kibbutz, now richer by fifteen new members from Lithuania, who had reached the country in the very midst of the turmoil, and poorer by six tents, which had been stolen. The rioting and murders and destruction were traumatic for the Jewish community in the country, but on a material level there were immediate advantages. The planters in the Jewish villages now preferred to hire Jewish labor, and there was much employment in Rehovot.

After life on the hill had returned to normal, Enzo finally left for Italy on September 24. For six weeks he went from city to city soliciting funds as a loan. He mobilized the aid of friends, acquaintances, and relatives. And he did not disappoint.

The house on Cavour Street was still the center of the Serenis. Leah carried on the family tradition, and after she was married the young couple took up their residence there. Mimo, who lived in Naples, became the father of a daughter, and the entire clan breathed more easily for, true to his new Marxist faith, he had announced in advance that if the child were to be a boy he would not have him circumcised, and the Serenis trembled at the prospect. Never had such a thing happened in their dynasty for two thousand years. Mimo and his wife named the child Leah Ottobrina, in honor of the Russian October Revolution, and when Mimo went to get the birth certificate, the clerk in the registration office in Naples warmly shook his hand and praised him for immortalizing in his daughter's name the date of the Fascist march on Rome.

Enrico, too, finally got married and his chosen one again aroused in Enzo a spark of hope that, despite all, the Serenis might yet be united in the land of Israel. Enrico's wife, Dvora, a third generation Palestinian and the granddaughter of the Ashkenazi rabbi of Jerusalem, was studying botany in Rome at the time she became acquainted with the Serenis. Enrico met her at Mimo's wedding, and when he showed an interest in her, Mimo warned him: "She is not for you. She is a fanatical Zionist." But Enrico went his own way and presently he offered her the post of his assistant. When she agreed to move to Naples, he noted in his diary, "She consents to marry me."

One evening, as they were engaged in their work late, Dvora humorously suggested to the revered professor, who seemed to have no time for anything except his work, that he seek a wife by means of an ad in the papers, and he responded with a marriage proposal. In honor of the event they climbed to the top of Mt. Vesuvius that same night and Dvora named three conditions for their marriage: that their sons be circumcised, that they have Hebrew names and speak Hebrew, and more conditionally, that in time they settle in Palestine. Papa and Mama Sereni received their new daughter-in-law with open arms, and the Jewish matrons of Rome had another opportunity to gossip. Here was further proof of the eccentricity of all the Serenis. Whoever heard of a man taking a wife of whom no one knew anything, one with no dowry, and without a preceding engagement period? Enzo, it is true, visited the family of his in-laws-to-be in Tel Aviv and his report was reassuring — the new member of the family stemmed from no ordinary class, but was of genuine Jewish aristocracy. But the Roman ladies were not appeased: "What's the rush?" they wondered. Enrico wanted to have the wedding at once so that he could take his wife with him to a scientific congress in the United States which he was about to attend, and like a true Socialist believing in liberty, fraternity, and equality he set the wedding day for July 14, Bastille Day. The wedding was held in Rome's large synagogue, and the rabbi dwelt discursively on the nineteenth-century German Socialist Moses Hess, who had urged the establishment of a Jewish state in Palestine in his *Rome and Jerusalem*. The wedding photo shows Papa and Mama Sereni beaming with delight — all four of their children had now established families, and the continuity of the dynasty had been assured.

9

A Treasurer
without Money

The bloody events reechoed throughout the world. Italy demanded that England surrender her mandate over Palestine and entrust it to a Catholic power, either France or Italy. The Jewish community in Palestine applied itself to reorganizing its forces, since England appeared too weak or unwilling to protect Jewish lives. If the entire Jewish settlement work was not destroyed it was mainly due to Jewish self-defense. It was therefore essential to strengthen this defense, which hitherto had been the task of the Histadrut alone, and to establish it on a broad basis together with other groups within the country. Despite the lack of trust between workers and bourgeois elements, and between left and right, an agreement was reached to establish a centralized defense command. The general conclusion was that more attention should be paid to security needs, the construction of strong stone structures in the settlements, better telephone communications, and setting up security fences.

Enzo shared the prevailing feeling of bitterness against the British. As a first security measure he urged the consolidation of Jewish settlements into contiguous blocks. "From now on we must consider the strategic factor in our settlement work as a matter of life and death," he wrote after he returned to Palestine early in November. The condition of his own kibbutz was, in fact, pitiful. The central barrack went up in flames shortly after the rioting, under unexplained circumstances, and only the tent camp remained, surrounded by Arab villages. It was essential to build at least one stone structure. The housing situation was shocking. All the members, Ada and Enzo included, now lived in tents, some of which were torn, that were not sufficient to provide for the new immigrants. A third inmate, for some reason dubbed a "primus," was added to each tent housing a couple. Ben-Asher was the "primus" in the Serenis' tent, and the hours of their sleep were diminished, for when Ben-Asher started a discussion there was no end to it. Outside the wind howled, and in the darkness of the night Enzo and Ben-Asher discussed the hereafter, the immortality of the soul, and the nature of God.

Finally they received an allotment of 560 pounds from relief funds raised abroad, and an additional 50 pounds for fencing in the camp, on condition that they move it to a neighboring hill that was higher and more extensive and overlooked the entire vicinity.

Ever since its establishment the group was known as the Rehovot unit of the Kibbutz Meuchad — a federation of kibbutzim. Now that they received de facto recognition from the national institutions, it was time to provide it with a permanent name, and, on February 15, 1930, after the general meeting had discussed routine matters of investment and construction, Sereni, in his capacity of secretary, announced that it was necessary to choose a permanent name for their collective. Several suggestions were made, and it was decided that the name be chosen by a majority vote of those present. Of the seventy-eight members who were present, forty-four voted in favor of Givat Brenner — Brenner Hill — in honor of Joseph Chaim Brenner, the author who best articulated what was in their hearts — despair, disillusionment, along with a belief in the return to Zion. Enzo proclaimed solemnly: "The name of our settlement is Givat Brenner." Everybody rose and appropriately welcomed the new name — with the singing of the "Internationale": "Arise, ye prisoners of starvation, arise, ye wretched of the earth. . . ."

Jewish-Arab relations, which for years had been considered of secondary interest compared with the main task — building the Jewish national home in Palestine — acquired a new signifi-

cance after the riots, but Enzo remained faithful to his ideas on
the subject. "We have always thought, and after the riots especially, that the welfare of the entire population of the country
was based on intensified economic development that is vital for
democratic political development. The Arab peasants and the
Jewish immigrants are alike interested in an agrarian democracy
based on intensive agriculture, which can be achieved only with
the investment of much capital, and the only source of such
capital is the Jewish people. Accelerated Jewish settlement in
the country therefore implies also accelerated Arab development.
. . . Let us say this once and for all, the Jewish and the Arab
workers have been joined forever. Together we will rise, together we will deteriorate. The Jewish worker will not have an
eight-hour day if the Arab workers toil ten and twelve hours a
day. The Jewish worker has no future in the villages without a
distinct improvement in the working and living conditions of
the Arab worker, and this will not come about without the
organization of the Arab workers who are now used as a whip
against the Jews."

His opposition to Vladimir Jabotinsky, the leader of the Zionist Revisionists, whom Enzo met while still in Rome and whose
energy and intelligence he admired, stemmed not only from
Jabotinsky's conflict with the labor movement, but also from a
certain personal, Italian allergy to "exaggerated self-assurance,
theatrical poses, bombastic formulations, militaristic training,
and the advocacy of physical violence." One duce was enough for
him.

Within the kibbutz Enzo insisted on individual freedom for
himself and for others, in matters of opinion, conduct, and
needs. He defended the right of the individual to be different.
When a member of the kibbutz petitioned the general meeting
for a week's leave because he needed dental care and a friend of
his in Tel Aviv was willing to do the work gratis, a number of
members opposed his request on the ground that personal friendship does not justify special privileges. And what if some other
member will make friends with an employer? it was asked. To
this Enzo replied that equality does not mean equality in tooth-
aches, and the member was granted his leave. But when he pro-

posed that the acceptance of new members into the kibbutz
should be done by means of secret ballot, since open voting leads
to hypocrisy, causes disputes, and is therefore not truly a free
vote, the meeting voted against him in no uncertain terms.

His insistence on freedom for the individual within the collective was the chief motive for Enzo's consistent advocacy of the
building of large kibbutzim that grow and absorb new members.
The sectarian, closed, and suffocating atmosphere prevailing in
small, "organic" kibbutzim such as were advocated by Hashomer
Hatzair, with their public confessions and constant examination
of what goes on within the members' souls shocked him. "The
morbid atmosphere of intimacy suffocates the individual instead
of liberating him; it places him under the inquisitorial supervision of the 'community,' which is basically not public opinion
but the opinions of a few, of the leaders. Such an atmosphere
produces results exactly opposite to those intended. If a kibbutz
does not remain open in the broadest sense of the word, not only
to new members but also to new ideas and habits, it is threatened
with petrification."

During the early days of the kibbutz, Enzo and Ada were the
only married couple within a community of singles, and, true to
the tradition of Italian Jewry, he was displeased and wished to
see the kibbutz consist of families with many children. In this
regard he was in the vanguard, for Ada was again pregnant. He
opposed with all his might those kibbutzim that encouraged
birth control for economic reasons. Why was the kibbutz established, he argued, if not for the future generations? For the same
reason he disapproved of the free sex without family obligations
that was then prevalent among the pioneers, especially those
from Germany. "The family cell is not only the basic unit of
present society, but is the only one that will survive, for it is
founded on a deep need. It is possible to do away with a clan,
with municipal organization, with the state, and supplant them
with other forms, but not with family life based on monogamy,
unless one wishes to destroy one of the greatest achievements of
human society. It is true that the economic collectivism of the
kibbutz does away with the bourgeois family which is based on
economic unity, but one must not undermine the monogamous

basis of the family if one does not wish to do away with love altogether. . . . A group that is founded on a high degree of intimacy does not tolerate the existence of other, deeper bonds, and it is no accident that dreams of intimate community arise and prosper in youth movements as a substitute for and sublimation of sex, and vanish as soon as normal sexual development occurs."

In March 1930, Ada and Enzo's third child, a son, was born, and they named him Daniel.

Ada seldom spoke up at the kibbutz meetings, and then only about practical matters that touched her directly, such as the problems of the clothing supply room where she worked after a brief period as an orange picker. It was tiring and thankless work, mainly because of the constant shortages. Her predecessor, true to the accepted policy in kibbutzim, would economize as much as possible and purchase as much as possible, buying the cheapest work clothes, which fell apart after a few launderings. When the members had no work clothes it was decided to buy cloth and hire a tailor to make the required thirty-two pairs of work pants. The tailor chosen undertook to do the work for the lowest price. The only trouble was that he did not know how to cut the trousers and all thirty-two pairs were unusable. In desperation, attempts were made to avoid a total loss by the addition of patches to the seats, but all in all it was a nightmare. When, contrary to her wish, Ada was elected to take charge of the kibbutz clothing supply, she acted in accordance with the principle that poor people cannot afford to buy cheap goods, and when the time came to replenish the supply of work clothes, she purchased the best and most expensive English cloth available. Members of the kibbutz were outraged. Complaints were heard from all sides, as well as resentment against her aristocratic manner. But the pants lasted a long time.

The problem that weighed most heavily on the kibbutz was that of equality. The young women who came from Germany brought with them much more attractive clothing than the girls from Lithuania had, and there was envy all around. Ada made a revolutionary suggestion, that the kibbutz should introduce an individual allotment for clothes and everyone should decide individually how to spend it. Naturally, the kibbutz rejected this suggestion, which smacked of private property.

As against Ada's restrained behavior, courtesy, and inner calm, Enzo was regarded by the members as a bit of a wild man. He couldn't sit still in the dining hall and wandered among the tables, helping himself to food on others' plates. Meeting some members of the kibbutz in town he would invite them to join him in an ice cream bar, then vanish when time came to pay. In matters of cleanliness he was also an exception. The abandonment of conventions and the harsh physical conditions caused most pioneers, even those from Germany, to disregard orderliness and sanitary habits, contrary to the middle-class upbringing at their homes in Europe. When the kibbutz discussed the cultural situation in March 1930, Enzo opened the discussion with two subjects that particularly annoyed him: the unsanitary condition of the sanitary establishments and the state of the library — the lack of respect for books, which frequently were damaged or disappeared. Cultural life in the kibbutz, he declared, expresses itself not only in study circles and attendance at lectures. The passion for Ping-Pong instead of reading on rainy days when one didn't go out to work, the meager attendance at general meetings, and the lack of interest in what went on about one were indicators of the state of culture within the kibbutz. The past year had been successful both in terms of absorbing new members and no defections, yet during the present year especially there had been a sharp decline in the cultural level.

The kibbutz was in a state of constant flux. Candidates for membership were accepted and others were rejected. Some were absorbed and others not. During the early days of Givat Brenner's existence, the status of candidacy for membership lasted three months. Later it was argued that this was too short a period to get to know a person well and the term was extended to five months. In most cases the discussion on whether or not to accept a new member was conducted openly and in the presence of the candidate, and this was not always an inspiring sight. All the shortcomings, weaknesses, and personal problems of the candidate were revealed publicly. It was therefore not surprising that on one such occasion the candidate got up in the middle of the discussion and announced that he was leaving the kibbutz since he now realized that some people in it did not approve of him. Against the acceptance of another candidate it was argued that he was chronically ill and the kibbutz was not in a condition to undertake such a burden. But for Enzo such considerations were irrelevant. "The question of accepting chronically ill candidates for membership," he declared, "is tied up with the entire idea of the kibbutz. . . . If a person wants to live in our society, there should be a place for him in our midst even if he is ill." In the matter of discussing personal traits of candidates, which were at times influenced by personal prejudices, Enzo's stand was clear: "The kibbutz strives to be a mass movement and not a place for the elect. It is not necessary to delve too much in psychology. I do not want to know the spiritual traits of a member, but only his actions. We do not wish to create a society where only the elite can live."

This conception of a constantly growing kibbutz also produced negative phenomena on a day-to-day level, such as disorder and improvised administration, and hindered both social and economic consolidation. It also failed to provide newcomers with the sense of moral support and belonging that they needed, especially immediately after their arrival in the country. But Enzo feared a stratified society. "Though it may appear cruel," he said, "the secret of the open kibbutz lies precisely in that it does not permit the creation of unquestioned traditions. Its eternal youthfulness lies in that it does not permit the creation of a rigid style of life. It is not only ready to absorb more people but is also wide open to new trends and currents which each new stream of immigrants brings with itself."

Those who did not agree with thinking of this kind, or could not adapt themselves to the constant changes, left the kibbutz; but even among those who stayed, many longed for the more familiar and known crystallized community life. This was especially true among the members who came from Germany. In the summer of 1930, ten of them left the kibbutz at one time, and many felt that the cause of their departure was the attempt of Givat Brenner to fuse emigrants from Germany with those from Lithuania. Most of the Lithuanians believed in the fusion of the emigrants from the two countries, but some of them suspected the Germans of trying to make Givat Brenner the center for all emigrants from Germany, and perhaps even to displace the Lithuanians. Others complained about the patronizing attitudes of the Germans, who boasted of their western culture and love of art and music. At work the relations between the two groups were more or less satisfactory, but in free hours life proceeded on two separate levels. This separation even invaded the central dining room, with the Germans sitting on one side and the Lithuanians on the other, while Enzo dashed between the two, proclaiming he was not only neither of the East nor the West but not even a Roman. Years of growing pains passed before the true fusion of the two groups began with the first intermarriages.

Culturally Enzo was closer to the Germans, but in his heart he preferred the Lithuanians because of their attitude toward work, their being at home in Jewish traditions, their realistic approach to things, and their knowledge of Hebrew. His own command of Hebrew was far from perfect. Rich, colorful, and full of literary allusions as his Italian was, his Hebrew was meager and strictly matter-of-fact. This no doubt accounted for his zeal for the language. He insisted that the kindergarten teachers and the women working in the children's home be able to speak good Hebrew. Again and again he stressed that in Palestine one must speak Hebrew even if, for a time, this narrowed one's cultural horizons. He himself conquered the difficulties presented by Hebrew literature. Since ordinarily there was little time for reading, he would do it whenever and wherever possible — in the dining room, riding on a bus, before the opening of meetings, in the midst of any turmoil — partly because he loved reading and partly in order to demonstrate to himself and others that living in a kibbutz did not mean that one had to deteriorate culturally.

In his occasional entries as secretary of Givat Brenner — mostly on stationery bearing the name of Dr. Sereni, Court Physician in Rome — Enzo Sereni, Ph.D. and sometime promising student among Italy's young scholars, wrote, with not a few Hebrew spelling errors, about seventy-three pairs of sandals and

twenty-seven pairs of work shoes that were made in the kibbutz
shoe shop, of the completion of the two-story stone building that
cost 220 pounds sterling more than had been budgeted for it, of
cows that suffered from inadequate protection from wind and
rain, and poor bedding.

Members of the kibbutz criticized his system of work, but,
after a dozen ballots, he was again elected to the secretariat of
Givat Brenner in the autumn of 1930.

And yet, despite all the criticism of Enzo's work methods,
despite all the problems growing out of the absorption of new
members, the debts, and unemployment, the balance sheet at the
end of 1930 showed much to be proud of. A year and a half
after the illegal occupation of the first parcel of land, Givat
Brenner now had in its possession over twelve hundred dunam
of land, properly registered in its name. Its membership had
grown five-fold to 150, plus twelve children. On top of the hill
there now stood a two-story stone house and a four-room house
built of cement blocks. A large wooden barrack was purchased
for a dining room. There was a water tank with a capacity of
150 cubic meters, and a well pumped by an electric motor had
been dug. Givat Brenner now had a shower room and a modern
bakery, a tractor, eight pure-bred cows, wood- and metalwork-
ing shops, a smithy, and a shoe shop. Forty dunam of irrigated
orange groves had been planted, and 400 dunam of field crops
were cultivated. A large tree nursery, a vineyard, and thirty
dunam of vegetables, as well as a grove of pines and another of
eucalyptus where the original tent camp had been, completed the
agricultural scene. And all this had been accomplished largely
with the kibbutz's own funds.

10

Fate Strikes
at the Sereni Brothers

Mimo did not conceal his leftist views from his family, but no
one knew of his involvement in the Communist underground,
the active cell that he led, his secret trip to Paris to consult with
leaders of the Comintern, or his part in the publication of the
underground paper *L'Unita*. The full truth was known only to
his wife, Xenichka, who went by the underground name
Marina and was his loyal assistant in all his doings. When an
underground comrade who was to visit them on September 15,
1930, failed to appear, she became deeply worried, and, in fact,
the police appeared at their apartment that very day. They
found Mimo at home and his wife bathing the baby. They made
a thorough search but failed to notice the unnaturally bulging
bosom of the young mother, where she had concealed documents
and manuscripts.

But Mimo was arrested and was soon transferred to Rome to
be tried before a special tribunal. Xenia and their infant daughter went to stay at the Sereni home on Cavour Street.

At the time Mimo was arrested, Enrico was at a scientific
conference in Venice, and upon the advice of friends did not
return home. Enrico was not a Communist, but a liberal Socialist, but he too was active in the anti-Fascist underground.

Enrico was now the father of a daughter — Ada — and
while he was in Venice his wife and child went to stay in the

Sereni home where they remained after a friend informed Dvora that Enrico had to go underground temporarily.

The two daughters-in-law with their infants found a rock of support in Alfonsa. All the time her two sons lived in Naples, Alfonsa would often take the midnight train there, loaded with baskets of salamis and baked goods. She would reach Naples in the morning, visit with her children, help her daughters-in-law, and return home at night. She never stayed overnight in Naples as a matter of principle. And when Dvora expressed doubts about whether it was right always to take things from the parents without giving anything in return, Enrico would reassure her that this was the family spirit: children repay parents with love, and in their turn will give to their children without expecting anything in return. This was a chain that linked one generation with another.

Enrico came to Rome for a brief and secret visit and Dvora and he decided to cross over to France separately and to meet in Marseilles. Dvora had a passport but the child was not named in it; any contact with the authorities on this score was liable to arouse suspicion. She therefore got the child through the border inspection wrapped up as a bundle, and little Ada cooperated and did not utter a sound. In Marseilles, Dvora waited with mounting desperation for days for Enrico's arrival. He finally came, having crossed the border through the mountains at night. But they were virtually without means, for it was impossible to withdraw any substantial sum from the bank in Rome without attracting attention. They therefore decided to go to Palestine and wait there to see to what extent the Fascist authorities were interested in Enrico.

Though some Jews had been removed from their posts in recent years, they had been removed as anti-Fascists, not as Jews, and Professor Sereni still served as court physician. When Mimo was arrested, Professor Sereni appealed to the Queen to intervene on his behalf. He obtained a promise that Mimo's sentence would be lightened if he were to deny ever having belonged to the Communist party. Together Alfonsa and Samuele visited Mimo in prison by special permission to discuss the royal suggestion with him. From his mother's tone — and for him she

was the determining personality — as she said, "I must tell you
. . . there is a possibility . . . if you deny . . . ," it was
clear that she did not approve of the suggestion. After all, it was
she who had taught her son that a person must stand behind his
convictions. Mimo refused to make such a denial and was sentenced by a special tribunal to twenty years' imprisonment, in
the presence of Uncle Angelo Sereni who, as a lawyer, was
permitted to attend the trial. Stunned by the sentence, Xenia
knew only that she must stand by Mimo no matter what, and
every day, throughout the years of his imprisonment after he
was removed from isolation, she wrote him a long letter in code
by means of a system of dotting certain words in scientific books
which he was permitted to receive. With a prophetic eye for the
future of communism, Mimo utilized the time of his imprisonment to teach himself Chinese, in addition to Russian — in
which he was already fluent.

In Palestine Enrico and his family were received jubilantly.
The noted professor of physiology was invited to lecture at the
Hebrew University in Jerusalem. He toured the country as a
VIP, and nobody except Enzo knew the true reason for his sudden visit. Alongside Enrico, with his thin, carefully tended mustache and his stylish clothing, the external changes in Enzo were
doubly noticeable. Shorter and thinner than his brother, Enzo
was sunburned and dressed like a laborer, his shoes had practically no heels left, and in the kibbutz he walked about barefoot.
Enrico, a cosmopolitan product of European culture, had no
wish to settle in Palestine. When the director of the aquarium in
Naples assured him that there was no danger and asked him to
return to his scientific work, he went back to Italy. Ada Sereni
and the three children accompanied him ostensibly for a family
visit.

The situation in Givat Brenner had meanwhile become cata-
strophic. There wasn't enough money for food, let alone to repay
debts. Italy again appeared as the sole chance of rescue, and
Ada's family visit was considered by Enzo as a suitable opportunity to conceal the true reason for her going there — to find
someone who would give 1000 pounds sterling to save the kibbutz from hunger.

Palestine was suffering from a depression, a consequence of the economic crisis that affected the entire world and of the drop in immigration. The Arab riots at the end of 1929 did not discourage Jews from wanting to come to the country but influenced the British government to put obstacles in the way of the immigrants. After the riots the British Colonial Office appointed an investigating commission headed by Judge Shaw. Its report, released in March 1930, declared that Palestine could not support an additional agricultural population and Jewish immigration could therefore be regarded as a direct cause of the riots. Should it prove, the report continued, that intensive agricultural cultivation was feasible in the country, it might perhaps be possible to admit a number of new immigrants into certain districts. On the basis of this report the government of England issued a White Paper in October 1930 that imposed limitations on Jewish purchase of land, set quotas for immigration permits based on the state of employment among Arabs, and considered the establishment of a legislative council for the country with an Arab majority. This was a bitter blow for the Jewish community, and especially for the labor movement, for the White Paper was signed by Lord Passfield, the former Sidney Webb, the father of English socialism, and was approved by Ramsay Mac-Donald, who had visited Palestine some years earlier as the guest of the Histadrut — the Jewish Federation of Labor.

Enzo, whose labor consciousness did not permit him to reconcile himself to British imperialism for some time, argued that it was as well that MacDonald's proclivity to falsehood and deceit had been revealed in all its coarseness and that the Jewish community had been shown clearly the hypocrisy of Albion (he did not use the term "perfidy"). The illusion, which part of the Jewish community had harbored for many years, that there existed common interests between the Jews and the British in Palestine had been unmasked. "Those who have been telling us — like the Revisionists — how much the British need us in this part of Asia, should better know, they and the rest of the world, that we have absolutely nothing in common with British imperialism."

In the meantime a new period of unemployment set in and in

Rehovot there was no work at all. At the meeting of the secretariat of Givat Brenner on November 30, 1930, Enzo announced
that the kibbutz could participate in a pioneering project at the
Dead Sea. The administration of the potash recovery plant at the
Dead Sea hitherto had refused to hire Jewish workers whom it
regarded as not tough enough. In order to prevent the elimination of Jewish labor from this basic industry, the Histadrut appealed to the kibbutzim to send volunteers for the work. Enzo
leaped at the opportunity, and even though the membership was
not enthusiastic he succeeded in persuading them. The following
morning some twenty members, led by Enzo, left for Jerusalem
by bus. In the city he obtained a free meal for them at the
cooperative restaurant and took them to the Wailing Wall. Thus
strengthened in body and spirit, the group went down to the
Dead Sea.

Until now only Arabs from Transjordan worked at collecting
the carnalite from the evaporating pans along the shore, and
they worked barefoot. The men from Givat Brenner worked in
shoes but these quickly disintegrated, their feet were covered
with sores, and morale plummeted. The situation was intolerable
and Enzo insisted that the management provide them with
rubber boots. In the end his demand was met. Boots were
brought from Jerusalem and the productivity of the workers
leaped up and far exceeded that of the Transjordanians. When
Enzo saw that matters were now under control he returned
home; on the way to Rehovot he fainted from pain for his feet
too were covered with deep wounds.

Enzo sent letters of alarm to Ada in Italy — we can't hold
out — but Ada could only act slowly in the matter of obtaining
funds. After she felt her way among friends and relatives, there
remained but one source — Papa and Mama Sereni. They gave
her a loan of 1,000 pounds, but without much enthusiasm, for
this was a very big sum for them, money that they had saved up
lira by lira thanks to Alfonsa's frugality and willingness to do
everything by herself. If it had been a matter of helping their
son alone, they would not have hesitated, but the kibbutz seemed
to be a bottomless pit.

Ada was still in Italy when Enzo received a telegram from

Naples: "Enrico died." After his return to Italy, Enrico had continued with his scientific work as if nothing had happened — only his and his wife's passports were taken away from them when they disembarked — and life returned to normal. On March 1, a Sunday, he and his wife were about to go for a walk with some visiting scientists from abroad. It was a rainy day. Enrico had no particular desire to go walking and decided to remain at home, but Dvora had been urged by her doctor to exercise a lot and she escorted the guests. Enrico loved to spend much time in the bathtub. Because of the danger from carbon monoxide at a time when all heating was done with coal, it was customary not to lock the bathroom door when someone was taking a bath and for someone to check every fifteen minutes by knocking on the door. The maid knocked on the door once and received a reassuring answer. But when she knocked again fifteen minutes later, there was no reply. She opened the door and found Enrico in a coma. A doctor who lived in the same building came within a few minutes and certified his death.

Alfonsa, who until now had been so concerned for the life of her oldest son that she did not allow him to participate in Umberto Nobile's flight over the North Pole in May 1928, which carried a number of Italian scientists to perform various scientific tests, immediately came to Naples, took matters in hand, cared for the baby, comforted Dvora, and brought both the daughter-in-law and the child to Rome where the funeral was held. In accordance with the custom of Italian Jews, Alfonsa and Dvora remained at home during the funeral, and Mother Sereni enjoined her daughter-in-law never to weep in the presence of little Ada, so that she could grow as a gay and healthy child. Alfonsa herself remained outwardly firm and took care of the child when Dvora returned to her scientific work.

Enzo at once went to Italy and, like all the Serenis, he was calm and restrained in the face of death. This may have stemmed from the constant bond of the Serenis with their dead. Samuele kept an exact record of the memorial days of the many Serenis who died in his time according to both the Jewish and the secular calendar, and they were remembered long after their deaths on their birthdays and death anniversaries, on the Day of

Atonement, and at family festivities, for death was not something unexpected and exceptional but an indivisible part of life.

On the face of it, the house on Cavour Street returned to its normal routine. Enzo collected and arranged the letters and diaries that Enrico had kept during most of his life, writing in them of everything — philosophy, literature, music, love, the family, the war — and after a few weeks he published an attractive, informative, and unsentimental booklet about his brother.

Enzo's return to Europe had been unforeseen, but now that he was there it was felt that it would be a pity not to utilize it. For some time there had been talk about his going to Germany as an emissary to the youth organization Brith Olim, but most members of Givat Brenner and also the secretariat of Hakibbutz Hameuchad opposed this. Enzo did not seem to be the right person to deal with German youth, known for their thoroughness and restraint. It was suggested by one of the leaders of Brith Olim that Enzo visit Germany to raise funds for the development of Givat Brenner. But Enzo had doubts about such a mission. "I do not wish to go to Germany merely to raise funds," he declared. "Even though this appears to be a practical plan, I do not think it is a good idea, nor does it lead to the desired goal. From my experience I am convinced that even funds can be obtained only when one gives something in return and one does not merely come making demands." In other words, he wanted to go there as an ideological emissary. It is true that he seemed to share some of the doubts about his suitability, for on March 17 he wrote to the secretariat of Hakibbutz Hameuchad that "I, too, have reservations whether I am the right man for work in Germany, despite my westernness — for not all people from the west are alike." Therefore he asked for an outright approval from Givat Brenner and Hakibbutz Hameuchad for his trip to Germany and insisted on an early answer. Givat Brenner agreed, hoping he would succeed in obtaining funds there. Hakibbutz Hameuchad also gave its blessing, and in April 1931 he left for Germany.

11

On a Mission
of Conquest

Young German Zionists who first saw the new emissary did not
know what to make of him. He was short, carried a bundle of
newspapers under his arm, dressed in a raincoat that descended
to his ankles, and wore a cap far too large for him — both
provided by Givat Brenner's collective supply room. From under
the cap, behind a pair of glasses, his eyes gleamed as if a light
had been lit in them, and he spoke rapidly about any and all
subjects. His listeners enjoyed his flashy remarks, the fluency of
his talk, and his tremendous knowledge, but he did not win their
confidence. For Enzo his stay in Germany and becoming acquainted with the Jewish youth movements there were like a
return to his own youth when he floundered between religion,
Zionism, socialism, and the final and painful decision to transform convictions into action.

That summer it was already possible in Germany to see
clearly the shape of events to come. The Weimar republic was in
a state of collapse after thirteen years of crisis-ridden existence,
and Hitler was now a figure to be reckoned with. Ridiculed in
the twenties because of the confused and megalomanic ideas
propounded in his book *Mein Kampf*, he was saved by the Wall
Street crash in 1929 and its consequences — the collapse of
German banks, the shutdown of industry, and unemployment
for millions. In September 1930, the impoverished masses

sought salvation in the two parties that promised basic changes
in the regime that had let them down: the Communists polled
four and a half million votes and the Nazis drew six and a half
million votes, thus becoming the second largest party in the
country with 107 seats in the Reichstag.

Enzo had no doubts that Hitler would come to power, like
Mussolini before him, and that only then would his true mission
begin. The only question remaining unanswered was when this
would happen. Meantime he remained in Germany as head of
the Hechalutz (Pioneer) organization, which then numbered a
mere 500 members. Ada moved from Italy to Berlin and the
family made its home in the commune on Alexanderstrasse, in a
large apartment in the workers' quarter. This served as a collective home for some of the local leaders of Brith Olim, Hechalutz, and other emissaries from Palestine. Membership in this
commune was subject to frequent changes as some went to
Palestine or were assigned to do organizational work elsewhere.
Economically, it was hard to make ends meet, for only a few
were employed and their wages were a mere pittance. The fur-
nishings were minimal. The Serenis' room contained only a bed,
and, of all things, a safe, a leftover from former tenants who had
been affluent. During weekdays the apartment had the cozy
atmosphere of a railway station, but on Friday evenings the
table in the common dining room would be covered with a cloth,
a hot meal would be served, and the commune became "a major
center in Berlin," as Enzo described it in his letters to Palestine.
He could not understand some of the other emissaries, members
of kibbutzim, who preferred to live in private quarters when not
at home. To him the very concept of "taking a rest from kibbutz
life" was inadmissible. "We must stress and insist," he declared,
"that here as well as in Palestine, the kibbutz is our way of life,
that without it we feel lost, and that whether it is easy or hard on
us, we must create also here, in the Diaspora, a kibbutz atmosphere." But aside from the principle involved, he regarded kibbutz life as providing practical advantages. Collective living
offered opportunities for frequent conversations and discussions
without having to resort to formal meetings. The members of the
collective went together to concerts and theater performances in

their free time. Here, Ada, too, was less occupied by her maternal duties, and for the first time in four years could do something for her own intellectual advancement.

The Jewish youth movements among which Sereni worked were a by-product of the German youth movement, the first to regard youth not simply as a period of transition between childhood and maturity but as a bearer of moral values in its own right. Youthful excitement expressed itself primarily in attempts to escape reality, the school and its harsh discipline, social conventions and philistinism in general. The escape was both physical and spiritual. The ideal was the Wandervogel — the migratory bird, abandoning the city and, rucksack on back, returning to nature, far from the suffocating environment of family and school, in order to create a new, pure, and liberated culture. The establishment of separate Jewish youth movements came as a reaction to social reality and was at first not based on ideological differences with the German youth movement. German youth, even when it was not anti-Semitic as a matter of principle, did not conceal its lack of enthusiasm for the presence of Jews, and even the most assimilated Jews felt more comfortable among themselves.

The graduates of the Jewish youth movements displayed a good deal of cultural snobbism. They judged a person by the level of his education, his familiarity with the worlds of music and literature, especially avant garde literature that had not yet become popular: Kafka, Proust, Kierkegaard, Thomas Mann. Their superiority stood them in good stead when meeting with Yiddish-speaking emissaries from eastern Europe, but drew a blank with Enzo who in short order was at home in Berlin's museums and libraries, conducted seminars on the German spiritual giants — Hegel, Kant, and Schopenhauer — and quickly demonstrated to his hearers that whatever they knew he knew better. For young Zionists who still hesitated to make a decision, Enzo was living proof that going to live in Palestine did not require a narrowing of horizons, that pioneering in the land of Israel need not lead to cultural deterioration.

He foresaw the economic fate of German Jewry where "hundreds of families which only yesterday could have been regarded as middle class gradually slip to the level of proletarians without employment, without an economic base, and without hope of regaining their former position. But while great numbers of Jewish professionals — doctors, lawyers, dentists — are without employment and without prospects for employment, thousands of young people pursue their studies for these professions, under pressure of some mysterious inertia that compels them even now to seek escape from the prevailing hell by means of private, personal solutions — save yourself, and yourself only, by means of your special merits."

The solution to the complex of German Jewry's problems, the only remedy for their individualism which, Enzo felt, bordered on madness, would be a movement that would organize the Jews as a unit and seek a collective answer for all Jews — and that meant Zionism. Here was the final conflict between absolute assimilation that would erase every Jewish trait and Zionism, which called for inner renewal — and both ways were painful. Numerically the two camps were most unequal. Zionism was upheld by less than two percent of the Jewish population in Germany, which numbered 530,000. "Anyone who has an opportunity, as I have, to see German Jewry in this time of crisis, beholds the full tragedy of this Diaspora not only in its day-to-day life but also historically. . . . One shudders when one realizes that every individual who has been won or lost for the cause may be decisive one way or another. Even small, everyday deeds acquire historic meaning." Therefore there was no contradiction between Enzo's aspiration to great deeds and his practical activities in the small Hechalutz organization and in youth movements ridden with intellectual complexes, in meetings with small groups, and in conversations with individuals.

Enzo's command post was in the large house of the Zionist Organization in which the Zionist "big shots" allotted the basement to the youth movements. Here were the cover organization Hechalutz and on either side the offices of Brith Olim and Kadimah, Zionist placards on the walls, heaps of leaflets, stormy meetings and loud debates, the clacking of typewriters, and overall that earnestness of which only young people are capable. He drove them hard, just as he drove himself in writing circulars, publication of pamphlets, preparation of speeches, writing numerous letters, all in that special style characteristic of Zionist youth movements: the language of intellectuals studded with such Hebrew organizational terms as *sicha*, *kvutzah*, *madrich*, *hachsharah*, which could not easily be translated into German. As long as Enzo was in Berlin (and he traveled extensively) there was rest in the youth headquarters only on those occasions when some organizational leader or some wealthy matron invited Enzo out for a fancy dinner, a temptation that he could not resist, and sometimes even plotted. But among the youth there were some with puritanical tendencies who looked askance at the emissary's acceptance of such invitations and regarded them as not good scouting, not proletarian, not in the pioneering spirit.

At first the youth movements advocated premarital sexual abstention, and the intimacy of group life served as a substitute for love relationships. But as they became more closely involved with Palestine, socialism, and pioneering, and especially as a consequence of the frequent, mixed agricultural training periods, they developed a strong sense of independence and liberated themselves from their puritanical notions. This led to sexual relationships at a relatively early age. Some of the couples developed lasting relationships, but there was also a lively interchange of partners that astounded Ada, who dwelt in her letters to the Serenis in Rome on the exaggerated sexual freedom that prevailed among the youth in Germany. Enzo, too, was displeased by this phenomenon, which he regarded as a form of sexual exploitation of the women without a corresponding assumption of responsibility by the men. And, as was his habit, he interfered in personal affairs: here he promoted a match and there he frowned on a liaison. This met with some dissatisfaction. There were those who considered that their personal affairs were none of his business; others regarded it as hypocrisy — here was a married man openly flirting with other women; who was he to preach morality to them?

It was known that Enzo kept in his desk a snapshot of Lonnie, a delicate blonde girl of seventeen whom he had met briefly during his work in Koenigsberg. For some time she was not

even aware of his feelings, and after she was informed by
friends she remained reserved, though she felt flattered that
Enzo, the new star in Germany, was interested in her, still a
high school girl. Many months later, after Hitler came to power,
he met her again in Switzerland, and confessed his feelings to
her. But nothing came of it all and he was brokenhearted. It
would seem that for a man who married a schoolmate at age
twenty-one, one love story is not enough to fill his entire life,
even though he be a doctor of philosophy and the father of three
children, especially so if he is a sensualist and of turbulent
temper.

After some hesitation, Hitler decided to run for the presidency
against Hindenburg on March 13, 1932, and when the ballots
were counted the aged president received 49.6 percent of the
vote and Hitler 30.1 percent; the remaining votes went to the
Communists and other small parties. The irony of it was that
Hindenburg, the protestant, Prussian, conservative monarchist
was backed by the Socialists, the trade unions, and the Catholics, whereas Hitler, the Catholic beggar who spoke in the name
of the middle class was supported by the industrial magnates,
the landowners, and the upper class in general. Because Hindenburg was .4 percent short of an absolute majority, it was necessary to hold a runoff election to choose a president, and Hitler
crisscrossed Germany in an airplane — a daring innovation in
electioneering — and promised everything to everybody: work
for the unemployed, prosperity for the businessmen, a big army
for the militarists. In the new elections that took place on April
10, 1932, the Nazis increased their vote by two million to a total
of thirteen and one-half million. But Hindenburg still obtained a
majority. Berlin was rife with persistent rumors that 400,000
brown-shirted SS troops were preparing a putsch, and Hindenburg issued a decree to disband them as soon as he was re-
elected. For a moment it seemed as if the tide had been halted.
      In view of what was happening in Germany, anti-Fascism
acquired new significance and Enzo renewed his ties with the
anti-Fascist underground, especially the group centering on
Carlo Roselli and the organization Giustizia e Libertá, which

had its base in Paris. Emissaries of the Italian underground from time to time also came to Berlin under assumed names, and with Enzo's assistance transported "material" from Berlin to Italy, but no one in the Hechalutz organization knew the full extent of his involvement in anti-Fascist work. Though by nature an extrovert who talked freely and without restraint, he also had within him areas that were tightly locked from public view.

Early in 1932, during the mass unemployment, a group of Jewish boys came to Recha Freier, a resident of Berlin and an independent social activist, and asked for help: they had been discharged from their jobs because of their Jewishness — could she assist them in obtaining other work, or help them get to western Germany where they would try to obtain work in the mines? Recha Freier, who became a Zionist under the impact of posters proclaiming that "Jews and dogs are not allowed," which she saw one day in the public park of her native town Norden, found little sympathy among the Jewish bureaucrats who felt that the problem of these boys "will be solved automatically when the economic crisis passes." It then occurred to her that it might be an idea to send these boys to the labor settlements in Palestine where they could train for their future. Enzo was the first person to whom she divulged her plan. From time to time he used to lecture to a group of girls who met in her house and she regarded him as spokesman for the entire kibbutz movement. Enzo caught fire at the thought. "Do so," he urged her. "You will cause a revolution in the Zionist movement in Germany."

At Enzo's suggestion Recha Freier addressed herself to the Histadrut, asking whether the kibbutzim would accept boys and girls aged 15 to 16 for a period of training lasting two to three years. The answer was affirmative and Kibbutz Ein Harod agreed to accept the first group. But the reaction of the Jewish organizations that had been asked to help financially was less than cool. Some spoke contemptuously of "a children's crusade" and of the meaningless fantasies of an eccentric woman. Even Henrietta Szold, who directed the social welfare department of the Vaad Leumi, the national council of the Jews in Palestine, reacted negatively to the plan, declaring that it would be wrong to bring children to a country that had its own problems with abandoned and backward children. Some partial assistance came from Dr. Lehman, director of the children's village Ben Shemen, who allocated twelve immigration certificates for the first group of boys, and the money for travel expenses and maintenance was collected by groups of women in Koenigsberg and Berlin. In the fall of 1932 the boys departed from the Anhalt station in Berlin leaving behind them their weeping parents. Youth *aliyah* to Palestine had begun, yet to many intelligent people it seemed contrary to human nature.

Meantime the Nazis gained control of the universities. Students persecuted Jewish professors and those of leftist opinions, and high school students were drawn to the symbols and the discipline that prevailed among Nazi youth. It became difficult for Jewish youth to meet in large numbers without risking a collision with Nazis and their young followers.

It is not clear what was the main reason for Enzo's wish to leave Germany in the fall. He wrote about "irresistible personal reasons." Early in the summer he sent Ada and the children to Italy. It might have been the suffocating sense of oppression in Germany that caused him to do so, or perhaps it was the realization that he would have to return to Germany after Hitler's certain rise to power and that it was desirable to rest up before this coming greater challenge. It is also possible that he had had a surfeit of the work, that something snapped within him and he lost patience. His formal explanation was not revealing: "I believe that in light of the present situation it is not desirable that I should remain here. I have brought matters to a certain conclusion, and it is necessary to carry on from here, but others, new and fresh to this scene, will be needed. My part is over."

Whoever wished to be an emissary of Zionism in those days when the title of emissary evoked admiration and respect and when the term Zionism was pronounced without quotation marks, had to love the Jewish people, but even more he had to love to travel. Since the beginning of Zionism its emissaries led a nomadic existence, and the biographies of the founders of Zionism read like a timetable. Enzo loved to travel, to discover new worlds, to meet new people, to challenge new foes. He loved first encounters and impressions. When he was in Germany he covered the entire country, then went to Danzig, and to Poland (during his first visit to Warsaw, the first thing he asked to see was the porters' synagogue), to Lithuania (including a visit to the Mussarniks, a moralistic sect at the *yeshiva* at Slobodka), to London to attend the sessions of the Zionist Executive (we'll be happy at your coming, but you must provide your own travel expenses). There were repeated trips to Austria, Switzerland, Czechoslovakia, and Holland, where he found a severe economic crisis, Communist stirrings, and a disembodied Zionism — the kind he had known so well in Italy — as well as great possibilities for obtaining funds for labor settlement in Palestine, if only the right person were to be sent there. He went on behalf of the pioneering organization Hechalutz to France, but in Paris, the fortress of Jewish assimilation, they wouldn't hear of it. And he traveled for his own sake — Dr. Sereni, philosopher, historian, lover of art, of people, and of good food.

12

A Zionist Pimpernel

All through the years of his travels over Europe and between Europe and Palestine, Enzo had planned his journeys with the precision of a migratory bird to bring him to Rome in the spring and autumn so that he could spend Passover and Rosh Hashanah with his parents. Thus, at the end of September 1932, he was again in the Sereni home on Cavour Street. It had been built to last for generations but there now remained only a single wing. Mussolini's grandiose plans for Rome called for a broad avenue from Palazzo Venezia, where he lived and from whose balcony he used to address the masses, to the Colosseum, and all structures that blocked the right of way of the future Via di Fori Imperiali or abutted on it were torn down.

The Executive Committee of the Histadrut finally became reconciled to Enzo's leaving Germany after all appeals to him to prolong his stay there were turned down. It was more reluctant to give its consent to having his talent wasted in Palestine on ordinary agricultural labor or in petty bickering with creditors on behalf of Givat Brenner. The genial suggestion was then made to send Enzo to the United States to repeat the miracle he had accomplished in Germany in sparking the flame of Zionist pioneering among the Jewish youth. Enzo readily agreed that work in the United States was important — but without him. "I feel broken down and exhausted after a year and a half of dashing around and constant activity," he wrote. "I must now spend some time at home. I want to do ordinary labor, to be with family and friends, to live in peace, to read, to write."

When Enzo returned to Givat Brenner early in November, he found the housing situation as bad as when he left. The crowding was terrible; the large house which had been intended for members was being temporarily used as the children's home; the sanitary conditions were abominable, as usual. A commission sent by Hakibbutz Hameuchad to inspect the kibbutz at the end of 1932 concluded that Givat Brenner must improve internal arrangements and especially look to the improvement of the kitchen. But it expressed satisfaction with the financial situation. Within one year short-term debts had been reduced from 4,200 pounds to 1,900. The woodworking shop now employed twelve members, the dairy enterprise was thriving, the tree nursery was developing well, and the kibbutz also operated a restaurant in Rehovot which served one hundred regular customers. Enzo successfully parried efforts to saddle him with assignments for the kibbutz or the labor movement. He now worked as a laborer in an orange grove and read much, but he wrote little. He even wrote few letters, partly because of the shortage of stamps in the kibbutz, yet it was little things like this that made it difficult to get used to kibbutz life after his return. Chana, Hagar, and Daniel quickly resumed their place in the life of the children's home, but Enzo was sorry to see them refuse to speak Italian, which they had learned during the few months they had spent with the family in Rome.

At a general meeting Enzo spoke of the need to introduce Hebrew into all areas of kibbutz life and called for political education work. "Our life will become boring if we do not take an interest in politics," he declared, and recommended the establishment of a number of study groups for the winter months which should take up the Arab question, the history of Fascism, and kibbutz problems. Despite the economic crisis that affected most of the world, he found the country prospering economically, and was "astounded at the American tempo at which it was developing. Wherever I turn after an absence of a year and a half, I see new things, new plantings, new people, a vital eagerness, a striving after advancement and well-being. Who cares if not everything that is being done is economically sound, good, or inspiring. For the first time we Zionists have the feeling that vital, natural processes operate here — not merely the heroic pioneering will of the few, but the obstinate and everyday will of little people, who do not aspire to great things, the way we did, but are capable of constructive effort no less than we are, and if their efforts are not as inspiring as ours, their scope is much greater."

On January 30, 1932, the doom of the Weimar Republic was sealed. Hindenburg appointed Hitler chancellor. Though the new government still bore the trappings of a coalition and out of eleven ministries only three, and not very important ones, were in the hands of the Nazis, Nazi rule was assured. That evening Enzo met Ben-Asher deep in thought. "It is necessary to go to Germany," he said. Indeed, Enzo had come to feel an almost physical bond, a close family relationship, with German Jewry, which had deluded itself with dreams of assimilation. The physical labor for which he had longed when he was in Germany did not heal his restlessness. While still in Germany in the fall of 1931, Enzo had made a pact with Eliezer Liebinstein (Livneh), a member of Kibbutz Ein Harod who had preceded him there, that they would both return to Berlin when Hitler came to power, an event that both were sure would occur soon. Thus it came about that in April 1932 Enzo, Liebinstein and Beilinson, who also wished to be in Germany to witness these fateful days, left for Europe. This time Ada and the children remained in Givat Brenner.

Despite the gradual decline of the democratic regime, and Hitler's open talk of his hatred for the Jews, the events of the spring of 1933 came as a deep shock and a nightmare reality for German Jewry, including, as they did, the quick elimination of all Jews from the legal profession and from government employment, the savage incitement against them in the press, the vandalization of Jewish institutions and attacks on individuals in the streets, and, after the burning of the Reichstag building on March 27, the full-scale mass terror against Communists, Socialists, and Jews. German Jewry beheld their entire world being destroyed before their eyes. Four generations of assimilation had bound them deeply to German culture and now their sense of belonging was undermined to its foundations. Zionism, which until then had attracted only a small part of the Jewish community, and not the most admired at that, became the main focus of the masses who sought escape and support and encouragement.

The day after April 1, which had been proclaimed a boycott day, when Nazi pickets prevented by force the entry of Aryan buyers into Jewish stores and attached posters on Jewish establishments to the effect that "Buying from Jews will endanger your lives," twelve hundred persons called on the Palestine office in Berlin in person or by mail, asking for information about the possibility of emigrating to Palestine and the chances of getting established there. Yet among the counselors at the office there was not one personally familiar with conditions in Palestine.

Upon his return to Germany Enzo found this situation: masses streamed to pioneering Zionism and were seriously interested in emigration. There were possibilities for rescuing tens of thousands and of transferring millions of marks; there were large-scale opportunities to influence political development and to be at the center of history instead of at its edges. The youth organizations, which had previously squabbled over ideological fine points, suddenly forgot these and united, as soon as Hitler came to power, into a unified movement. Hechalutz, the organization of pioneers that had numbered no more than five hundred during Enzo's previous stay in the country, now grew to two thousand, and additional thousands were willing to join. As was usual in Zionism, ideological conviction exerted influence, but hard times were much more effective.

At Zionist meetings there was an atmosphere of revolution. The younger generation whom the Jewish establishment had systematically directed to mercantile professions as if everything were progressing peacefully, demanded the removal of the leadership that had misled them. But the youth movements were incapable of absorbing these masses because of their educational structure, and Enzo stressed that the chief purpose of Hechalutz

at this time was to establish mass centers for young people who
had not passed through some Zionist youth organization.

The first group of pioneers left for Palestine after the events
of April, and Enzo saw them off at the Anhalt station in Berlin.
Hundreds of visitors crowded around those who were departing,
members of their families were excited, and mothers wept while
the curious Aryan onlookers wondered at the meaning of it all as
the crowd sang "Hatikvah." Before Hitler's rise to power, pioneers would leave for Palestine in small groups after prolonged
periods of training, intensive study of Hebrew, and psychological preparation. Now more immigration permits to Palestine
were granted by the British authorities. (The British government allotted one thousand immigration certificates for the Jews
of Germany as an advance against the quota for 1933–1934,
and the number of candidates for immigration grew by leaps
and bounds.) "It is no secret," Enzo wrote at that time, "that the
new immigrants do not fulfill the requirements we made in the
past, but they passed a short training period and we may assume
that they will become acclimated in the country."

But despite his satisfaction with the success of the Hechalutz
organization, which had become a decisive factor in Jewish life
in Germany and, numerically, the largest Jewish organization in
the country, Enzo was not satisfied with the mere technical organization of emigration and demanded thorough education of the
prospective immigrants. "We cannot succeed if we do not retain
the educational character of our movement," he wrote. For
though need is the driving force of Zionism, despair and a sense
of feeling lost are merely the symptoms of Jewish helplessness in
the Diaspora, not a guarantee for success in Palestine. Immigration to Palestine must therefore be fitted to the needs of the
country. "Even in this difficult hour we must allot most of the
one thousand immigration certificates to pioneers," Enzo argued.
"This may seem cruel, but even if the British were to grant ten
thousand certificates instead of the one thousand they are giving
us now, we would still say: Let the young people go, for even if
they suffer less than the older ones, they are better fitted for the
task in Palestine. Children can later bring their parents, but not
the other way around." He was convinced that he had a moral

right to demand preference for pioneers in the allocation of immigration certificates only on condition that they remain pioneers after they came to Palestine and went to live in kibbutzim and *moshavim*. Therefore he also demanded that the immigrants go in organized groups as it would facilitate their acclimatization in Palestine and continuation of life as laborers. (This problem, whom to save first, whose survival has priority, pursued the leaders of Zionism in Europe all through the period of the Holocaust and again and again required decisions affecting the life or death of others, the kind of decision that no man should ever have to make.)

In this atmosphere of confusion, helplessness, and dread of the morrow, Recha Freier's plan to take children to Palestine without their parents appeared less unrealistic, and when Enzo came to Germany in the spring of 1933, Recha went to Palestine to examine the possibilities for placing children in the labor settlements. Enzo gave her a letter of introduction to Zev Orbach at Givat Brenner and urged him to accompany her on her tour of the country. "You must work on this project intensively," he wrote to Orbach. "Without exaggerating I can state that there exist opportunities to raise tremendous sums, for no other project is as close to people's hearts, but, naturally, it is possible to raise funds only for projects that are well founded and make a serious impression." Kibbutz Ein Harod expressed its willingness to take in the first group, and other settlements followed. The Federation of Labor gave its full assistance, and visionaries began talking of transferring ten thousand children, but Henrietta Szold still had doubts whether it was desirable to place children in labor settlements.

To hasten the placement of the youngsters, Enzo transferred through clandestine channels the first sums that were collected in Germany for the construction of the youth center in Ein Harod, but matters still moved slowly and cynics in Berlin derided the entire plan as a "movement to transfer sixty children to Palestine." Only after the Zionist leadership formally adopted the plan did things begin to move. Henrietta Szold agreed to take over the leadership of the office in Jerusalem in charge of the project, and the British authorities consented to grant a special allotment of immigration certificates for children and youth under eighteen years of age. The sixty children who had waited for an entire year finally left and reached Haifa on February 19, 1934. The youth organizations in Germany were happy to send their younger members to labor settlements in Palestine, but the children's parents were at a loss. In spite of Hitler and the persecutions and the "Aryan laws" it required great determination for Jewish parents to send off their children to a tropical and undeveloped country that seemed to them no less dangerous than Germany. Thus only five thousand children left for Palestine before World War II broke out, and the vast majority of parents hesitated and could not become reconciled to the thought of parting from their children. On the contrary, many parents felt that, especially during these difficult times, families should remain united, a fortress against the onslaughts of the outside world, and bear their fate jointly — and together they were turned into ashes scattered on the fields of Poland.

Zionism as a whole was confronted with a terrible dilemma. On the one hand there was the powerful desire to summon world Jewry to take drastic steps against the Nazi persecution of Jews. On the other hand there was the fear that an outright anti-German policy, especially a call for a boycott of German goods that arose spontaneously and received spontaneous support throughout the world also among non-Jews, would endanger the rescue activities of the Zionist institutions which, for the time being, enjoyed relative freedom of action in Germany. Early in August 1933, on the eve of the eighteenth World Zionist Congress, the Zionist administration in Germany sent a secret letter, also signed by Sereni, to the Zionist headquarters in London, asking that the Congress be called off "in order not to draw so much attention." "Until now," the letter stated, "and for a variety of reasons, the work of the Zionist Organization, Hechalutz, and the youth movements has not been forbidden. Our legal existence has enabled us to organize thousands and to transfer large sums of money to Palestine. There is apparent a tendency on the part of the authorities to facilitate the export of capital and the extension of our activity, as a result of which Zionist influence in the Jewish community is growing daily. It is clear that if the Zionist Congress meets, it will have to express sharp protests against the government of Germany, which, in turn will react with a prohibition of Zionist activity and the export of funds, and even the lives of a large number of German Zionists may be jeopardized."

The Congress was held in Prague in the latter part of August, and it did not endorse the calls for a boycott of Germany as demanded mainly by delegates from America and those representing the right-wing opposition.

The Germans, too, regarded systematic emigration abetted by favorable regulations for the withdrawal of part of the emigrants' wealth, as a desirable way of solving the Jewish question, and Palestine, in the nature of things, the most likely place for the absorption of the Jews. In addition to their desire to get rid of the Jews, this decision was also motivated by the boycott of German goods that was effectively conducted in numerous western countries precisely at the time when the Nazis were anxious to encourage exports in order to do away with mass unemployment.

The aims were similar but the interests were not parallel, and the Zionists reached an agreement with the German emigration office regarding the transfer of Jewish capital to Palestine. Negotiations began in May 1933 and general agreement was reached in July. Potential emigrants would deposit their funds in a joint account in Germany. A parallel trust fund would be established in Palestine and importers of German goods would pay to this fund the cost of their imports. The immigrant to Palestine would then be reimbursed from this fund in Palestinian pounds the equivalent of their deposits in Germany. This would also eliminate brokers' fees and other expenses, which amounted to about ten percent.

But even while these legal transfers went into effect, Enzo took charge of transactions of another kind. It is impossible to determine what were the sums transferred through secret channels, but they were considerable and ran into many millions of marks. (It is estimated that until 1939 the equivalent of fifty million pounds sterling of German Jewish wealth was rescued, about a third of this sum by legal means.)

The smuggling operation was carried out with Enzo's system, that is, with the greatest measure of improvisation, without superfluous bureaucracy, with the aid of hasty notes on scraps of paper, and with great personal daring. Sometimes the money to be smuggled would be concealed on the persons of individuals going abroad or in their baggage, in tubes of tooth paste, or under double bottoms of suitcases — tricks that any freshman smuggler would be ashamed of. One of the most common tricks was to reserve two places on a train going abroad to Denmark or Switzerland, to hide the money in one of the reserved seats and to occupy the second one, which might be in a different car, and then to await the results. If the searches at the border were strict and the money was discovered, then it was ownerless. If it was not discovered, then it was taken out from its place of concealment after the train was out of Germany, assuming, that is, that it hadn't meanwhile been discovered by one of the conductors, or another smuggler.

Enzo loved the craftiness and the excitement, the danger and the challenge to fate involved in this game of hide and seek. The easiest way to take money out of the country was through Jacob Robinson, the representative of Lithuania at the League of Nations who, because of his diplomatic status, was not subject to search at the border. In any case it is a fact that Enzo succeeded in transferring the funds destined for Palestine almost in their entirety. He, and Liebinstein, who was his partner in matters of smuggling, succeeded in crossing the border many times without being caught, although they were both citizens of a foreign country. They assumed that they were both so well known to the police that the latter did not believe they would further endanger themselves with smuggling. It is also possible, of course, that they were not apprehended because the Germans did not want to do so for reasons of their own, taking into account their usefulness in encouraging Jewish emigration.

From a certain standpoint those were Genesis days, and even the Nazis were still learning their trade. The secret police were still in the process of organizing themselves on a national scale, and punitive measures were irregular and depended on the whims of the local officials. Operation of concentration camps was largely improvised. The Nazi terror was brutal but still lacked the characteristic German efficiency. Violence would come in waves, now intensified and then dying down for a while. When all the political parties except the Nazis were abolished, and all the German youth movements gave up without a struggle, the Zionist youth movements and Hechalutz continued their regular activities without interference on the basis of a "Fuehrerausweis" signed by Baldur von Schirach, leader of German youth activities, a name that did not ring any bells in anyone's mind at the time. Most of the Nazi organizations whose titles later aroused a shudder were still in the beginning of their careers. The conferences and major meetings of Hechalutz and other Zionist youth organizations were required to have special permission from the secret police, which usually sent one of its own men to attend. The representatives of the authorities were well known and did not try to conceal their presence. It would seem that the Germans were not nearly as misled as the Jews imagined them to be, but they attached little importance to these games of subterfuge when compared with their central aim: to get rid of the Jews as soon as possible.

Hitler declared clearly: "I don't know whether within two or three centuries my name will be praised in Germany for what I sincerely hope to achieve for my people, but I have no doubts about one thing — that within five centuries I will still be praised everywhere as the man who once and for all uprooted the curse of the Jews from the world." This he declared as early as March 1933, but the Jews of Germany failed to grasp the full significance of his words and clutched at every shred of hope. After he had been in power for a year, the mood of the German Jews, who immediately after Hitler's rise to power streamed into the Zionist movement, seeking within it answers to their spiritual confusion and economic distress, changed. With remarkable adaptability they became accustomed to the new situation and after the first wave of anti-Jewish decrees and racial laws that removed tens of thousands of Jews from their economic foundations had subsided, there set in a measure of relative tolerance, and the government provided for a number of exceptions to every anti-Jewish law. With the profound optimism that characterizes Jews, everyone hoped to be one of the exceptions. The decline in interest in Palestine had an additional cause, which Enzo sensed with deep concern: the Zionists were incapable of responding to the needs of the masses and did not justify the trust that the Jews of Germany reposed in them during the early days of Nazi rule. This disappointment with Zionism, Enzo felt, was not a consequence of the lack of immigration certificates to Palestine — people will wait patiently, if they know what they are waiting for — but of a mounting conviction that the Zionist movement lacked constructive plans for the mass absorption of German Jewry. (Of the 200,000 German Jews who were supposed to go to Palestine, according to Dr. Ruppin's plan, only about 53,000 immigrated to Palestine by the time of the outbreak of World War II.)

Alongside the disillusionment with Zionism there were attempts to return to the old economic positions and to revive assimilationist efforts. There appeared an organization called "Land and Labor," which argued that also in Germany Jews could change their economic pursuits and pass over to productive labor and thus once again find their place within the German nation. Whereas in the spring they had sought Jewish values and sensed a Jewish national revival, they now drew back from making decisions and waited to see what would happen next.

The period of rapid Zionist advances of early 1933 came to an end and was not likely to recur in the near future. In Enzo's opinion "German Jewry was doomed to slow but unavoidable demise, since it was impossible to reverse the economic processes which would be the cause of this decline, but this would not come about dramatically as in the spring of 1933 but would rather resemble the slow death agonies of the Jews of Poland or Lithuania. But since Jewish consciousness was much weaker in Germany, the role of Zionism would be more difficult and complex and the assimilationist tendencies would be more powerful." Indeed, in 1934 a substantial part of German Jewry still believed

that a common destiny united Jews and Germans, and nationalist elements in German Jewry weighed the possibility of an
understanding with the more "moderate" Nazis of Gregor
Strasser's type. Even after Strasser was murdered by his Nazi
comrades, there were some Jews who proffered declarations of
loyalty to Germany on the order of "Germany is our homeland,
and its happiness is our happiness. We look forward to the day
when we will be called, when our loyal youth will have an opportunity to demonstrate its loyalty. . . . We stand prepared for
Germany."

In April 1934, Enzo returned for a short stay in Palestine, by
way of Rome, naturally. Givat Brenner had become the main
absorption center for newcomers from Germany, having received
about 160 of them among its total membership of three hundred.
At a general meeting called to discuss "shortcomings in our life,"
he declared: "The Zionist movement seems incapable of master-
ing the tide of history, and the kibbutz movement, including
Givat Brenner, did not succeed in gaining control of the mass
influx. Many kibbutz members who have now lived in Givat
Brenner for months participate in the physical existence of Givat
Brenner but are not a part of the kibbutz experience and their
membership in Givat Brenner is a mere formality. What does the
newcomer find here? Who will talk to him? Whom will he meet
in the common dining room? There is much tumult and noise,
but what will he find aside from the noise? Does anyone among
us show interest in his concerns? When a member leaves the
kibbutz he mostly does so not because of material circumstances
but because he hasn't found anyone who will share his concerns."

Enzo regarded Givat Brenner as the yardstick for the successful absorption in Palestine of the newcomers from Germany;
and were this to fail, the entire tremendous effort of the preceding year would have been wasted. As one who had returned
from outside, he could take a fresh look at kibbutz life and he
found it wanting. He observed that many of the new members of
the kibbutz responded to the demands of collectivist life not out
of conviction, the way the founders did, but merely as a form of
submission to the accepted conventions of kibbutz life. He even
hinted that there existed "a kind of spiritual terror of the Bolshe-

vik kind, which expressed itself in moral pressures on the individual members and the creation of an atmosphere where
individuals refrain to act as they would wish to for fear of public
disapproval of certain types of behavior as being not truly in
accord with kibbutz or pioneering principles and therefore to be
shunned. This leads not only to hypocrisy but also to inner du-
plicity in the minds of unsophisticated members and to a climate
of pressure against those who do not adapt themselves to the
demands of the majority, and finally to abandonment of the kibbutz altogether." Time and again he complained about what he
regarded as the two chief shortcomings in kibbutz life of which
he had talked so frequently in the past: the open ballot that
compelled some members to vote as they thought was required
of them; and the lack of a kibbutz constitution that defined the
duties of the individual to the community and guaranteed his
rights and thus restrained the hidden tendency in kibbutz life to
educate the individual by mechanical means.

When Enzo was at home in Givat Brenner, life there acquired
a different tempo. From his travels he would bring gifts for all
the children in the kibbutz, and take an interest in their education; he would carry Daniel on his back and take his daughters
for long walks; he would tell stories and play roughly with the
children on the lawn, or take all the children of Givat Brenner for
hikes; he would dash from one meeting to another, confer with
the leaders of the community, deliver lectures, take an interest in
the well-being of everyone, then disappear as suddenly as he had
arrived.

Yet with all his criticism and concern for Givat Brenner, it
was now the center of his life, as the Sereni home had been in
the past, and though preoccupied with many activities in Germany, he always kept the needs of Givat Brenner in mind.
While he was in Germany there came to him parents of children
who had settled in Givat Brenner who begged that they themselves might obtain immigration permits. But the possibilities of
absorbing parents into Givat Brenner were not self-evident.
Some members feared that it would place too heavy an economic
burden on them; others doubted whether a collectivist community was a suitable place for conservative older people who were

religiously observant and lived in the world of yesterday. Enzo opposed this attitude unyieldingly.

An incubator, agricultural machines, equipment for the laundry — all these Givat Brenner received from Germany where Enzo raised the funds for them in his own unique ways. In Germany he looked for a doctor to take charge of the vegetarian nursing home that was about to be set up in Givat Brenner at the initiative of the poet Jessie Sampter, a native of the United States and an invalid confined to a wheel chair who then lived in Rehovot and donated all her capital on condition that she be allowed to live in the nursing home all the rest of her days.

Enzo decided to return home in the fall, and this time there could be no doubt about the urgency of his decision. For a year and a half he had worked at a hectic tempo, constantly on the road, bearing responsibilities, and often in personal danger. He could look back at his accomplishments with pride. Never had the Hechalutz organization in Germany prospered as under his leadership. It now had 15,000 members, 3,800 of whom were undergoing training. Since April 1933, some 2,200 emigrated to Palestine and about two-thirds of these joined kibbutzim.

He left Germany at the end of September in order to be able to spend the High Holy Days with his parents, but this time no longer in the Sereni house on Cavour Street. During the summer of 1934 the last wing of the house had been torn down, and now there were only ruins. But though the house had been destroyed, the projected Via dei Fori Imperiali did not reach it. It is quite possible that the demolition order had been issued as punishment for the Sereni family whose children were known anti-Fascists. The land on which the house stood remains unoccupied to this day.

The Sereni parents lived in a rented apartment; Mimo was still in prison. But Enzo did not hesitate to ask for money from family — this time for the construction of a school in Givat Brenner. When he tried to get a large hall where he could address the Jews of Rome and warn them of the danger threatening Italian Jewry (some seven thousand of whom were members of the Fascist party) no less than the Jews of Germany, he was brushed off with the usual alibi of Jews in the Diaspora that

"talk about the danger only intensifies it." Enzo was thus compelled to address a limited audience in a small room and his
words aroused general resentment: Didn't Mussolini's regime
grant asylum to thousands of Jewish refugees? Didn't he permit
free passage through Italy for Jews on their way to Palestine?
Hadn't he proclaimed, again and again, that he would never
allow anti-Semitism in Italy?

13

On a Solitary Island
without Jews

Some members of a kibbutz are doomed not to become farmers. No sooner had Enzo returned to Givat Brenner and worked for a short while in the orange plantation than he was involved in administrative duties. When he was asked to take the job of kibbutz secretary for external contacts, he rejected the suggestion with the argument that it would be a mistake both for him and for the kibbutz. But his refusal had only a limited effect, and at a general meeting of all the members of the kibbutz he was elected to the post of secretary for the internal affairs of Givat Brenner.

He derived some satisfaction from the organization of cultural activities. A study month was proclaimed and it enjoyed the participation even of heads of families and others who had lived in the kibbutz for years but had not hitherto taken part in its cultural activities. A special barrack was put up to serve as cultural center and here the kibbutz library, which Enzo regarded as one of the best in the country, was housed. All this was cause for elation.

The housing situation, however, was intolerable. Givat Brenner now numbered four hundred members. Half of them lived in tents of varying age, some of which could not be used at all during the winter. The fugitives from these tents found temporary shelter in the nursing home, which was still not quite finished. Fifteen others were housed in the huge packing crates in which the immigrants' possessions had been brought from Germany; nine others had no regular housing. The older members refused to take a third party into their family quarters. To alleviate the situation somewhat, a temporary structure of cinder blocks, not cemented together or plastered inside, was put up and quickly gained the name of "the death wall." An investigating group from the health organization of the Federation of Labor came to examine sanitary conditions in Givat Brenner after the outbreak of a typhus epidemic and condemned what they saw. In the entire camp there were only eight toilet booths. The bakery was filthy. Garbage was dumped in open places and flies proliferated. The shower room could, with difficulty, accommodate only one hundred persons and had no hot water installation. The verdict was that unless improvements in the sanitary arrangements were made, it would be impossible to recommend Givat Brenner as a place that could absorb youthful emigrants from Germany.

Enzo fought stubbornly against the prevailing filth and neglect. He'd go about the kibbutz grounds with a box of matches in his pocket, rake up the trash and set it on fire, to the accompaniment of ironic remarks from aesthetically less sensitive members. Disturbed though he was by the unsanitary conditions prevailing, he was troubled even more about the cultural absorption of the young people who were soon to come to the kibbutz. "There is no educational value," he argued, "in merely providing the newcomers with a place to sleep, if we do not also provide educators, and I will regard it as a great failure if we do not succeed in finding teachers in our midst and have to seek them outside." Apart from the question of prestige, his concern had a more solid basis, for numerous elements in Germany, as well as in the World Zionist Organization, were still opposed to sending the youth immigrants to labor settlements and would have preferred special institutions for this purpose.

Visitors from outside who came to Givat Brenner did not share Enzo's concern. Sir Arthur Wauchope, the High Commissioner for Palestine, was deeply impressed, and even David Ben-

Gurion, whose relations with Hakibbutz Hameuchad were then strained, was enthusiastic when he came on the occasion of a festival to welcome the newly arrived youngsters from Germany.

But Enzo remained troubled, particularly about the children. Collective upbringing was still in its infancy; the teachers lacked experience and there were frequent changes in staff. The children had no peaceful place to retreat to in their parents' room, and their overall cultural level was unsatisfactory. True, they had a close relationship with nature, but their aesthetic sense was wanting. "I gave them a number of pictures to choose from," Enzo related, "and they invariably picked the ugliest ones." At a meeting he offered his opinion that the minds of the children were primarily concerned with two things: the struggle for power and categorizing the newcomers as either "elegant" or "nonelegant." It was true that their attitude toward work was positive — they were not lazy, but work as such played no role in their lives. It simply did not interest them. Enzo believed that the root of this attitude was the children's total lack of fear of authority. A kibbutz child never felt the need to submit to someone or something. Yet children do not always wish to be persuaded; sometimes they want to be compelled.

His post as secretary for the internal affairs of the kibbutz required him once again to deal with financial matters and covering deficits, except that now the sums involved were much larger and the opportunities to plug up temporarily gaping financial holes in the budget were more numerous. But the debts also increased with the growth of Givat Brenner. One hundred and fifty new people had joined it since the autumn of 1934, and Enzo now talked of the possibility of a kibbutz of two thousand members; nor did he conceal his ambition to make Givat Brenner the largest kibbutz in the country.

When he announced that an additional forty people, including an organized group from Lithuania, were about to join the kibbutz, many voices opposed this both because of the housing shortage and because of the difficulties encountered in the absorption of many who were already there, either socially or culturally. "We are told to absorb new immigrants," many argued.

"But why do we ignore members who have already lived with us for two years and are still strangers to our life-style, our hopes, and particularly to our language?"

Indeed, the influx of a large number of newcomers led to manifestations one had never dreamed could arise in the early days of the pure pioneering spirit. One such was a member who malingered and even knew how to raise his temperature artificially. When confronted with this, he said in his defense that he had seen others doing the same thing. The meeting that dealt with his case demanded that he be expelled from the kibbutz. The man argued that expulsion from the kibbutz would drive him to leave the country altogether. Enzo pleaded that the meeting deal with the culprit mercifully, especially since the charges against him were not adequately proved, but by a great majority the meeting voted to expel the man.

Minutes of membership meetings of that time present a somewhat distorted image of affairs: low attendance, and when members came, it was not to listen to enthusiastic reports of achievements, but mostly to express bitterness at the situation, to criticize, and to voice demands. Ada, who was still working in the clothing store, complained of the growing amount of work; eighty members had still not been assigned private cubicles and their belongings lay around on a table or under it; nearly everybody lacked sufficient linen and work clothes, and some even lacked dress clothes. Every woman in Givat Brenner had one dress for the Sabbath, but the budget of the kibbutz could not provide them all with dress shoes. It was the custom of the kibbutz to buy one pair of women's dress shoes in each size, and if someone had occasion to go to the city, she would borrow a suitable pair from the stockroom. There were times when one could see the following scene at the bus station in Rehovot — a woman returning from the city taking off her shoes at the station and handing them to another about to go to the city.

Ada, who had made friends with the Weizmanns in nearby Rehovot, would occasionally visit them. They were living in a modest home which they had temporarily rented from Jessie Sampter before they built their permanent home on a hill overlooking the Weizmann Institute of Science. One day she hap-

pened to be alone in Vera Weizmann's room and stood in deep
wonder before the shelf on which stood Vera Weizmann's shoes,
twelve pairs, all beautiful and all belonging to one woman. For
years afterward, Vera Weizmann used to recall the look of wonder on Ada's face at the sight of so much individual wealth.

With all his love and concern for his family, Enzo used to
decide for himself whether or not to go on his various missions
and Ada's wishes in these matters were given only secondary
consideration. Early in 1935, he was approached with a proposal to go to South America on a fund-raising mission, and he
reacted to it coolly. Another suggestion was that he go to the
United States on behalf of the pioneering Hechalutz organization. What he really wanted at this time was to complete one of
his favorite literary projects, a study of the young Marx, and to
"find himself somewhere on a remote island without Jews, instead of going to America." Ever since Moses, Jewish leaders
have experienced this sense of weariness with their people, but
not many of them have had an opportunity to find solitude on
Mount Sinai.

The absorption of the Jewish immigrants from Germany, and
the transfer of their money to Palestine, which caused an economic upsurge in the country, was one of the chief topics of
discussion at the nineteenth Zionist Congress, which met in
Lucerne, Switzerland, and at which Sereni was a regularly
elected member on the Labor party list. When Meir Grossman,
head of the Revisionist state party, accused the Labor faction at
the Congress of underhanded dealing with Hitler's agents and
deriving personal benefits from the moneys transferred, Enzo for
the first and only time took the floor in defense of the efforts of
the labor movement in Germany. He spoke of the thousands of
young Jewish pioneers who were brought to the Socialist kibbutzim, against which Grossman had raged. "I know," Enzo
declared, "that in the process of these rescue activities we have
been compelled to resort to means and activities that were sometimes distasteful to us. We also knew that the process of liberating German Jewry through an exodus cannot be accomplished
by means of verbal protests and proclamations but only through
concrete action. And we knew there are some who were inter-

ested that the transfer should be arranged in a way that would benefit plutocrats and individuals. When I hear their outcries against our work, I wonder, are these people really so altruistic?"

But at that time Switzerland was the scene of consultations much more important than the Zionist Congress. The League of Nations meeting in Geneva was confronted with a host of problems arising from Italy's invasion of Ethiopia. England and France were willing to enter an agreement with Mussolini granting him the fertile areas on the plateau and leaving to Haile Selassie only the mountainous region that since ancient time was the core of the kingdom; this proposal was made secretly without consultation with Haile Selassie. When it became public, it aroused a storm of indignation. Negotiations were halted and Mussolini proceeded with his invasion. The League of Nations voted economic sanctions against Italy, but not a single power took up the defense of Ethiopia with arms.

In Palestine the Ethiopian war raised melancholy thoughts. If this could happen to a long independent Christian country that was also a member of the League, what fate awaited the Jewish community in Palestine, which was still building its national homeland under infinitely more difficult conditions? If treaties were disregarded and promises ignored, what defense was left to the weak? Only not to be weak, and to accumulate as much strength as possible! In principle, Enzo was opposed to Mussolini's imperialist war, yet a certain spark of Italianness remained within him. He was exasperated with friends who doubted the military abilities of the Italians or ridiculed their "macaroni" army and barely concealed his satisfaction with the advances of the Italian army in Ethiopia. When a friend asked him bluntly, "Don't you admire the duce just a little bit?" he thought long and answered: "Once upon a time there was something to Mussolini. He was a good guy, but lost his way. A pity!"

The Italian settlement in Palestine grew apace. Nino Hirsch, who ten years earlier had vowed to follow Enzo, now arrived and joined Givat Brenner. There also came Alfonso Pacifici, his wife, and four children, whom they wanted to educate in the Promised Land, especially their six-year-old son. Pacifici settled in Jerusalem and encountered great economic difficulties. More than ever he was convinced that salvation for the Jewish people would come as a result of greater devotion to the Jewish faith. For a time Enzo used to be a frequent visitor at his former mentor's house, but relations between them deteriorated as Pacifici expressed his displeasure that Enzo not only abandoned religious tradition himself but also influenced others to follow in his ways.

Dvora Sereni, Enrico's widow, returned to Palestine with her little daughter and took employment in the experimental station at Rehovot as an expert plant pathologist. Enzo tried hard but unsuccessfully to persuade her to join Givat Brenner. Mimo, the youngest of the Sereni brothers, was released from prison after five years, under the terms of an amnesty that Victor Emmanuel proclaimed on the occasion of the birth of his grandson and direct heir to the throne, but he had to report twice daily to the police headquarters in Rome. As required, he reported regularly while secretly planning his escape. The Communist underground provided him with a false American passport as well as expensive luggage to enable him to cross the border in the guise of a wealthy American tourist. Right after one of his appearances at the police station he shaved off his beard and, together with his wife Xenia and their little daughter, escorted by a Communist party agent, went to Milan. There the family boarded the express to Paris, and by the time it was necessary for Mimo to appear at the police station he was already across the French border. Since the elder Sereni enjoyed the protection of the court, the regime did not persecute him. The Serenis continued to help Mimo financially and in other ways whenever there was an opportunity to smuggle out such assistance. Xenia tried to earn some money by taking in sewing, but, like her husband, she was deeply involved in political activity. As much a zealot as Mimo, she declared that "I cannot imagine true family life if husband and wife are not bound together by common convictions and activity." This activity was the center of her life, as it was also of Mimo's, and was more important to them than their being together, or even their two little daughters, the second one being born after they fled from Italy.

Xenia Silberberg — Xenia Sereni's mother — followed her

Jewish friends to Palestine, where she settled in Kibbutz Na'an. This presented her daughter with a fateful question: Was it right for her, a member of the Communist party, to maintain personal relations with persons who were not Communists? And when it was explained to her forcefully that "those who are not with us are against us," she decided to break all relations with her mother. This step would no doubt cause pain to her mother, but since revolutionists are not to be daunted, she wrote her a farewell letter: "Precisely because you have devoted your life to bringing me up strong in body and in spirit, I know that you will not condemn my decision; on the contrary, you will admire my determination and will yourself support me during this difficult time. I will not write to you, nor you to me, but you know that you are and always will be my mother, and all my love, everything that a person feels for one's mother, I feel now as in the past — more than in the past."

Xenia Silberberg did her daughter's bidding and stopped writing to her.

Enzo Sereni at Givat Brenner

Enzo on his Bar Mitzvah in Rome, spring 1918

The Sereni family during World War I

*Enzo and Ada Sereni and their oldest daughter, before their
departure for Palestine in 1927*

The three Sereni brothers: Enzo, Enrico, and Emilio

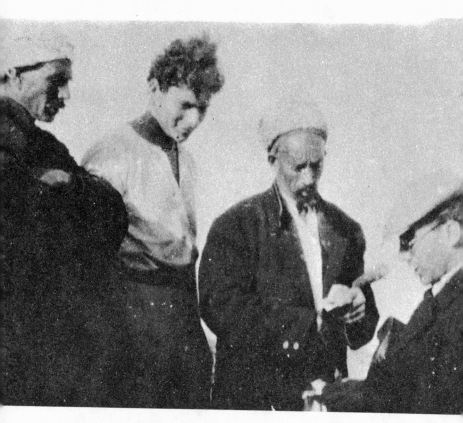

Enzo while secretary of Givat Brenner, with Arabs from the neighboring village Zarnuga

During World War II in Iraq as emissary on behalf of illegal immigration

*Enzo on the eve of his last mission, together with Ada, Hagar,
Daniel, his mother, his sister, and her family*

14

A New World with the Same Old Troubles

By the time Enzo returned to Givat Brenner from the Congress at Lucerne, the suggestion to send him as emissary to the United States to work with the pioneering organization Hechalutz had hardened into a decision and he accepted it. The Secretariat of the Executive of the Histadrut, which would deal with his going to the United States, wanted him to leave as soon as possible. Zalman Rubashov (later Zalman Shazar, president of Israel), discussing the condition of the Zionist movement, pointed out how effective emissaries like Sereni could be in America, for it was believed that there lay a secret treasure to which no one thus far had found the key.

It is true that in the United States the Jewish Labor movement in Palestine had a number of devoted admirers centered about the Poale Zion party, and each year since 1922 the Histadrut had sent a delegation to the United States to lead the annual campaign for funds. But the influence of these delegations was chiefly limited to eastern European immigrants in America, people who vividly remembered the Diaspora and the poverty and oppression of the sweatshops during their first years as immigrants, and if they had not personally experienced these, then they had heard about them from their parents. Largely Yiddish-speaking, they were bound by innumerable strands to Jewish culture and tradition. Many of them had served their labor Zionist apprenticeship in the same Socialist-Zionist movement from which came Ben-Gurion, Berl Katznelson, and Golda Meyerson (as Golda Meir was known at that time), and not a few of them reached the United States via Palestine where they could not make a go of it. The emissaries of the Histadrut visiting the United States found friends and ideological sympathizers who were loyal supporters, but not candidates for emigration to Palestine. This generation had already made the great effort of becoming acclimatized to a new environment in their lives, and they would lack the energy as well as the impetus to make another such effort.

The children of these immigrants, born and educated in the United States, regarded themselves first of all as Americans, and Zionism did not interest them. The youth groups advocating pioneering in Israel were minute, immigration to Palestine was virtually nil, and none of the delegates sent by the Histadrut found a common language with them. For these reasons it was decided to send Enzo, an intellectual and a man of western culture, dynamic, unconventional, who had demonstrated his magic in Germany.

It was clear why Enzo was wanted in the United States. But why did he consent to this assignment less than a year after his return from Germany? Of course, the highest authority of the labor movement in Palestine imposed the mission on him; nevertheless, he would not have accepted it out of a sense of duty alone. There must have been a number of other motivations: curiosity about a new world and a new culture; inner unrest; lack of satisfaction with what he was doing in Palestine. It had been suggested that he be given some assignment in one of the institutions of the labor movement, but this, at best, would have been an assignment of secondary importance. Although he was liked by the chiefs of the labor movement and his talents were recognized, he remained an outsider and did not belong to the inner circle; he was too different, too independent and unpredictable. Perhaps the determining fact was that he had faith in his mission, and regarded himself as one to whom a higher power had entrusted the task of arousing the Jewish world to the idea of the return to Zion.

The financial condition of Hechalutz in the United States was pitiful — it didn't have a penny to its name, a reflection of the attitude of disdain felt toward it by the leadership of Zionism in America, including the Poale Zion. It was regarded as a barely tolerated by-product that might serve to adorn a mass meeting or solicit contributions for the Jewish National Fund. The very idea of pioneering immigration to Palestine from America seemed absurd. Altogether the Hechalutz organization numbered some two hundred, and of these some scores had joined it not out of devotion to the idea of pioneering but because they were socially maladjusted at home.

On January 28, 1936, Enzo sailed on the *Majestic* from Southampton to New York by himself. The original plan had called for the family to accompany him, but this was modified at the last moment. Ada and the children returned to Givat Brenner until Enzo could look over the situation and make the necessary arrangements for them to join him. On the eve of his departure he appealed to the Executive Committee, "Do not leave me penniless," yet from the day of his arrival in New York, financial problems relentlessly pursued him.

For the Jewish community in Palestine was again undergoing an economic crisis as a result of the Ethiopian war and the fear of political upheavals along the Mediterranean. In addition, the war in Ethiopia and the failure of the halfhearted attempts to impose sanctions on Italy revealed the helplessness of the democracies, France and England, when confronted with totalitarian regimes, and there were numerous indications that Arab-Jewish relations would again deteriorate and lead to a new wave of clashes. It was therefore not surprising that the Executive of the Histadrut could not be bothered with such peripheral matters as the problems of its emissary in the United States, whose letters often remained unanswered.

Alone in a strange country, he had no one with whom to consult, and "one of the main difficulties here, more than in any other country, [is] that the new emissary [is] at once expected to establish contacts with various elements and to provide them with directions and information. This is unavoidable and the demands on him are justified. Isn't he the man from Palestine, the one who is supposed to know everything and able to solve all problems?"

Enzo assumed his duties with gusto. He met with Stephen Wise, one of the leaders of American Zionism, who promised to obtain $10,000 for Hechalutz, and although the promise was hedged with conditions, Enzo at once began making plans. At the first formal meeting of the Hechalutz executive committee he projected the publication of books, including anthologies on Brenner, Borochow, and Gordon, and the transformation of the Hechalutz bulletin into a regular monthly dealing with informative as well as cultural matters. He proposed that more stress be placed on active training instead of organizational activities. "We must change the lives of the members of Hechalutz from the ground up, and this can only be done on training farms," he insisted. In his opinion there were altogether only between sixty and seventy members who were real candidates for immigration to Palestine, and they needed a suitable farm for their training; although he had doubts about the financial feasibility of such a project, negotiations were begun for the acquisition of a training farm.

Cream Ridge, a run-down farm-resort of 140 acres in New Jersey, boasting a brook, a swimming pool, a dining room seating two hundred people, and a hotel with twenty-three bedrooms, was finally chosen. It was a bargain at $12,500 and was purchased with a downpayment of $1,000, a sum taken from funds contributed by the potential immigrants to cover their travel costs. The rest was covered by a mortgage to be paid off at the rate of $60 a month. Shortly after the acquisition of Cream Ridge, a summer seminar was held there under the guidance of Enzo and Zalman Rubashov. Of the seventy participants only about fifteen were members of Hechalutz, the rest being members of the League for Labor Palestine and Junior Hadassah. The seminar ran up a deficit of $800, but Enzo was satisfied. It was addressed by renowned lecturers who lent it prestige, and the participants became supporters of Hechalutz. In the United States even those modest results were a major accomplishment, since the first objective was the creation of a periphery of supporters for the pioneering movement.

Enzo was the last man to be content to stew in the small pot of the miniature Hechalutz and its troubles. He aimed to penetrate new circles of the young Jewish intelligentsia, to gain a foothold among university students, and thus create a reserve for Hechalutz. He had a clear idea of what he wanted: "I limited my activities to one part of American Jewry, the part that not only spoke English but also lived in its culture. To this day a large part of American Jewry not only continued to use the Yiddish language, but also tried to keep alive the Yiddish language and culture. But in this they did not succeed and despite their stubborn attempts to win for their ideals the loyalty of the generation that was American born, they failed. An abyss separated parents and children. From the very start I gave up the idea of entering the Yiddish-speaking world, My own biography and the environment in which I grew up made me incapable of acting among them. I pinned my hopes on the English-speaking, assimilated Jewish youth."

Joe Criden, whom Enzo astounded during their first meeting when he came out to greet him totally nude after taking a shower, was captivated and was persuaded to come to New York to work in the Hechalutz office for a ridiculously low wage. Even this token fee was often borrowed back a day after it was paid out in order to buy postage stamps needed by the office. Though Enzo was a merciless employer, his vitality swept young people along as in a whirlpool and caused them to follow him as Hassidim follow their *rebbe*. But since punctuality was not one of Enzo's chief attributes, Joe was assigned the job of seeing to it that he appeared on time at meetings. Once, when on their way, they passed a movie where a western was being shown — one of Enzo's favorites — and he dragged Joe inside. Both appeared a couple of hours late at the scheduled meeting. "It's nothing," Enzo decided. "So we missed a meeting."

When Ada and the children arrived in New York, the Serenis and the activists formed a commune. Ada refused to live in any of the dreary hotels that had been recommended to them and went to look for quarters more in accord with her taste on Riverside Drive. She found a large apartment, suffering a good deal from neglect but facing the Hudson, whose rent, divided among ten to fourteen tenants, would have been reasonable. So far as the uniformed doorman was concerned, Ada was Mrs. Beth Hechalutz who received much mail. What he could not understand was why the people living in such a roomy apartment on the seventh floor so frequently borrowed from him nickels for subway fare. For Enzo, communal living was a matter of principle; Ada wanted it so as not to be lonely in the big city and not to be tied to the house during Enzo's absences on his travels.

Ada looked after the cleanliness of the two rooms in which the Serenis lived, the kitchen, and dining room. The other rooms were kept more or less tidy by the other members of the commune, whose number averaged ten. Ada cooked only for her family, but when members of the commune returned home at night hungry, they would consume whatever they found in the refrigerator. In an effort to save her supplies from the hungry locusts she would tag various containers with notations "This is for the children," but even this didn't always work.

Wherever he went Enzo sought out concentrations of Italians and observed how the process of their Americanization eroded their old world traditions and values, the same process that affected the Jews. With the assistance of some trade unions an interview was arranged for him with Fiorello LaGuardia, then mayor of New York, and it was a sight to behold, the excited meeting of these two short Italians gesticulating and simultaneously talking in loud voices.

Of the anti-Fascist circle of his youthful days Enzo found in America Max Ascoli who came to the United States in 1931 on a fellowship from the Rockefeller Foundation. Without first informing him of his plans, Enzo appeared late one evening in Ascoli's house far from the center of New York. Despite the embraces and the joy of reunion, their conversation became heated within a matter of minutes. Enzo told Ascoli about his mission in Germany and praised Hitler's political talent. Ascoli was at that time a close friend of the journalist Dorothy Thompson, who was one of the first to arouse the American public to the dangers of Nazi rule. "You American intellectuals," Enzo exclaimed, "you and your Dorothy Thompson, you don't understand Hitler. He has political intuition. Your Roosevelt can't

measure up to him in this respect." "But Hitler wants to eliminate the Jews," Ascoli protested. Enzo, who loved to float trial
balloons to test their effect, argued, "Who knows? Hitler's anti-
Semitism might yet lead to the salvation of the Jews." And
Ascoli was convinced that Enzo had not changed at all during
the intervening years, that he was still courageous, devoted to
his ideals, but hopelessly immature. "When will you finally stop
being a high school boy?" he chided him. The heated debate
ended as it usually did with Enzo, with an embrace and friendly
backslapping.

By spring Enzo felt at home in America and had established
numerous contacts. "If I were to summarize my feelings and
impressions of my first few months here, I'd say that it is necessary to approach life here without any prior judgments and
without comparing manifestations of Jewish life here to what
may appear to be similar circumstances in other countries."

But the affairs of the Hechalutz organization in America,
which seemed important at the time Enzo left Palestine, became
irrelevant when compared to the wave of troubles that engulfed
Palestine in April 1936. In 1929, many regarded Moslem fa-
naticism as the chief cause of the rioting, but now there was no
longer any doubt about the political nature of the outbreak, nor
that it was organized by a nationalist movement, nor that it
aimed to nullify the Balfour Declaration, suspend Jewish immigration, prohibit the sale of land to Jews, and eliminate the
Jewish community in the country. Murder on the highways,
attacks on the railway, setting fire to Jewish homes, and ambushes in the countryside threatened the physical existence of
the Jewish community, and the prolonged Arab strike was also
intended to undermine the *Yishuv* economically. These events
aroused great interest in the United States and many young
Jews who were influenced by the anti-Zionist propaganda of the
Communists were eager to learn about the roots of the problems
affecting Jewish-Arab relations. Enzo decided to publish an anthology devoted to the Arab problem, which was also the chief
theme of his public appearances.

The anthology *Jews and Arabs in Palestine: Studies in a
National and Colonial Problem*, edited by Enzo Sereni and R. A.

Asheri, was published in the summer of 1936 by Hechalutz Press and contained essays by Chaim Arlosoroff, David Ben-Gurion, Moshe Beilinson, Yaakov Chazan, Hayim Greenberg, and Enzo Sereni. It is true that many of these essays, including Enzo's, had already appeared in similar form some three years earlier in Germany when Enzo was an emissary in Berlin. But at that time the views they expressed were lost in the turmoil of activity, whereas now they aroused a response when copies were dispatched to prominent Zionists in Palestine and throughout the world, since the problem of the relations of Jews and Arabs had been brought into sharp focus both because of the bloody events in Palestine and the keen sensitivity among western Jews to issues of human justice.

In his forty-page essay, "Toward a New Direction in Zionist Policy," which contained the essence of his views since he had settled in Palestine, Enzo argued for an autonomous Jewish community within a pan-Arab framework.

The characteristic feature of the struggle of the Arabs against us [he wrote] is that it is a struggle of desperation. Time is acting for the Jews, and against the extreme Arab nationalism. . . . Jewish immigration, restricted though it is by British officials, has already grown to such a political, economic, and moral force that no power in the world will be able to destroy it. Setbacks can occur. This may mean a slowing down in the tempo of the building. . . . But no Arab or Jewish power exists that can destroy Jewish immigration, just as there exists no Jewish power that can halt the process of Arab development which has been accelerated or even brought into existence by our immigration. Looking at the matter realistically, this is the starting point for the Jewish-Arab policy that must come into being as soon as the Arab national movement is convinced of what we already know, that they cannot annihilate us. . . . Our task then is to find the basic program for a possible Arab orientation. . . .

The heart of Enzo's argument was that "the only political escape from the contradictions between the interests of the Jewish immigrants and those of the Arab population of Palestine" was an overall "Arab pattern" in which Palestine would be included. With the coming of millions of Jews to Palestine, "it would follow that not only a dislocation in the relationship of power would take place, but also that the present Arab majority would be reduced to a minority. . . . But the inclusion of Palestine with our consent in an Arab pattern offers the possibility of a solution. In this pattern the Arabs will be a strong majority and they will not have to fear that we will surpass them in numbers. The problem of the dislocation of power in Palestine loses its point. It is however insoluble within an isolated Palestine. Within a Palestine set within a large Arab pattern the problem is no longer existent. . . ."

He admitted that such an orientation did not offer an immediate solution to the Jewish-Arab conflict: "The Arab forces who will support our aims are certainly not yet at hand or they are unknown to us in their inner nature." And yet, he added, "there exist even at this moment certain concrete political and practical tasks within the frame of this orientation. . . . In order to fulfill them it is necessary to rid ourselves of certain ways of thinking that are customary in Zionist circles":

We can and must stop trying to influence the Arabs by the argument of the economic advantages that we are bringing to their country. This resembles the method of argument used by our assimilationists in the Diaspora who always are astounded that the gentiles are against us, notwithstanding that we have brought wealth and plenty into every land.

We must free ourselves from the way of thinking of those who appeal to the Arabs on the basis that we have a mission to fulfill in the Arab world, or who point to our common past in Spain and in the Orient. We must appeal to the concrete political reality of today, with an eye to the future.

Zionism, he argued, had only two choices: revisionism, which meant a determined drive to establish an independent Jewish state in Palestine with the aid of British colonial rule; or a policy oriented on the Arabs that would strive to establish an authoritative body that would determine the political rights of the two parties, based on an agreement between them. No middle road existed, and what might appear as a middle road actually amounted to supporting one or the other of these alternatives without the courage to admit it. In truth there existed only one road, for revisionism had become a utopia impossible of realization, and should the masses adopt the Revisionist point of view, they would end in a state of demoralization and despair, as always happened after pseudomessianic hopes had been aroused. There thus remained only one alternative, different from what the early Zionists had visualized, one that would require compromises but preserve all the vital elements of Zionism.

American Jewish youth appreciated Enzo's frankness in thus presenting before them the problem of Arab-Jewish relations in Palestine, and his demand that the Arab interests should command the same attention that is devoted to Jewish interests corresponded with their humanistic convictions. But people of the older generation, who were close to the Histadrut, were shocked and found ways to inform those concerned with their attitude toward this emissary who, from the moment of his arrival, did not try to adapt himself to the mode of activity prevailing among Labor Zionists and did not conceal his impatience with meaningless discussions about matters of prestige and his distaste for pointless activity. The Executive Committee of the Histadrut in Tel Aviv began receiving letters about Enzo's public addresses on the Arab question which differed from the accepted stand of the Histadrut.

"We are informed in these letters," wrote a member of the Histadrut Executive, I. Mereminski, to Enzo, "that our representative dealing with youth education declared in an address that we must not use the name Eretz Israel but should refer to the country as Palestine, that there must be no talk of Arab gangs but only of protagonists of a nationalist movement, that he unequivocally stated that we 'wronged the Arabs,' that we must not fight for the priority of Jewish products, that the Tel Aviv port must not be referred to as a Jewish port, etc. All these letters expressed resentment and asked the same question: Either the Histadrut conceals from us things that are known to its emissary Sereni, who declares that Jews are wronging the

Arabs, or Sereni expresses personal views, which is his perfect right, but not when he talks in the name of the Histadrut. I know that you always succeeded in preserving the independence of your views and attitudes without these interfering with your work along the lines of Histadrut policy, and with much concern I am awaiting your elucidations which will enable all of us here to answer the complaints reaching us from America."

Enzo felt offended. Shouldn't he have been told who the authors of these letters were? Didn't the members of the Executive of the Histadrut have confidence in his ability to draw the line between what should and what shouldn't be said? As for the facts: Enzo had participated in a Labor Zionist conference where Yiddish was spoken. Since he didn't know Yiddish he chose to speak in German. "Naturally I spoke of Palestine, and when I was asked why I don't use the name Eretz Israel, I answered 'Now I am speaking German and in German the name of the country is Palestine. And we should learn something from this, that in the consciousness of non-Jews, what to us is Eretz Israel is to them Palestine. We must reckon with this fact and draw appropriate conclusions.

"In the course of my address I touched on the nationalist character of the Arab strike. I expressed the opinion that although we condemn the acts of the Arabs we must admit that some of them are marked by courage. Isn't it permissible to express these views in a discussion of the Arab problem at a Labor Zionist meeting?"

He went on to point out that he did not speak of wronging the Arabs and merely called attention to the fact that the Arabs did not want us even if we never wronged them. "I tried to understand why the Arabs oppose us and why honest and sincere Arabs in particular are against us. I tried to explain this by the national character of the Arab movement which at this time prefers political freedom and self-government to economic advantages. . . ."

When Beilinson died on November 19, 1936, Enzo's sense of aloneness became more pronounced, and he sensed a vacuum which no one else could fill. And Beilinson, too, during the last weeks of his life, had spoken of his concern over the lack of

talented people to continue the work and expressed the fear that
Enzo, too, might drift away, or that Ada might become accustomed to the easy life in the United States and refuse to return to
the kibbutz. Or that possibly Enzo's troubled conscience on the
question of the Arabs might lead to a break between him and the
movement.

The age difference between the top leadership of the labor
movement and Enzo was not great, yet he belonged to another
generation. Golda Meir, who was in the United States on a
mission for the Histadrut at the same time that Enzo was there,
felt this difference between herself and Enzo, and once asked
Saadia Gelb, one of the leaders of the Habonim organization, to
explain to her why Enzo was regarded as part of the youth
movement, and not she; why he was invited to address youth
meetings as one of their own, while she, who was his senior by a
mere six years, was only invited as a guest of honor. It was true
that in addition to his personal charm, which always attracted a
stream of devotees, he was primarily influential by means of the
frankness with which he talked to the youth about the Zionist
cause, thus making them feel they were partners in the work.
When Golda, who grew up in Milwaukee and knew American
Jewry well, heard Enzo discuss the Arab problem, she was concerned. She feared that the enthusiasm of young American Jews
might be blunted and they would come to entertain doubts about
the Zionist work as a whole. Years later she admitted that Enzo's
frankness did not diminish their interest but might have been
the very thing that attracted them and convinced them more
powerfully than other arguments.

It is hard to determine how many people joined the Halutz
movement on account of Enzo, how many went to Palestine
under his influence, or simply became more closely interested in
Palestine because of him, or for whom the encounter with him
marked a turning point in their lives. They did not number in
the thousands. Prevailing circumstances in the United States in
1936 were not conducive to this. But in one point Enzo differed
from the other emissaries who came before and after him: he
left a lasting imprint.

Financial matters were an endless source of dispute between

Enzo and his assistants. In his opinion all moneys — his own, that belonging to members of the commune, his family's money, the funds of Hechalutz and Habonim — were all intended to serve the needs of the cause, and he did not distinguish among them. He went out on coast-to-coast lecture tours to raise money for Hechalutz and he took money belonging to members of Hechalutz that was intended to defray their transportation costs to Palestine as a loan for the purchase of a training farm. His American assistants were not accustomed to this kind of book-keeping. Saadia Gelb, who was responsible for the management of the Habonim summer camp, concluded the season without a deficit and was proud of this achievement. Among assets left over from the summer camp was a used tender. Enzo suggested buying it for the use of Hechalutz. "It cost eighty dollars? OK, I'll give you seventy." When months passed and this sum was not paid, Saadia, who believed in separate accounts even for organizations dedicated to the same cause, called Enzo to a hearing before David Wertheim, the national secretary of Poale Zion, who ruled that Enzo must pay this sum. He agreed. But did he pay? Never.

And just as he was stingy with the salaries of the people who worked for Hechalutz — most of whom received fifteen dollars a week, a sum that one could subsist on only if it was supplemented with free lunches cadged from friends and relatives — so was he demanding of them where their work was concerned: and he was still more demanding of himself. No matter how early in the morning any of his assistants came to the dim and cluttered office of Hechalutz on Broadway, Enzo was already there, deeply immersed in newspapers. In an attempt to get to the office before Enzo at least once, Ben Halpern on one occasion went to the office directly from an overnight trip by train. He came in, dozed off for what seemed a few minutes and, when he awoke, there was Enzo at his desk at seven-thirty. They were often exasperated by him, yet they obeyed him, even in important personal matters. Thus Enzo decided that Joe Criden, one of his assistants, should get married. Joe agreed in principle but pointed to a lack of a candidate. Enzo promised to find a suitable bride on condition that Joe marry her. One day he brought to the office a girl named Ruth and said, "This is the one you will marry." At first a bit suspicious of Enzo's role as matchmaker, the two became acquainted nonetheless, and in the end they married and are living happily together to this day.

Enzo did not know English well when he came to America, which did not stop him from addressing audiences in the language from the day he disembarked. He learned English while working. He regarded his morning perusal of newspapers as one of the best ways of learning the language and when the office staff would come in the morning he would greet them with something like the following: "I just read in the *New York Times* on page twenty-three that . . ." The *Times* is a bulky paper with many pages, and his staff would test him; he invariably remembered with the precision of a computer the page, the column, and the exact content of what he had read. He would read on the bus, in the subway, on trains, between meetings, and would infect those about him with his reading fever.

On the eve of Yom Kippur he was seen leaving the Labor Zionist offices in a hurry, while leading Daniel with one hand and holding a black bound volume in the other. Shlomo Grodzensky, the editor of the Labor Zionist Yiddish weekly, ran after him to wish him a Happy New Year and asked him what was the book in his hand. A prayer book, he said. "You mean you plan to go to the synagogue?" Grodzensky wondered. "Yes, but only on the Day of Atonement." "Why so?" Grodzensky wanted to know. "Because the Day of Atonement is our only religious holiday. All the others are national in character."

Another time, when he strolled with Grodzensky in the streets, Enzo asked him: "Should Zionism fail — don't stare at me like that, do you have a guarantee that it won't fail? — whom would you join, the Communists or the orthodox Agudas Israel?" "Agudas Israel, naturally," Grodzensky replied. Enzo slapped him on the back. "Now I know that you are a real Zionist," he said.

In letters, reports, and articles Enzo tried to analyze the situation of American Jewry and to find the answer to a question that he regarded as basic: Do those laws of Jewish dynamics whose existence Zionists have always maintained were characteristic of Jewish fate throughout the Diaspora operate in America too? Only a few years earlier many believed that the development of the Jewish situation in America would not parallel that in other countries; now there were signs of growing anti-Semitism and a feeling that Jewish cultural and social integration did not succeed, and that Jewish community life proceeded without establishing fruitful contact with the outside world. In short, it was realized that the melting pot, which many hoped would do its work, did not function as expected.

To a certain extent this change in awareness was influenced by the fate of German Jewry, hitherto the epitome of successful civil and cultural assimilation. Events in Germany undermined the faith in the stability of political and economic positions especially among German-Jewish immigrants, who constituted the aristocracy within American Jewry, less so among immigrants from eastern Europe, who were confirmed in their belief that Europe was forever a place destined for trouble. Nevertheless, the exaggerated belief that "It can't happen here," was undermined, and Jews went about imbued with an unspoken fear that everything could indeed happen also in America, and perhaps even more so than in Europe.

Enzo was especially critical of the Zionist movement which in America, as in the Italy of his youth, remained essentially philanthropic. "After the great effort of American Jewry during World War I, the Zionist movement lost all traits of a national movement and became a mere agency for collecting funds for their persecuted brothers. It regarded Palestine as a problem in relief. Palestine's popularity corresponded to the success of practical work there, but there was no true ideological involvement, no youth, and no new personalities."

He was particularly critical of the Labor Zionist movement. "We repeat, with greater talent, precisely those errors which had become a misfortune for the Zionist movement as a whole. In order to attain adopted campaign quotas, we disregard what methods we use in our propaganda. True, for the moment we can mark accomplishments, but we are cutting off the branch on which we could depend during difficult times which may come in the future, when Palestine should be closed to us for a long time, or some other country — Russia, for instance — should appear as a competitor in absorbing immigrants."

Enzo felt that the labor movement erred doubly in that it did not learn how to speak to different groups in American Jewry, to each in its own language, but limited itself to one segment that was temporarily the most important numerically and also financially and politically, but that had no followers and no future.

Emissaries of the Histadrut would return to Palestine with glowing reports of the warm and affectionate reception which they encountered in America. Enzo responded with anger to their reports. He protested against their exaggeration and high rhetoric and tried to explain the true situation to the labor movement in Palestine: "Those circles which are close to us are old-time veterans of socialism in America. It is true that they are leaders of the trade union and political labor movement now, but winning them is of little value from the standpoint of the future, for they are a childless generation that has no continuation. I don't think that my pessimism is exaggerated. In another fifteen to twenty years, when this older generation passes away, we will have no one to turn to in the United States, and our disappointment will be all the greater for it will come after years of financial affluence."

Shortly before the Serenis' departure from the United States they arranged to celebrate the last Seder night together with a small group — the members of the Riverside Drive commune and five or six invited guests from the outside. It was decided that if anyone should invite any other guests, he was to inform Ada in advance, but Enzo ignored this decision. He casually invited whomever he met in the city, and shortly after Seder it became apparent that there would be more than one hundred guests, for whom there were neither chairs, dishes, nor food. Ada proceeded to boil eggs in tremendous quantities and the commune members bought additional matzoth. To the Seder came Hayim Greenberg and Zalman Rubashov, Joachim Prinz and Golda Meir, and many more. Rubashov recited the Haggadah in traditional fashion. People sat on the floor and ate anything they could get; it was a mad, unplanned evening but one that people remembered with pleasure for years to come.

On May 15, 1937, Enzo and his family left for England, leaving behind them the new world with its old problems.

15

With a Club
against Guns

After the American interlude Enzo felt the need to replenish his
spiritual and intellectual resources, which had been exhausted
by day-to-day organizational work. In London, he immersed
himself in research work on the development of British involvement in the Middle East, a subject that had interested him for
some years, while Ada and the children returned ahead of him
to Givat Brenner. The focus of his research was the British
acquisition of the shares of the Suez Canal, and the political
intrigues that preceded this, but he also began gathering material for a study of Sir Laurence Oliphant, the English adven-
turer and mystic who, at the end of the nineteenth century,
settled in Haifa and was also active in the work of ingathering
Jews to Zion. But by September 1937, he became impatient to
rejoin Ada and the children. "As the children grow, matters
pertaining to parent-children relationships which cannot be
understood rationally are becoming increasingly clear to me," he
wrote. "The heart has a logic of its own, and I often feel guilty
for having neglected parental duties whose value I only now
appreciate."

The Sereni children (Chana was now eleven, Hagar nine, and
Daniel seven), who in their short lives had knocked about between the family home in Italy and communes in Germany and
the United States, were again growing accustomed to kibbutz

life. Daniel, black-eyed, intelligent, impulsive, and undisciplined, became the darling of the kibbutz; but upon his return from America he had forgotten virtually all his Hebrew and had to go back to the first grade.

When Enzo returned to Givat Brenner in the winter of 1937, the problem of a school building was at the center of attention, but there were still not enough children to justify the maintenance of a separate school, and the talk was about a joint school with neighboring Kvutzat Schiller that would also serve workers' children in the neighborhood. But one condition was paramount — that the school building be in Givat Brenner. It was Enzo's ambition that Givat Brenner become the largest kibbutz in the country, and when he mentioned the fantastic figure of a membership of two thousand, this aroused much general merriment. He obtained a loan from Aunt Ermalinda Sereni for the construction of the school. Aunt Ermalinda was a close friend of Maria Montessori, the progressive Italian educator, and was interested in all educational problems. She also used to send books and educational toys to the children of Givat Brenner. She now came to the inauguration of the school, a tall and elegant old lady; but she refused to remain in Palestine — her roots were too deep in Italy.

As has been the custom in kibbutzim to this day regarding emissaries returning from abroad, Ada went back to work in the kitchen, and she proposed some radical innovations in the eating habits of the kibbutz. Instead of the huge and noisy central dining room, she visualized a number of small and more intimate dining rooms, to which the food was to be brought from the central kitchen and picked up on a self-help basis. (It was a plan that anticipated fulfillment by half a century.) After her turn in the kitchen, Ada went to work in the preserves factory, a project that had begun modestly, canning the surplus vegetables grown by the kibbutz during the summer. Refrigeration facilities were still unavailable and the kibbutz used to distribute the surplus cucumbers among the unemployed in Rehovot. Vegetable growing was only one-fourth as profitable as outside employment, because of competition with cheap Arab produce; still the kibbutz vegetables more than once saved Givat Brenner from

hunger. It was therefore decided to preserve part of the crop for
the dead season. At first they pickled cucumbers in brine in
accordance with old-time recipes; then the kibbutz sent a member to train in the art of vegetable and fruit preserving. The
project was primarily intended to solve the problem of employment for the older members, and it was not prospering. In the
spring of 1938 its treasurer asked the kibbutz to invest a further
1,500 pounds for the mechanization of this enterprise, and many
members expressed their doubts: why assume additional expenses? Sereni was angry. "This constant belittling of an enterprise that we built is intolerable. Where in the world is agriculture developed with the savings of the settlers only? But here,
the moment there is a deficit we tend to despair. Fruit trees are
uprooted or a project is restricted. We have grown old. One
would think that Givat Brenner was built entirely on deficits.
But one must not renounce a vision. Our future will depend on
diversification."

The kibbutz approved the necessary investment by a large
majority, but many months passed before this decision was carried out. The full development of the enterprise occurred only
when, during the war, the Mediterranean was closed to commercial traffic and Palestinian industry developed rapidly. Rimon, as
the canning plant was named, then worked full blast to supply
orders from the British military forces stationed in the vicinity.
In time Ada became the director of the project, the first assignment in which she demonstrated to the kibbutz, many of whose
members had at first regarded her as merely someone attached
to Enzo, that she had individual administrative talents of her
own.

When the days began to grow shorter and the heat less oppressive it was a sign that autumn was not far off and, in Enzo's
private calendar, it was time to visit his parents in Rome for the
holidays. The public reason for the trip is now forgotten but in
September 1938, Enzo was in Italy, where he had an opportunity to observe how the country followed in Germany's footsteps,
a development that he had foreseen and predicted earlier, and in
so doing had enraged the Jews of Rome. Now the ground was
being prepared for the promulgation of race laws.

All through 1937, many statements had appeared in Italy that dealt with the alleged sharp contrasts between the Jewish and Italian spirit and stressed the bonds between bolshevism, free-masonry, and the Jews. Early in 1938, Mussolini's government denied all rumors about an impending limitation of Jewish rights and insisted that what was planned was merely the limitation of Jewish influence in the cultural and economic life of the country to the proportion of Jews within the Italian population.

The Jews, eternal optimists, found this reassuring, and were therefore shocked when, on July 15, 1938, they read a statement by many professors declaring that Italians belonged to the Aryan race, which had to be protected from alien influences, especially that of the Jews, who belonged to another race. This position was formally adopted by the Fascist party. One of the few who raised his voice against such racism was Benedetto Croce, Enzo's teacher, but his protest was suppressed. There were rumors that the king opposed the racist policy; however when the time came for him to sign the racist laws, he did so without protest. As a first step, Jewish children were prohibited from attending government schools, and Jewish teachers and professors were discharged from their posts. Many professions, such as government employment, banking, insurance, and employment by the Fascist party, were now closed to Jews. The vast majority of the Jews of Italy were stunned into silence. Some four thousand Jews quietly converted to Christianity. As a result of royal intervention Professor Samuele Sereni was among the two thousand protected Jews; these included the families of those who gave their lives for the Fascist cause, held decorations for wartime services, or had participated in the occupation of Fiume. Despite Enzo's pleas, his parents could not make up their minds to leave Italy and go to Palestine, but his sister Leah, her husband, and their three children did decide to leave, and Enzo obtained the precious immigration certificates for them.

Even while Enzo was still in Europe others made plans for him. Leib Yaffe, the Director of the Keren Havesod (the fund that financed Zionist activity in Palestine) begged the kibbutz to send Enzo on a three-month mission to Egypt. The secretariat of Givat Brenner refused. "For years now," they wrote, "Sereni has been on the go. There always are weighty reasons compelling both him and us to respond to urgent demands. But we have resolved that this time we must not agree that Sereni should go out on further missions. For the near future he must remain at home. This is essential both for him and for us. Sorry."

This firm decision lasted exactly two weeks, and the Keren Havesod arranged the matter directly with Enzo. His chief task on this mission was to work for the national funds among rich Jews in Egypt, especially in the Italian-Jewish community in that country. Some of the fugitives from the Italian racial laws had found refuge in Egypt, and Enzo tried to transfer them to Palestine. His dream of long ago, when he saw himself as the vanguard of Italian immigration to Palestine, was now fulfilled — thanks to Mussolini. Italian Jews now arrived — relatives, friends, acquaintances. Were it up to Enzo, he would have taken all the younger immigrants to Givat Brenner, and for the older ones he would have built a community on private adjoining land.

A stubborn struggle developed around the young Italians who had undergone Zionist training. Enzo, as noted earlier, wanted them in Givat Brenner where they would be under his care. But here an obstacle arose. Most of these young immigrants were religious, in the specific Italian sense of integral Judaism. Ever since the early thirties these Zionist-oriented young people met in youth camps that stressed selective religious observances alongside ordinary camping routines. As a result of these camps, study groups were organized in the cities and there arose a kind of vaguely religious youth movement whose yearning to go to Palestine became more marked as the Jewish situation in Italy deteriorated. When the first exploratory group came to Palestine to examine the situation there, it quickly became aware of the real conditions as these had been shaped by the conflicts between the various religious trends and by the gulf that separated the religious from the secular communities. Alfonso Pacifici made a special trip to Italy to persuade these young people to settle as a group in Jerusalem, while Enzo fought to have them in the kibbutz, for he feared that without his guidance and protection they would not be able to withstand conditions in the country. "I am sufficiently Italian," he said, "to understand their moods, and enough of a Palestinian to be able to bridge the differences between them and the Palestinian community." Pacifici remained isolated and for a long time was embittered against Enzo who, he felt, caused the young immigrants to become estranged from Judaic views, where were the only ones, in his opinion, that could have led to a fruitful integration of the various trends within the nation.

But now a new problem arose. Givat Brenner at first refused to accept the Italians because of their demands for a kosher kitchen and Sabbath observance. Social life in Givat Brenner, it was felt, was complicated enough as it was, consisting as it did of Lithuanians, Germans, Americans, and graduates of local youth groups; there was no need to complicate it still further. And it was only after frequent appeals from the secretariat of the Hakibbutz Hameuchad, and an educational campaign by Enzo and Ada, that the general meeting of Givat Brenner decided, in December 1938, to accept a group of twenty for one year's training.

Their observance of kashruth — dietary laws — at once isolated the Italians from the other kibbutz members. They did not eat in the large dining room, which was also the main social meeting ground, but in a pitiful barrack, together with the aged parents of kibbutz members who also observed kashruth. The Italians resented the arrogance of the kibbutz old-timers, and these in turn mimicked the "Italians who live in a ghetto and eat spaghetto." Enzo invested much time and energy in this group, wishing to spare them a repetition of his own experiences. The newcomers had lived under a restricted totalitarian regime, and as a countermeasure Enzo urged them to read Benedetto Croce, whose books were forbidden in Italy. Every time he met one of the Italian group outdoors in the kibbutz, he would ask: "What are you reading these days? What books have you exchanged in the library?" He gave them courses in the history of socialism, translated for them from the writings of J. C. Brenner because of his rejection of illusions; he organized Bible courses for them and urged them to attend kibbutz meetings and listen to news broadcasts in Hebrew on the single radio set owned by the kibbutz. Every Saturday he would sit with his Italians, on the lawn in the summer and in his room in the winter, and teach and encourage, explain, fool around, and drink wine with them, and they would bring to him all their problems — personal, economic, ideological. He felt responsible for every one of them. And still they were confused. They were sensitive to the derision aroused by their religious devotion. Contrary to Enzo's hopes their example did not influence the kibbutz in the direction of traditionalism. For years he had been the only one in Givat Brenner who went to a synagogue on the Day of Atonement and actually fasted, instead of attending a lecture on the significance of the fast. The circumstances prevailing in the kibbutz affected the Italians. At the end of the year's training a few left Givat Brenner and joined religious kibbutzim; the rest gave up their kashruth and Sabbath observance and went over to the main dining room.

Enzo thus became a kind of high commissioner for Italian affairs in the country. Whether they were pioneers or bourgeois, he felt responsible for their integration and personally attended to the needs of each of them. Together with Augusto Levi, a lawyer from Florence and president of the Zionist Organization in Italy since 1933 who came to Palestine in 1938, he formed an organization of immigrants from Italy as a framework for rapid acculturation. The Italians, who brought with them their treasured furniture and old books and their ancient and revered family heirlooms, clung to each other in the cities, tried to live near each other, and remained isolated from their environment partly as a result of circumstances and partly out of a sense of aristocratic superiority. The organization of Italian immigrants had its headquarters in a small room on Lilienblum Street in Tel Aviv, and here they met during the first difficult months. Enzo would listen to them with paternal patience, knowing from his own experience that many of the new immigrants, and not only those from Italy, experienced the first period of acculturation as a disease, as a form of dizziness, when a person loses his spiritual equilibrium and sense of security and is then nervous and supersensitive and consumed by doubts. He understood them and loved them.

Meanwhile, as the danger of a world conflict became more

real, the British attached increasing importance to the strategic value of the Arab countries, and the Arabs exploited their growing political weight and pressed Britain to rescind the plan for partitioning Palestine, which grew out of the recommendations of the Royal Commission under Lord Peel. The conclusions of this commission were announced in 1937 and surprised everyone. It was impossible to reconcile the aims of the Jews and the Arabs, the commission concluded, and Palestine was therefore to be divided into three parts: an Arab state, a Jewish state, to include about one-fifth of Palestine, and an enclave connecting Jerusalem with Jaffa that was to remain under British mandate. This proposal aroused the wrath of the Arabs, who were not inclined to compromise now that the international situation was so favorable for them — active support for the Arab national movement from Hitler and Mussolini and a policy of appeasement on the part of England's prime minister, Chamberlain.

Among Jews this partition plan aroused a tremendous debate. Some regarded it as the end of Zionism, while others considered it as the beginning of salvation. Within the Labor party itself there were sharp differences of opinion. Ben-Gurion held that it was desirable to accept the plan and to establish this minute Jewish state, which could serve as a decisive way station on the way to a greater realization of Zionism, and meantime could absorb one hundred thousand Jews a year for the next fifteen years. Berl Katznelson, though opposed to the plan, because it could not assure either independence or security, nevertheless was concerned for the unity of the labor movement. In any case he did not believe the plan was realizable. Itzhak Tabenkin stressed the idea of the unity of Palestine; its chief value, he believed, lay in its large undeveloped areas and the Jewish community had no right to renounce them for future generations.

To stress their opposition to the partition plan, the Arabs intensified the disturbances which they had sporadically engaged in since 1936, until these became a regular armed uprising. Roads were blocked, the railways sabotaged, telephone lines disrupted; they attacked from ambushes, set fire to fields, blasted water installations, and attacked Jewish settlements. In September 1938, Givat Brenner was attacked and British military reinforcements were rushed to the neighborhood. The kibbutz maintained a round-the-clock guard. Some settlements saved themselves from Arab attack by their own armed defense. In the midst of this overall insecurity, Enzo announced that he would not stand guard with a firearm as a matter of conscientious objection. This Gandhian gesture accorded with his pacifist view that Arab-Jewish relations would be solved by peaceful means only.

There was some logic in Enzo's refusal to take up arms against his Arab friends, but there was also a certain selfishness in it, for it was clear that an unarmed Jewish community invited Arab attack, and it was not likely that Enzo was willing to sur- render Givat Brenner without a battle. (The quantity of weapons at Givat Brenner's disposal was in any case pitiful — seven rifles for the entire kibbutz.) Had an ordinary kibbutz member announced that he refused to take up arms, it is prob- able that he could not have remained as a member. But since it was Enzo who made his declaration, his plan to go on guard duty armed only with a club was met with tolerant smiles, as a quixotic attempt to halt the world's march to war with a wooden cudgel.

The British invited representatives of the Arab countries — Iraq, Saudi Arabia, Egypt, Transjordan, and Yemen — as well as representatives of the Arabs of Palestine and a Jewish delega- tion — to London to seek an agreed solution to the problem of Palestine. The conference took place in St. James's Palace in February 1939. From the very start it was obvious that England acted out of the conviction that it was preferable to sacrifice the Jewish interests in order not to incur the hostility of the Arabs. The Arabs refused to sit at the same table with the Jews, and the discussions were conducted on two separate levels. The final recommendations that emerged from St. James's were that an independent state with an Arab majority should be established in Palestine after a transition period of not more than ten years. During this time no more than 75,000 additional Jews were to be admitted into the country, an all-out campaign against illegal immigration was to be conducted, and severe restrictions on the sale of land to Jews were to be imposed. But even these recommendations did not satisfy the Arabs.

The general reaction, expressed by Ben-Gurion and Tabenkin, was militant: the British plans should be opposed — by force if necessary.

Enzo reacted as follows: "It is true that we all aspire to Jewish independence; we all want Jewish power. But it is also necessary to provide an answer to the basic problem: how does Jewish independence square with the Arab desire for independence in this country? Zionism cannot be realized in a vacuum, and we must provide an answer to how we intend to link our cause with the cause of the renaissance of the Arab nations." His opinion was clear: "We are interested in the political — and not only the religious — rights of the Arabs in this country. If we have the courage to go along this road, it may not prove immediate salvation, but it can serve as a guide that, after many years, may lead to the triumph of our political and settlement struggle."

On August 30, 1939, at a general meeting in Givat Brenner, he spoke on many aspects of a situation that was rapidly deteriorating. A world war was likely to break out at any moment, and the country was not prepared for it. For the time being there was no plan to transfer children from the cities to the countryside. It was not desirable to waste money on the purchase of gas masks since it was not probable that there would be gas attacks on agricultural settlements. The purpose of the meeting was to imbue the members with a realization of the urgency to prepare for war, to take over the unused land in the vicinity of the kibbutz, to cultivate it to raise food for times of emergency, and to utilize contacts with friends and relatives outside to obtain funds for the kibbutz.

Two days later World War II broke out with Hitler's attack on Poland. Plans for resistance to the British became pointless. Despite all differences, it was obvious that the war against Nazi Germany was a struggle common to both the British and the Jews, or, as Ben-Gurion phrased it: "We will fight alongside the British as if there were no White Paper, and we will fight against the White Paper as if there were no war." Italy was still neutral, but everyone realized that this was not to last long. Only now did Alfonsa and Samuele decide to move to Palestine. Despite Enzo's frequent appeals, and the fact that he had prepared immigration certificates for them, Papa Sereni, sixty-nine years old and fragile after a heart attack, and Mama Sereni, sixty, still active and at the peak of her strength, had kept on postponing the fateful step till the last moment. It was hard for them to part — and they knew that at their age this would be a parting forever — from Rome, from their way of life, from the family graves.

In November 1939, they finally reached Givat Brenner and took up their residence in an apartment that had been prepared for them in the house of the Roccas, their daughter and son-in-law. Enzo was now truly happy — the circle that had been breached thirteen years earlier was closed again, and the Sereni-Pontecorvo settlement came to life on the soil of the land of Israel. He only grieved that his oldest daughter could not feel more warmly toward her grandparents. She did not understand their doubts and could not adapt herself to their unfamiliar ways of thinking.

In addition to the Sereni parents there came at this time uncles and other relatives, and it was Enzo who provided them with immigration certificates and looked after the placement of their children in institutions of the youth *aliyah*. Although his personal ambition was to concentrate the Italian colony about Givat Brenner, this was not realized. Nor was the immigration large: up to 1940, only some five hundred Italian Jews came to Palestine, slightly more than one percent of Italian Jewry before the deluge.

16

The Deluge

The fate of Europe hung in the balance; Britain was besieged; European Jewry was in mortal danger. And Enzo found himself far from the center of events in a country that benefited from the war. For the time being the Arab riots in Palestine subsided, the economic crisis passed, the political tension relaxed. Enzo found a justification for going to Europe.

On the plane in which he flew to Italy there was also a refugee from Poland who had reached Palestine without an entry permit and whom the British were now returning to Greece. A high Italian official who was on the plane asked for an explanation of the refugee's plight and Enzo intervened to explain how persecuted Jews were denied the right to enter the only country that could absorb them, adding a bit of the history of Zionism and the founding of Givat Brenner. The Italian official and his aides wondered how it came about that a Palestinian spoke such pure Italian with a distinct Roman accent.

"It was not easy to explain to my courteous fellow passengers," Enzo later wrote, "about the complications and manifestations of Jewish psychology that had brought me, a son of an ancient Jewish family, to become a resident of Palestine. How could I explain to them how it came about that years back I had heard within myself a great voice that I could not silence, which called on me to return to a nation that I suddenly felt was my people?"

This was Enzo's first encounter with Italians since the promulgation of the racial laws. The Italian official assured him that his attitude toward Jews had not changed for the worse since the new laws went into effect, but these assurances aroused within him sad reflections about the nature of Zionism. Was it true that Zionism and anti-Semitism were perversely parallel in their relation, as both friends and foes of Zionism sometimes maintained out of a distorted understanding of the problem? "I know what our answer is, that Zionism, like socialism, is not a tragic and pessimistic idea. It recognizes the prevalent evil and offers a positive solution to it. It does not accept the idea that hatred of the Jew is an eternal law, just as socialism rejects the eternity of classes and war."

He found Mussolini's Rome far different from the Rome of his youth. It was beautiful as befit the capital of an empire, but as he wandered about its streets he felt a certain strangeness. Everything was orderly and organized and as if catalogued. Stranger still were his encounters with Jewish friends whom he hadn't seen in years. Some happily informed him that the anti-Semitic propaganda had virtually ceased. Others begged him to stop sending them Zionist literature: "These things are dangerous because they remind others of our existence." More than a third of Italian Jews had converted to Christianity, and Enzo hardly knew whom he despised more, those who bought admission tickets to Italian society through conversion, or the church that collaborated in this game of finding the "true faith."

The Italian Jewish middle class, which in the past he had been proud of because of its deep moral sense, its model family life, its civic pride that stemmed from its deep roots in Italian society, had "demonstrated its total corruption with the outbreak of the first tempest. . . . Its rabbis abandoned it at the first sign of danger, and there was hardly a soul to raise a voice in protest. The story of Italian Jewry was coming to an end and sinking without glory, without a flame announcing the coming of redemption, or even one to light up its end."

From Rome Enzo traveled to Paris, whose charm was not

lessened by the cold-war winter. When, on the day after his arrival, he went to a bomb shelter at the sound of the warning siren, his friends laughed. They regarded it as a pointless caution, not unlike the gas masks that had been distributed to the children. Ordinary people who sympathized with the left felt defeated after the signing of the Stalin-Hitler Pact, but the Communist leadership, including its Jewish members, were reconciled to the Soviet line. Communist discipline proved stronger than Jewish awareness. Among Parisian Jews Enzo found an Olympian calm. The Hechalutz organization was dying. A few of its members went to Palestine. Some others had mingled with the working class during the popular front days. Some joined the army and some found their place among the middle class. Jewish youth movements were at a standstill. Of the two hundred thousand Jews residing in Paris, a mere six thousand belonged to the organized community, which was virtually paralyzed.

"It's a terrible picture," he wrote at that time. "Zionism is no longer a serious factor in the life of Diaspora Jewry. Its sun has set. We could not transform Palestine into a refuge for Jews not seeking a place of refuge. This, in my opinion, is the true significance of the British White Paper. The Jewish masses have lost their faith in the possibility of a solution of the Jewish problem in Palestine. . . ."

At the end of March he went to Holland, which he knew well from his frequent visits when he worked for Hechalutz in Germany and whose landscape he loved. Now signs of war were everywhere. The military were all about, in the streets, in the trains, in the villages; there were barbed-wire obstructions and guards on the highways and bridges and alerts for German spies. But despite the nervousness and the economic hardships there was confidence in the allied victory and faith in the small but well-equipped Dutch army.

During the last day of his stay in Holland he witnessed the departure of a train full of refugees from Poland who had managed to reach Amsterdam by way of Kovno, Riga, and Copenhagen. From Amsterdam they were to proceed in sealed cars to Marseilles whence they would sail for Palestine. At the sight of the calm Hollanders, who looked with amazement at the large crowd of Jews who had come to see the train off and sang "Hatikvah," he was reminded of the first group of Halutzim who left Germany shortly after Hitler came to power. But then the departure had symbolized the start of a great migration; now this train marked the end of an era, the last to escape before the curtain went down, and the shadow of the future was all about.

As usual Enzo was involved in many projects simultaneously: negotiations with a VIP, meaning a very rich person, for the construction of a canning factory in Givat Brenner; assignment of immigration certificates; contact with Dr. Weizmann about raising a large loan for the Keren Havesod in the still neutral countries — and also plans for the expansion of the convalescent home in Givat Brenner. As ever, he did not forget the kibbutz children and wrote to their teacher requesting a suggested list of presents for each individual child. ("But, of course, it must not cost too much.")

And to the kibbutz he wrote: "I am staying in the modern 'American' hotel, in a spacious room which I can never dream of in Palestine. . . . But I am in the midst of a destroyed community. 1939 will no doubt be remembered as a fateful year in Jewish history. In 1933 one could still hope and live in illusions. Now all that is past. Refugees from Poland bring tidings of the total destruction of Jewry in its last historical center. Every Jewish refugee has the face of a hunted animal seeking escape from mighty forces that have determined to erase the name of Israel from the world."

Early in April 1940, Enzo returned to France by way of Brussels. In Paris life proceeded as usual — the same professional smile on the hotelier's face, the same inane remarks by the waiter. But on the day after his arrival, on April 9, this calm vanished as news was broadcast of the German invasion of Norway and Denmark. The illusions of the sitzkrieg evaporated. His first thoughts were of the activities he had planned to conduct, but these required calm, and now the entire population of Paris was in a state of shock and helplessness.

On May 10, the sirens announced to the inhabitants of Paris that the Germans had invaded Holland and Belgium. The hour of the great battle had come and the French people awoke from their sleep. Paris was denuded of soldiers and General Gamelin announced: "The hour which we had awaited for months has struck and found us ready." But when the first news of the German breakthrough in the Ardennes came, Paris was panic-stricken. Yet, "Such is the force of habit," Enzo wrote, "yesterday the French insisted that the decisive battle would be along the Maas or the Albert Canal in Belgium. Today the talk is about Flanders." And as the news of one defeat after another kept coming in, he sensed how deeply European he was, and how much he loved France and its glorious history, which had given mankind the belief in human equality and brotherhood: "Never have death and sacrifice seemed so unavoidable if we are to assure our lives as at this time. . . . If we wish to live, we have to be prepared to die and to kill. If we will know how to live and to die properly, we will not be lost." Such was the change in the man who so recently had tried to protect peace with a wooden club.

But when he returned to Palestine, the British had prepared a surprise for him — a detention camp. On June 10, 1940, Mussolini declared war on allied nations, and all those holding Italian citizenship in areas ruled by England became enemy aliens. Thus it came about that many citizens of Italy in Palestine, including Enzo, were taken to a camp near Acre. The regime in the camp was quite liberal, when compared to the concentration camps mankind came to know later. The detainees were not bothered excessively, and Enzo utilized the brief period of his incarceration to organize courses and lectures. The British action aroused a wave of protest in the Jewish world, and Dr. Weizmann sent a strongly worded letter to the British Colonial Office: "The Jewish Agency had offered its cooperation to the British Government in determining the loyalty of Jews of Italian origin, but unfortunately the government preferred to resort to detention without discrimination, which causes unnecessary hardship to innocent people, and is of no use against a fifth column." In his letter Dr. Weizmann specifically mentioned Dr. Lattes and Dr. Sereni, "whom I know well personally and in whom I have complete faith." To strengthen his argument, Weizmann added, not quite in accord with the facts, that the Sereni family had particularly suffered from Mussolini's persecution, that Enzo's father had been dismissed from his post as royal physician and exiled to the Lipari Islands.

Most of the detainees were freed after a week on the guarantee of the Jewish Agency, and Enzo bore no resentment against the British. He sought ways to enter British military service, to the surprise of many of his friends.

Ever since the outbreak of the war, and even before that, representatives of the Jewish community pleaded with the British authorities to establish a Jewish fighting force both to defend Palestine and to fight alongside British forces against Hitler wherever it should be necessary. But the British response was, at best, noncommittal, and mostly outright negative, mainly for fear of Arab reaction. Having rejected the plan for a separate Jewish force, Britain finally agreed in the autumn of 1939 to establish mixed Jewish-Arab technical and sapper units, the aim clearly being to keep the Jews out of actual combat duties.

The attitude of the Jewish community in this regard was not uniform. There was eagerness to fight the Nazis, to defend the country against possible German invasion or Arab uprisings inspired by the Axis, and to add weight to the Zionist political struggle by means of mobilization of its manpower. But there were also those who feared for the fate of the Jewish community in the country if large units of armed Jews were to be sent to battlefields abroad.

The attitude of the British toward military cooperation with the Jews fluctuated with the state of their military fortunes. Whenever they were more sympathetic to Jewish requests it was an indication that their military situation was imperilled. Thus it came about that it was not till 1940 that they agreed to the recruitment of two battalions — one Jewish and one Arab — within the framework of the Royal West Kent regiment, when pressed by Churchill to do so during a particularly difficult time. Opinions within the Jewish labor movement in Palestine were divided. Ben-Gurion and Moshe Sharett regarded such Jewish units as the basis for a future Jewish military force and hoped to break through British hostility to Zionism by means of such

military cooperation. Tabenkin, a leader of Hakibbutz Hameuchad, on the other hand, demanded that young men of military
potential should be husbanded for the defense needs of the community, which was threatened by invasion from Syria, now that
the Nazis had gained complete control of western Europe.
Eliahu Golomb, the central figure in Haganah, the Jewish defense organization, did not agree with these distinctions and felt
that both forces could serve as nuclei for the armed strength of
the Jewish community in case of need.

Enzo appealed to Moshe Sharett, the political secretary of the
Jewish Agency and chief liaison between the Jewish community
and the British authorities, and expressed his readiness to go as
an ordinary soldier wherever necessary. Sharett, who held Enzo
in great affection, persuaded him that this would be a hasty step
and advised him to wait for special assignments and important
projects and promised to call on him when the time came.

The opportunity came some weeks later when British and
Italian forces clashed in North Africa and Marshal Rodolfo
Graziani's army penetrated Egypt as far as Sidi Barani. Enzo
felt that anti-Fascist propaganda among the Italian prisoners, as
well as in the Italian colony residing in Egypt, was just the
thing for him. Here he could have the best of two worlds: to act
on behalf of the Jewish people as well as for Italian independence.

Sharett kept his word. In September 1940, Enzo was on his
way to Egypt, equipped with a British passport in the name of
Dr. Frederic Simmons, which had been provided him by the
British Intelligence Services. Alone in the car, except for a
British officer and his orderly, Enzo wrote: "Do I regret my
decision? Of course not. As always, whenever I have to make a
crucial decision, my first reaction is the instinctive one, what one
must do to be true to oneself. Later come rational explanations
that confirm the instinctive response. These are a continuation of
the thoughts that troubled me when I witnessed the terrible
events in May in France. I then began to doubt many things that
I had before that regarded as sacred. I did not reject any of my
former convictions: profound hatred for war and for the false
belief that violence can decide the fate of nations and bring peace

and security anywhere. These remained firm. What I did revise was my faith in the absolute value of human life, in human life as the highest good which is not to be sacrificed at any price. . . . Is it indeed true that nothing is worth the sacrificing of young lives? That the call for such sacrifices is always a deception foisted by people with dark motives on naive idealists in order to use them as tools in the hands of evil and corrupt forces?

"Deep inside I am still suspicious of all rationalizations of the sacrifice of the individual for the sake of abstract and remote group interests. Even in the kibbutz I always considered the defense of the interests of the individual against possible pressures of 'public opinion' and 'higher considerations' as one of the chief tasks of any person who honestly seeks a society of absolutely free people. And if this is true in the limited society of the kibbutz, where the distance between the individual and the community is smaller than in any other society, isn't it so much more urgent in broader societies to remain on guard against the violation of individual rights in the name of all kinds of giant idols?"

17

In the Service of British Intelligence

The British imperial forces hardly snapped to attention when Enzo, the authority on Italian propaganda, reached Egypt. He met with Captain Strange of British Intelligence who wanted to get some idea about this little man with broad gestures, whose English speech reflected all the accents in the world, and who responded to practical questions with a pathos that was not at all Anglo-Saxon.

Captain Strange possibly was not much impressed by Enzo, or perhaps he wanted to test this new arrival. More likely he did not care if another member of his staff idled away his time in Egypt. In any case, Enzo was told to stand by and wait for instructions. When these finally came, they were highly disappointing: "Dr. Simmons" was asked to write three or four articles for *Giornale D'Italia*, an anti-Fascist paper that had been appearing since the summer of 1939 under British supervision for the benefit of the Italian colony in Egypt, which was largely Fascist, aiming to estrange it from the duce, and also for the Italian prisoners of war who were in camps scattered throughout Egypt. Four articles! Was it for that Enzo had abandoned wife and children, parents and country? But he swallowed the bitter pill, confident that his chance would still come. Who knows? Perhaps the British wanted first to test his abilities and loyalty.

The instructions that Enzo received were accompanied by guidelines that declared in no-nonsense military terms that "Italians, as a rule, do not love the Germans and fear them. Concentrate on the Italians' anti-German feelings.

"Refrain: from attacking the royal family. Various regions of Italy have different degrees of reverence for the king, but, as a general rule, though they regret the weakness of the king against Mussolini, they are monarchists at heart.

"Stress: the wealth of the Fascist leaders which they accumulated at the expense of the people, the futility of the conquest of Ethiopia, the near bankruptcy of the economy brought about by the regime.

"Accentuate: the basic corruption of the Germans and their inability to win the war.

"Avoid: mentioning that we are fighting to save democracy. Very few Italians are interested in this.

"Make it plain: that we are fighting to save Europe, if not the entire world, from German domination.

"Always remember: that Italians have a highly developed sense of humor, that they are rational, fanatical, proud, and dramatic. Exploit these traits in the style of your propaganda."

In the opinion of "Dr. Simmons," all of these assumptions were totally erroneous, and he did not conceal his views from the British officers whom he met by chance; this led to his being asked to offer in writing his own suggestions for the improvement of British propaganda among the Italians.

He minced no words in his critique. British propaganda has no chance of success, he stated, if it shows no regard for the Italians' national pride (and it is difficult for Englishmen, who have never experienced the humiliation of military defeat, to understand the inferiority complex of Italians in contact with strangers). Fascism has raised the status of the Italian colony in Egypt, and no patriotic Italian will cooperate with the British if their common labors are not based on belief in freedom, independence, and social justice. He recommended dropping leaflets on northern Italy, or smuggling them in through the Yugoslav frontier, and to avoid silly tales about the anti-Fascism of this or that nobleman (this was the period when the British flirted with

the Duke of Aosta, the royal Italian representative in Ethiopia)
or the imaginary conflicts between certain noblemen and Mussolini. Activity among Italians must be given a definite social
tendency. Catholic feelings could be appealed to in southern
Italy, but even there, there was no point in encouraging monarchist sentiments, since the royal family had lost all influence in
the south, and had been none too popular even before the war.
This was Enzo's credo all the time he was in Egypt, and it was
far too Socialist to suit the conservative tastes of the British
command in the Middle East.

Enzo waited, and perhaps for the first time in his life he had a
surplus of free time. He began to study Arabic ("I might yet
come out of Egypt equipped with another language, and a more
or less expert Arabist.") But the necessary peace of mind for
study was often lacking. These were the days of the British
attack in the western desert. At night there were air raids, the
sirens wailed — hardly a suitable atmosphere for academic pursuits. But Enzo persevered. He read all of Shakespeare in the
original and familiarized himself anew with Ezekiel and the
Psalms. He was preparing to tackle seriously the Book of Job. In
his letters to Givat Brenner there was no hint of dissatisfaction
with his situation, for that would have meant an admission of
defeat.

Traffic between Palestine and Egypt was lively and he had
opportunities to meet the volunteers from Palestine in the Jewish
soldiers' clubs in Cairo and Alexandria that were maintained by
the local Jewish communities, which, though assimilationist and
remote from Zionism, were proud of the "Jewish heroes" in
British uniform and reacted with excitement to the sound of
Hebrew speech and the sight of the blue-and-white flag.

Thus passed December and January. In February the British
went on the offensive and drove out the Italian forces from
Egypt and occupied Cyrenaica and part of Tripoli. In the process they took 113,000 Italian prisoners. But still Enzo was kept
on ice. And when in mid-February he was informed that he
would have to discontinue his writing for *Giornale D'Italia*, the
only activity which provided him some satisfaction, he decided
that it was time to do something about it. "After four months

with the service," he wrote to his superiors, "I must conclude that there is not much point in continuing my present duties which do not keep me sufficiently occupied and, what is more important, do not give me the feeling that they are essential." He stressed that his dissatisfaction did not reflect on the attitude of his superiors, but that he had not volunteered for the sake of the kind of work he was doing. He had not thus far had an opportunity to meet Italian prisoners of war, and the duties he was performing could easily have been handled by someone else.

In reply he was asked to submit recommendations and he sketched his plans: that a special office be set up in Greece or, preferably, in Yugoslavia that would establish contacts with Italians and organize sabotage and propaganda in Italy itself. "I am prepared to go to Italy myself to establish contacts, but should it be regarded as more useful that I organize the work here before going, I will gladly do so." He also recommended that parachutists of Italian origin be dropped in Italy and pointed out that under favorable circumstances such parachutists had a reasonable chance to be in Italy for quite a while without being apprehended. As an alternative to this recommendation he suggested that he be sent to southern France where thousands of anti-Fascist Italians lived and whence it was possible to establish contact with Italy. He also expressed willingness to do educational work among Italian POWs and to go anywhere for this purpose, be it in India or South Africa, as long as it involved genuine activity.

The British were not overly impressed: there was no dearth of Jews with mad ideas who were willing to risk their lives behind enemy lines. And meantime they decided to send "Dr. Simmons" on home furlough, always a calming experience.

The encounter with the ruling elements in Egypt — corrupt, satiated, given to intrigues, and consumed by greed — on the one hand, and with the mass of people — ignorant, pitiful, fatalistic — on the other, with their concealed or open admiration of Hitler, convinced Enzo of the remoteness of the vision of workers' solidarity that was supposed to solve the problem of the region. It was a different Enzo who returned from Egypt, and he was not shy about declaring this publicly. At a conference of the

Central Committee of Mapai which was held in March 1941 in Ayanot he declared: "I was in Egypt for a few months, and I must say that I have cooled off toward the Arabs. I have a lower opinion of them now than I did before. There are greater political experts than I, and they might feel otherwise, but in my encounters with the British I sensed that even though they are now willing to make concessions to the Arabs and to enter into deals with them, they feel a great contempt and anger toward the Arabs for the troubles they cause them. This presents a great opportunity for us, for the English now realize that there are peoples and peoples. Now is the time to explain to the British, especially within the framework of the army, the aims of Zionism."

Enzo was convinced that the day of small nations had passed. "This new imperialist war has raised again the question of the division of the world, and now is the time to clarify what will be the future of the Jewish people after the war. At the end of World War I, the answer was in the spirit of the period: independence for small nations. It is not so now. If the democratic forces on whom we can rely are agreed on anything it is that the favorable attitude toward small nations of 1918 will not recur." The solution, therefore, would have to be a larger state. We must declare that at the end of the war we aim to transfer the bulk of the Jewish people to Israel and to proclaim: we are liquidating the Diaspora. Now, while the war is still on, we must educate the Jewish people toward such a transfer."

Enzo's solution to the Arab problem was not the same in 1941 as it was in 1935: "To bring order into the world it is necessary that there should no longer exist any minorities, and to demand a population transfer also for Palestine."

Meanwhile Hitler, who allowed Mussolini to take a drubbing at the hands of the Greeks, finally decided to come to his assistance and concentrated German forces along the Greek border as well as in Greece itself in the form of a fifth column. Thousands of German officers infiltrated Greece in the guise of tourists and were informed of every move of the British there. In the British military camps in Egypt it was clear that Greece would be the next arena and the volunteers from the kibbutzim asked Enzo,

before he went on home leave, to consult with the Jewish authorities whether to demand to be sent to Greece. Enzo advised
against making such a demand, either because he foresaw the
forthcoming debacle in Greece or because he felt that the major
battle would take place in Libya. But his advice was futile, and
2,500 men from the Palestinian units were included in the ex-
peditionary force of 62,000 that was dispatched to Greece.
Early in April Enzo cut short his home leave, hastily returned to
Egypt, and then went to Greece.

What was the purpose of this journey? Ada did not want to
know about the nature of Enzo's missions, fearing that, should
Palestine be occupied by the Germans she might not be able to
withstand questioning under torture. Speaking to Palestinians in
Athens, Enzo darkly hinted that he was there on behalf of
British Intelligence. Some assumed that he was there on a mission of the Jewish national authorities to warn the Jews of
Greece of the danger facing them in the event of a German
occupation and to seek ways for their evacuation. To some
friends he said that he was examining possibilities to cross over
to Italy by way of Yugoslavia. But whatever the true nature of
his stay in Greece, events moved too rapidly and the Greek Jews
could not prepare to meet the danger approaching them. The
military struggle ended before it had hardly begun.

The British defeat in Greece came simultaneously with the
collapse of the front in Libya which, except for Tobruk, was
taken by Rommel, and it was a terrible blow to British prestige.
It seemed as if no force could halt the Germans; in Palestine
Arab admiration for the Nazis mounted and there was confidence that here was finally someone who would settle their score
with the Jews. Within the Jewish community black moods prevailed. "I can well imagine how concerned you are these days,"
Enzo wrote to his parents after the interlude in Greece. "But
without disregarding the seriousness of the situation, I am not
only certain as always about the final outcome, but I also have
faith about developments in the coming months. Patience. There
will no doubt be some difficult weeks ahead, but don't forget that
ever since Hitler missed the bus in London one year ago, the

outcome of the war has been decided in our favor." Through the anti-Fascist underground in unoccupied France he learned that his brother Mimo was alive and well. And except for his serious concern for the fate of the 1,400 Palestinian soldiers — among them about one thousand Jews — who were taken prisoner by the Germans during the hasty British evacuation of Greece, and worry about Ada, one could have said that he was in an elated mood, for he finally had work that he found satisfactory.

Whether through a change in the attitude of the British authorities as a result of their recent defeats or the influence exerted by Enzo's Italian friends in the British service or simply an accidental bureaucratic fluke, Enzo's luck changed when he returned from Greece. He was appointed a member of the editorial staff of *Corriere D'Italia*, an anti-Fascist paper that succeeded the defunct *Giornale D'Italia*, and he was permitted to contact Italian POWs. He began setting up a network of anti-Fascist agents and prepared plans of activity for the anti-Fascist movement in Egypt. In short, he became active. He defined his main work as "of a literary-journalistic nature for which I am quite suitable. Of course, in order to write much I must read much, books of all kinds, both old and current, and I always found this quite satisfactory. . . . My writing seems to meet with approval; in any case I am becoming accustomed to simple writing, and this is my greatest problem, for I am used to the Italian scholastic style with its long and involved sentences."

There were few Italian anti-Fascists in Egypt, and these were mostly Masons and Jews who squabbled among themselves. Ever since Mussolini came to power, the small anti-Fascist groups in Cairo and Alexandria had operated under conspiratorial conditions. Only after Italy entered the war, and especially after Italy's defeat in Libya, did their weight begin to amount to something. In 1941 these small groups came together and appeared before the British authorities as a united movement with a membership of one thousand and with a plan of action: to assume responsibility for all Italian propaganda, including publication of *Corriere D'Italia*, radio broadcasts, and a school for POWs; to establish contacts with anti-Fascists abroad and to

coordinate activity with them; to organize action in Italy to fight
against Fascist elements; and to recruit a legion of Italians to
fight alongside the Allies for the liberation of Italy.

In the latter part of May "Dr. Simmons" was sent, together
with Dr. Umberto Calosso, an Italian Catholic, a man of *Giustizia e Libertà* and an editor of *Corriere*, to visit a number of
Italian POW camps — Mustafa near Alexandria, Helwan,
Ganfieh, and Ajami — to gauge the mood among the prisoners,
to hear their reactions to the paper and the radio broadcasts, and
to seek candidates for special tasks within the scope of organized
anti-Fascist activity. It was not a pleasure trip. Within the camp
at Helwan there were rumors that anti-Fascist agents were operating in the neighborhood, and the prisoners met their visitors
with insults. Those who consented to talk with them protested
that the paper was too pro-British and anti-Italian. The only
articles that were regarded as objective were a series of fifteen
installments on the Third French Republic. The chief obstacle
in gaining the confidence of the prisoners was the fear of both
officers and enlisted men that they might be regarded as anti-
Fascist by their comrades and that they might be informed on in
Italy and their families made to suffer as a consequence. For
they were fully convinced that the Axis would gain an early
victory and daily awaited the arrival of German parachutists to
liberate them. In the report that "Dr. Simmons" and Dr. Calosso
presented to Colonel Thornhill, their chief intelligence contact
officer, they declared that *Corriere* was well read though not
liked and that the prisoners were hostile to the radio broadcasts
and resented the attacks on Mussolini. They recommended
greater freedom of movement for the prisoners, or at least for the
officers among them, concentrated cultural work, lessons in English — and the removal of two statues of nudes that had been
set up at the entrance to one of the camps to a less prominent
spot.

One of the assignments given to "Dr. Simmons" was to establish a network of local agents to keep an eye on Fascists in
Egypt. He recommended the recruitment of three or four Arabs
and one Italian to keep in touch only with the anti-Fascist committee but give no information to the Egyptian secret service. He

also objected to having hired informers, a situation that created a dangerous and corrupting atmosphere and suggested the employment of agents who, though working on a volunteer basis, would be reimbursed for expenses. And, in order to cause confusion in the enemy ranks, he recommended that printed matter be mailed to the homes of known Fascists, sometimes in the guise of Fascist material and sometimes with anti-Fascist content. For the POW camps he asked that anti-Fascist propaganda be smuggled in as prohibited literature, to encourage the prisoners to read it.

Once a week, on Sundays, Enzo would visit the home of Emil Najar, a young Jewish lawyer, which served as a discussion center for a group of intellectuals that included Moslem and Christian Arabs, Jews, Italian residents in Egypt, and sometimes Englishmen who found themselves temporarily in the country. Some were Socialists, other Communists, but all of them opposed British rule in Egypt and supported the Arab liberation movement.

Palestine was becoming ever more remote. Hebrew newspapers reached him seldom, and he had no time to go to the soldiers' club to read them. Letters from friends in Givat Brenner were rare, and the bond with the Jewish community in Palestine was weakening. "Sometimes I think that there is a danger that the means — joining the war effort in order to protect the Jewish people, human freedom, and the Socialist movement — could with many of us become an end and make us forget the center of our life: that there must be a land of Israel. And if such is the case with me, who in many respects find myself in a position more favorable than that of the rest of us, imagine the situation of an ordinary comrade, whose ability and will to retain his bonds with the Jewish cause in the midst of aliens and assimilationists is much smaller," he wrote in a letter to Givat Brenner, which was preparing to celebrate the thirteenth anniversary of its founding.

He battled against his spiritual drift away from Palestine and begged to be sent letters, kibbutz diaries, newspapers. Of Ada he begged for gossip, which she refused to supply — teachers' reports about the progress of his children. He showered questions about the welfare of his widespread family and offered advice.

Enzo's written output was amazing, especially so in Cairo's suffocating summer heat, which compelled even him to take the customary siesta. During the four months of his work for *Corriere D'Italia*, he wrote some eighty articles, sometimes two a day, under various pen names. In the first month alone he wrote, in addition to the series on the end of the Third Republic in France, about Italian forced labor in Germany, Wilhelm II, the imminence of American intervention, the difference between Garibaldi's red shirts and Mussolini's black ones, feuilletons in the form of letters to soldiers, an extensive essay on the anniversary of the murder of Matteoti, and a novella. In addition he helped with the translation of the English pamphlet "The Battle for England" into Italian.

"Extensive and tiring work, but useful," is how he defined his work since his return from home leave in a letter to Moshe Sharett. "It seems that *they* appreciate what I do and have discovered that I really know Italian; they also allow a certain latitude in matters concerning the social direction of the work here. . . . I may be going to Ethiopia for a few days in connection with the organization of the work there, in which case I will no doubt meet the 'friend.' I am trying to find out exactly where he is."

The trip to Ethiopia was postponed from week to week, possibly under the influence of a report submitted by one of the intelligence officers, who argued that it was not desirable that Jews should engage in anti-Fascist work in Eritrea. The "friend," General Orde Wingate, came to Cairo after his brilliant victory over the Italians in Ethiopia, in a state of depression and disappointment because neither he nor his men were shown appreciation for their great effort in liberating Ethiopia. In this mood of despair and helplessness, Wingate tried to commit suicide on July 9, 1941, by cutting his throat. He was rescued in time by Colonel Thornhill who occupied an adjoining room in the Continental Hotel.

The report about Wingate's attempted suicide spread throughout Cairo and Avraham Akaviah, his devoted secretary, wired the Jewish Agency in Jerusalem that Wingate was in serious condition as a result of "an accident." Sharett, who was a close friend of Wingate, at once came to Cairo and, together with Enzo, went to visit him in the military hospital. Wingate asked Enzo to leave the room and confessed to Sharett that it had been a suicide attempt in protest against British policy in Ethiopia. Later, as Wingate was recovering, Enzo visited him several times and discussed Palestine with him. Whenever British officers were in the room, Wingate warned Enzo in Hebrew to watch what he said in the presence of "these scoundrels."

Russia's entry into the war, on June 22, 1941, came to Enzo as a relief from a depression that had plagued him for months — now events seemed to have justified his faith in the Soviet Union, which he had not abandoned even during the days of the Hitler-Stalin Pact, and for which he was often attacked in the course of debates in Palestine. "For the first time it became clear to me that the war could end much sooner than one might have thought at its beginning. Now that it was no longer a war between the two imperialist blocs, there was greater hope for a new order in the postwar world, and prospects of greater unity within the labor camp in Palestine, which had been divided in its attitudes toward the Soviet Union. Now it was possible to mobilize forces for the struggle not only for the sake of the defense of Palestine or because there was no alternative, but also for the sake of a new world. The war could now become a struggle for the liberation of all oppressed people also in the consciousness of the European nations. The participation of the Jewish labor movement will now be of decisive value. I know that our participation will still meet with obstacles and disappointments. I am fully convinced that people who want to advance the cause of revolution must actively participate in the struggle, always emphasizing its revolutionary nature."

This faith in a coming Socialist world was also shared by the editors of *Corriere D'Italia* and was reflected in the paper and in the radio broadcasts, to the great chagrin of the British authorities in charge of these projects, who came from conservative British circles. Clashes began as early as June 20, when "Dr.

Simmons" had to explain to Colonel Thornhill how it came about that the article "A Letter to an Italian Soldier," which had previously been ruled out by the censor for publication in *Giornale D'Oriente* now appeared, three months later, in *Corriere*, with the same anti-British tone. "Dr. Simmons" could not understand what was wrong with encouraging Italian POWs with the words: "Let us laugh all together when they call us 'macaroni' and 'mandolini' and tell them that we prefer macaroni and mandolini to their beer and whisky and bagpipes. And if they talk to us about our defeat, we will not remind them of the black pages in their history, but with head held high tell them of the glory of those Italians who unified Italy, those men who truly belong to us."

Hardly had the "macaroni" incident subsided when the censor canceled a radio commentary that struck him as outright Communist because it mentioned Karl Marx, quoted the slogan "Workers of the World Unite," and referred to the centuries of oppression of Italian workers. And as if all this were not enough there appeared in *Corriere* a talk by Paolo Vitorelli (the pseudonym of Raffaello Battino, the editor in chief of the paper) under the heading "Radio Cairo Broadcast Yesterday," which had a definite leftist tone. The heading caused the censor to assume that this talk had been cleared by the radio censor, and Colonel Thornhill, a man of determined character, took a step that he regarded as logical: he removed all three editors from their posts. When they asked to meet with him, Thornhill declared that this was impossible since they were guilty of a serious violation of instructions. They had no choice but to appeal to him in writing.

In the clarifications and counterclarifications that followed, Colonel Thornhill touched on the heart of the issue, which was not the technical violation of censorship rules but the content of the article that spread Communist propaganda. The editors of *Corriere* were outraged, for each of them, in his own way, had been an opponent of communism for many years. They justified their attitude as follows: most of the listeners of the radio broadcasts were Italians living in Fascist Italy who risked their lives to listen to the broadcasts. Therefore it was not enough to feed them with general propaganda slogans and gossip about the corruption of the Fascist leaders. In order to fight Fascism effectively, it was necessary to oppose to it another ideal that stressed social, political, and ideological values; it was necessary to be not only against something but also for something — for social justice and democracy, values that were remote from communism.

But Colonel Thornhill reminded them that they were in the service of His Majesty's government. The three then made it clear to him that though technically they were "servants" of the British government, they had come as free men "to cooperate with the British government in the common struggle against Fascism. The Germans might be content with the services of Quislings working for them, but the British no doubt encouraged free men working with them." Stressing their innocence and determination to do the best they could, the three felt that they deserved full confidence as men whose intentions are beyond all suspicion and whose word is the word of gentlemen. On July 5, Colonel Thornhill finally informed them that "after full consideration of the explanations offered in your letters, I have decided to regard this matter as closed and to return you to your posts."

In the murky atmosphere prevailing in Cairo there was no end of intrigue surrounding the radio broadcasts. Miss Terni-Chialente, an author and journalist who was in charge of the broadcasts, at first opposed Enzo's radio work, not on personal or political grounds, but because of his Jewishness. It might arouse suspicions, she said, that Radio Cairo was under Jewish influence. This argument did not impress him, for most of the other participants in the broadcasts were also Jewish, and this argument was never raised against them. Enzo, the eternal optimist, told this to her frankly, hoping that an open discussion of the matter and work for the common cause would have overcome ancient hostilities which he believed stemmed from her sympathies for communism. A temporary modus vivendi was arranged and Enzo continued broadcasting.

But the Jewish question would not die and the machinations about it persisted. Professor Calosso, one of the editors of *Corriere*, secretly met with Lieutenant Colonel De Salis, who was his immediate superior in the intelligence service, and called the attention of the British to the large number of Jews serving in his department and in the anti-Fascist group. In the professor's opinion, this led to negative results. He quoted a British officer of Jewish descent who had not long ago returned from Ethiopia and Eritrea and who allegedly said that it was not desirable to send Jews for propaganda work in these countries. The professor's visit did not remain secret for long and a report of it sent to Colonel Thornhill reached Enzo.

Enzo's trip to Asmara, Eritrea, to intensify the anti-Fascist activity there was postponed from week to week. In anticipation of the trip he gave up his comfortable living quarters and now lived in a casual room. He was restless and his nervousness increased after his request for home leave had been refused because of the uncertainty of the Ethiopia trip. "What can one do?" he wrote home. "One can't always have one's way and it's necessary to take things as they come. This too will pass, as have so many other things. Does Father listen to the radio? Does he listen to my broadcasts occasionally? Does the paper reach you regularly? How does it look to you? I would like to have your criticism, though I'd have you know that here it is regarded as one of the best papers in Egypt." Finally the trip to Eritrea was definitely off and, for the first time in five months, Enzo was granted a two-week furlough.

On September 1, 1941, right after his return to Givat Brenner, Enzo reported to the kibbutz comprehensively about the political and military situation in the world, and heard an account of the recent conference of Hakibbutz Hameuchad held at Ramat Hakovesh. A number of emissaries of the kibbutz who had been in Poland at the outbreak of the war and returned home by way of Russia were present at this conference. Tabenkin congratulated them on their safe arrival, but Berl Katznelson regarded their abandonment of their trainees, and Diaspora Jewry in general, during this critical hour as a form of betrayal of their mission. He had asked them frankly: Why had they returned? Weren't there moments when one must be ready to sacrifice oneself? It is true that the Jews of Palestine did not yet know then about the extermination camps, but the tragic question that tormented the community throughout the war years and long afterward, whether everything possible had been done to rescue Diaspora Jewry, was already in the air.

As far back as early August "Dr. Simmons" and Dr. Battino had presented the British authorities with a detailed, fourteen-page memorandum on the problems of propaganda among Italians. This dealt with the newspaper, the radio broadcasts, the anti-Fascist "gruppo," and the argument regarding the undesirable influence of Jews in the work. "In answer to this one can say," the memo declared, that "Italy was perhaps the only country without a Jewish problem, and racism was an imported article there. It would be an error to think that if competent Jews are removed from the anti-Fascist group, its work would be more attractive to politically indifferent people or to Fascists. The only yardstick that should be applied to Jewish membership in the group must be their intelligence, ability, and anti-Fascist views. Jews who had become anti-Fascist only after the introduction of the racist laws, which affected them personally, must be dealt with as cautiously as with any other Fascists who had become converted."

Whoever read this memorandum in British Intelligence (the comment on it was not signed) did not agree with the views of its two authors. In his opinion, if the "gruppo" was to speak on behalf of the Italians in Egypt, its composition must be fundamentally changed. The ratio between Jews and non-Jews was important. In Cairo alone there were 515 Jews out of the 575 members of the group. "It is true that the Jews are our allies in the war effort, but would it be wise if they should constitute the leaders of the movement to unify the Italians, who, since 1938, have been subjected to anti-Jewish propaganda?"

From the text of the memorandum it appeared that its authors were not content with their functions and they suggested that the British authorities grant to the anti-Fascist committee an unequivocal representative status, like that of Free France, in order to enable it to engage in extensive activities, and above all, to define clearly the postwar world order desired, to guarantee absolute national independence to the Italian people, and to assure that Italy would not be placed in a position of inferiority and the errors of Versailles not be repeated.

It cannot be assumed that the authors of the memorandum were aware of the decisions of British Intelligence regarding them. Enzo was just then making preliminary steps for collaboration with the Italian anti-Fascists in the United States, most of whom centered about the Mazzini Society headed by his old friend Max Ascoli. In his reply Ascoli described to Sereni the problems of the Mazzini Society and the struggles of the Italian refugees in the United States. They, too, thought of setting up an Italian government in exile, contrary to the advice of Ascoli, now an American citizen, who regarded the chief function of the Mazzini Society to consist of shaping American public opinion rather than distributing posts in a nonexistent government.

The heat that radiated from Cairo's swarming streets was almost unbearable. At night the sirens wailed. Intrigues proliferated. But Enzo wrote energetically, an article or two a day. All his reserves of thought, memory, and information broke open — an article on Syria, the "land of contrasts," one on the significance of July 14, a critique of the autobiography of Cecil Rhodes, the problem of the second generation of Fascists, letters to soldiers, a chapter of his study "The Suez Canal and Modern Egypt." Writing about the sanctity of human life, he mentioned the polio epidemic "in my country" and talked about his fear lest his children be stricken. The superior worth of life occupied his mind all through the war, and he wrote of the danger that, in the midst of the great slaughter, the importance of individual life might be overlooked. The "V" sign, he often said, was not necessarily a sign for victory; it could just as well symbolize Vendetta, but above all it should mean *Vita:* we are the detachments of the victory of life over those who would destroy us.

The work in the newspaper, radio, and the anti-Fascist committee absorbed him and swept him along. It gave him wings and at the same time deepened the cleavages in his soul. "I am in a strange situation," he wrote, "between two worlds. Aside from the Bible, which is with me always, I have not seen a Hebrew book in months. I am in captivity among gentiles, I see almost no Jews, not our kind, anyway. Far away from home, centrifugal forces gain the upper hand in us and we tend to drift away from our Hebrew cultural sources. It requires a daily effort to overcome the surroundings and to remain true to ourselves. Unless suitable aids to such an effort are provided us, there is the danger that many of us will fall victim to the alien environment."

In light of the urge to escape from the nest of intrigue in Egypt and to participate directly in the world struggle, to activate masses and to lay the foundations for a new postwar Italy, the reality, British style, was especially disappointing. To restrain the excessive independence of the editors of *Corriere*, De Salis appointed a military officer to be the responsible editor of the paper. Galleys of all material had to be submitted to him before publication, and he held two editorial sessions a day with the civilian editors. "Dr. Simmons" informed De Salis that he could not agree to some aspects of the new management of the paper and hinted at his readiness to resign. As British supervision over the Italian propaganda work intensified, "Dr. Simmons," Dr. Battino, and the director of the radio broadcasts went to De Salis's office to present the resignation of the propaganda commission, but when De Salis suggested a postponement in order to clarify matters they agreed to it, and on September 27 "Simmons" and Battino were furloughed with pay while awaiting new instructions.

How great was Enzo's surprise when on November 5 he received a letter informing him that his resignation had been accepted: "In view of the work you have been doing it has been decided that you should receive salary for the entire month of October, two weeks more than is coming to you under the law. I am sorry to inform you that, on the basis of instructions from a higher authority received this morning, this decision is not subject to appeal under any circumstances. Sincerely, Lord De Salis, Lt. Col."

In vain Enzo argued that it was impossible to accept a resignation that had not been submitted. The doors of *Corriere D'Italia* were closed to him.

The immediate cause of Enzo's dismissal was his article "Perfidious Albion," which he had prepared for *Corriere* and which had been turned down by the British censor. This article deprecated the use of generalization about nations, such as "macaroni eaters," or "Perfidious Albion" and the simplistic arguments against the British because of their alleged sense of superiority. But it also contained undertones of "Brutus is an honorable man." Superficially this article was an appeal against age-old prejudices that Italians harbored about the British — an image of strange and eccentric gentlemen who come to Italy as tourists with their wives, an image of snobbish graduates of aristocratic private schools who regard the entire world as their oyster, of hypocrites who preach morality to the world while they deny Ireland its freedom and pursue bloody conquests. Enzo argued that it was necessary to see the English people in its entirety, to remember the British working class supported Marx and Engels, to appreciate English devotion to ideals and willingness to fight for noble causes. But it was also not hard to read "Perfidious Albion" as definitely anti-British. By itself the article would not have been cause for his dismissal had he been otherwise welcome. But by this time it was no longer a question of an article but of the author whom the British found too independent and too far left in his views, not only concerning Italy but also where England was concerned — and altogether too energetic and imaginative for their tastes.

When the British Intelligence authorities in the Italian division reached the conclusion that "Dr. Simmons" would not play the game in accordance with British rules, that is, quietly resign and go his way, they decided to act with greater energy. On the evening of November 26, Egyptian police arrested Enzo on the charge of maintaining a dual identity with the aid of a fictitious name and a forged passport. The British thus not merely tossed him out but handed him to the Egyptian police, which had its own account with the man who had set up a network of secret agents behind its back.

In the search of Enzo's quarters that accompanied his arrest a number of documents were impounded, some of which bore the name Sereni and others Simmons, proof of his use of a dual identity for which the penalty was two years' imprisonment and/or a fine of twenty pounds sterling. When he was led out of his room by two British soldiers, they ran into Dr. Battino and Enzo said to him in Italian: "Inform the British." He could not believe that the British would cooperate in his detention because of a transgression committed at their behest, for it was they who provided "Dr. Simmons" with both his name and passport and constantly refused to heed his recurring appeals that he be allowed to function under his true name. Now he was incarcerated and vanished without a trace.

By chance Moshe Sharett, the head of the political department of the Jewish Agency, came to Cairo the day after Enzo was arrested and was shocked to hear of it. Like most leaders in the diplomatic service of the Jewish community, he believed in British fair play. This belief was based on his personal contacts with the British command, especially in the area of cooperation in the war effort. Enzo's arrest was a personal blow to him, not only because of his fondness for him and because he regarded him as a potential future colleague in an independent Jewish foreign service, but also because he was the one who had sent Enzo to work for the British command, and he felt responsible for his fate.

At first the British darkly hinted that Enzo had been guilty of a serious security breach, and Sharett hesitated for a moment. But after he began to act energetically for Enzo's release and formally protested on behalf of the Jewish Agency, the British took steps to have Enzo released. It turned out that Enzo had engaged in a hunger strike the entire eleven days that he had been incarcerated, not in order to be released but in protest against his illegal detention, since he had never been informed of the cause of his arrest. He emerged from prison pale, gaunt, and barely able to stand, but with a gleam of triumph in his eyes: he had challenged fate and overcome it.

The British Intelligence office agreed to release Enzo after it became evident that his scandalous arrest had aroused great resentment in the Italian colony, in anti-Fascist circles, and among the Jews of Egypt and in Zionist circles. But in order to maintain its prestige, it insisted that Enzo be expelled from Egypt. Enzo protested against this ruling since it implied confirmation of a wrongdoing of which he was not guilty and which might have prevented his entry into Egypt in the future. After negotiation with the British, with Dr. Battino as intermediary, a compromise was reached: Enzo would leave Egypt voluntarily, a free man unescorted by police or soldiers to the borders of Palestine.

Before leaving Egypt Enzo sent a letter of farewell to the secretary of the British embassy in which he wrote: "I came to Egypt at the invitation of the British authorities, at a time when England did not have too many allies, in order to participate in the common struggle against Nazis and Fascism. As long as I am prevented from participating in this struggle, I see no reason why I should remain away from my homeland. . . . But I take the liberty of making a number of comments. Humiliating accusations have been leveled against me and slanders have been bruited about me in connection with my removal from the editing of the paper and my illegal and foolish detention. It is understandable — though in my case this seems strange — that in wartime it is permissible to detain a co-worker and to sentence him without trial and without giving him an opportunity to defend himself. There are times when exigencies of war impose such a painful silence. But there is no moral or legal justification for not holding responsible the person who had spread the slanders after their falsehood had been proved. War may justify silence; it does not justify false accusations. . . . I am too strongly aware of the need to destroy the Nazi-Fascist beast to be overcome by feelings of bitterness and resentment. . . . The little people who see in the big war only their petty interests will disappear and there will remain only the men of goodwill who will triumph in the battle against reaction despite the old politics of appeasement and the spiritual fifth column. I am convinced that we will yet meet again on this battle front; and I am always prepared to answer the call to contribute all my strength and even my life should that be necessary."

Enzo returned to Givat Brenner in December 1941. He was thirty-six years old and much more mature than when he had left fifteen months earlier. Members of the kibbutz saw a more restrained Enzo, more melancholy and refined, a man who had learned to bear sorrow. And he was enraged at Moshe Sharett because if even for only a brief moment he had been inclined to heed the British accusations. The Sereni clan received the wandering son with open arms. Ada, the children, the parents, Leah and her family, all sought his nearness, to talk to him, to listen to him. And he did not disappoint them. But though he told much, he did not mention the period of his incarceration, nor what his feelings were then.

For the time being he returned to his scholarly work — writing a history of Italian Fascism for the younger generation of Italians who did not know its roots. And his voice was again heard at membership meetings where was now discussed a problem that ten years earlier, during the time of hunger and unemployment would have seemed like a dream — the problem of labor shortage. As a result of the economic affluence kibbutzim now employed nonmembers, contrary to the kibbutz principle of self-labor and nonexploitation of the work of others. But if the employment of outsiders was unavoidable, Enzo felt, then it was at least necessary to make them aware that they did not work for an ordinary employer but in a collective labor enterprise that was always ready to accept the temporary nonkibbutz employee as a permanent member with equal rights.

Enzo often visited Berl Katznelson in his home in Tel Aviv. He talked to him of Egypt while Berl listened and looked at him with that special look of affection he reserved for Enzo. A number of plans were suggested for his activity in Palestine, and the members of Givat Brenner hoped that he would stay at home for a while. But those who knew Enzo sensed his restlessness.

18

Storming Baghdad

A desert separates Palestine from Iraq, and the Jewish communities in the two countries were ages apart. Iraqi Jewry had had almost no contact with the outside Jewish world for many years. During the reign of King Faisal after World War I, when England held the mandate over the country, the Jewish community enjoyed a brief period of splendor — they were elected to membership in the Parliament, held high office in the administration, constituted a substantial percentage within the liberal professions, and thrived in business. When Faisal, who was regarded as a friend of the Jews, died, extremist nationalists came to the fore and the situation of the Jews deteriorated under the growing influence of Nazism. Enemies of the British among the extremists were numerous — orthodox Moslems and ambitious military elements — and preferred alliance with Germany. In 1941, after a number of abortive revolutions, when it seemed to the Arabs that England was on the brink of defeat and that the moment was propitious for an outright revolt, the government of Raschid Ali al Ghailani repudiated its defense treaty with England and openly sided with the Axis countries.

Though Britain was then beset at home, in Africa, and in the Middle East, Winston Churchill sent a military expedition to Iraq and it gained an unexpectedly easy victory. Iraqi forces dispersed, Raschid Ali and his government fled, and the British stood at the gates of Baghdad. Passions that had been aroused by the conflict, the defeat, and the systematic Nazi propaganda burst loose and the people of Baghdad staged a pogrom on Jews. The British, standing at the gates of the city, found it politic not to intervene. On the festival of Shavuoth, the first and second days of June 1941, the Jews of Baghdad were subjected to a full-scale pogrom: murder, looting, rape, and destruction. About 180 Jews were killed during the two days and more than a thousand were injured, thousands of homes and businesses were looted, and only few among Baghdad's 100,000 Jews dared offer any resistance. This event deeply shocked Iraqi Jewry, which proudly maintained its awareness of having lived in the area long before its present rulers. A small number concluded that there was no longer any future for them in Iraq and chose to immigrate to Syria, India, and the West Indies. A few hundred managed to reach Palestine through illegal channels by means of their own efforts. A number of young Jews understood that the Arab rioters would have hesitated had they met with armed resistance and began to organize themselves in small armed groups without any assistance. But the majority, as had ever been the custom of Jews in the Diaspora, deluded themselves that the pogrom was a one-time outburst and that now that the British had returned everything would be peaceful again.

In March 1942 there came to Iraq Shaul Meirov (Avigur) who headed the Mossad, the organization for illegal immigration (Aliyah B) that had been established in 1934 as an independent body under the authority of the Executive Committee of the Federation of Labor. At first its activity was limited but by 1939 the Mossad brought into Palestine some 6,000 of a total of 11,000 illegal immigrants that entered Palestine that year in small and unseaworthy vessels. And later, before all avenues of escape from Europe were shut, another 7,000 illegals were brought to the country through all kinds of daring and desperate ventures. Mossad consisted of a small, tightly organized group of dedicated people who were accustomed to working in secrecy.

Shaul, a member of kibbutz Kinneret, an earnest and systematic person, came to Iraq in the uniform of a British soldier, provided with addresses of reliable Jews in Baghdad. He spent four days in the city and established the initial contacts. It was then decided by the Mossad to send a number of emissaries to Iraq to work there underground, under the leadership of one person who was to have a legal status. What was wanted was a person who could speak English and establish contact with British officialdom, a man of western manners who would also be an experienced youth leader able to communicate with oriental Jews. Enzo's name was suggested among a number of others but Shaul and others in Mossad had grave doubts about him. Under the conditions prevailing in Iraq, where both the British and the Iraqi authorities were extremely anti-Zionist, it was felt that a man was needed who was capable of working in great secrecy in conspiratorial conditions; Enzo, they felt, was too much the extrovert for such a mission, and his southern temperament was the opposite of that of a secret agent.

But in the end he was chosen for the mission. The Mossad did not have a superabundance of suitable candidates unassigned at that time. The Mossad's secretary drove out to Givat Brenner in the only car available to it in the entire country, armed with a handwritten note from Shaul informing Enzo that it had been decided to send him on a mission and that he was requested to report to Tel Aviv without delay. The secretary found Enzo engrossed in a book. He introduced himself, handed the note to him, and explained in a few words the nature of the assignment. Enzo asked no questions. "OK, I'm going with you," was all he said. To Ada, who happened to come into the room just then, he merely said, "I have received a letter from Shaul. There is something I have to discuss with him in Tel Aviv." He asked neither her opinion nor advice. He got up and went to accept a mission that would once again take him from his family, kibbutz, and country for many months.

Why did he consent so readily? Perhaps it was out of a sense of duty of one who regarded himself as mobilized for his entire life, or because of the moral authority of the Mossad, Haganah, and the labor movement. Conceivably he was also affected by a sense of frustration engendered by the sudden transition from active preparation of an Italian resistance movement on a worldwide scale to the calm of Givat Brenner, which was just then enjoying economic prosperity as a result of the war and the sea blockade. His mission in Egypt had ended in a defeat that was particularly difficult to bear within the narrow framework of family and friends who knew what had transpired. The mission to Iraq was thus simultaneously a fulfillment of duty, a challenge, and flight.

Enzo began practical preparations the very next day. He met with members of Mossad, with immigrants from Iraq who had come to Palestine after the pogrom, and with David Hacohen, the director of Solel Boneh, the construction contracting company of the Histadrut which would provide the legal cover for his stay in Iraq. Solel Boneh had contracted with the British to build some airfields and other security installations in Iraq, as well as an expansion of the refineries, and the British preferred Jewish workers, who were at least allied to them in the struggle against Nazism, over Arab workers who might be serving the Axis. Some four hundred Jewish engineers and technicians were then employed by Solel Boneh in Iraq, and traffic between the two countries was heavy. The representative of Solel Boneh in Baghdad had to attend to the needs of the workers who stopped in the city on the way to Abadan in the south and to Mosul and Kirkuk in the north. It was a post that did not require much work and was an ideal cover for underground work. Thus it came about that Enzo, wearing a British uniform marked "Special" — the British had insisted that all Solel Boneh employees be uniformed in order to conceal their identity — left for Baghdad by bus by way of Syria. He was in high spirits. His underground name was Ehud.

Upon his arrival in Baghdad he was introduced to the British officials who were in charge of the work of Solel Boneh, and he was pleased to be given permission to wear civilian clothes. He took a room in the Semiramis Hotel, one of the most modern and luxurious hostelries in the city, as befit his official status.

It very soon became apparent that he would have to make his own way and organize the work as he thought best. He had been given wide authority by the Mossad, and when he came to Baghdad Iraq was virtually an unknown territory. Except for a handful of people who had visited the country, Palestinian Jews

did not go there and in recent days not many Iraqi Jews had
gone to Palestine. It was therefore necessary to feel one's way as
in the dark.

His first contact with the Youth Rescue Organization consisted of a meeting in a café overlooking the Tigris, which also
served as a meeting place for the local Arab intelligentsia. Two
very young men met with him, one a high school student and the
second somewhat older, and both were suspicious of him as a
possible British agent. They introduced themselves as David and
Abraham. Enzo explained his view that, important as was the
defense of the Iraqi Jews, it was not a final goal in itself, that the
defense activities had to become part of broader Zionist work
and preparation for migration to Palestine. Their entire organization should join this movement, he declared, and he demanded
an answer on the spot. The young men hesitated and asked for a
week's time to think the matter over. They suspected that all this
might be a provocation. Enzo thereupon demonstratively flung
his documents on the table for them to examine. Altogether he
made an indelible impression on them and they agreed to meet
within three days.

At this time there arrived in Iraq two other underground
emissaries, Shmarya Gutman and Ezra Kaduri, both kibbutz
members. Kaduri was a native of Iraq who had come to Palestine as a child. The two were provided with forged Iraqi passports. According to the division of functions, Enzo was to be in
charge of general Zionist activity, Shmarya was to attend to
illegal immigration to Palestine, and Kaduri to take charge of
defense activities. These two new emissaries, who had to present
an appearance of local Jews, dressed, as was customary in Baghdad, in jackets and ties even in the summer heat, and could not
openly meet with Dr. Sereni, the formal representative of a
Palestinian concern, in order not to arouse suspicion that they
were Zionist sympathizers. They never entered the hotel where
Enzo stayed, and when it was necessary to contact him, they sent
a messenger. Enzo, too, visited them in the Jewish quarters
secretly, to the extent that he was capable of secrecy.

Many of the Jews of Baghdad still lived in the old ghetto, in
houses built around courts and with no windows facing the

street. All doors opened on the central court. All the houses abutted on each other, and in case of need it was easily possible to escape by way of the roofs. Each family inhabited a house of its own — parents, children, uncles all together — and when one of the sons married he continued to live in his father's house, space permitting. The Sehayek family, whose sons were the main pillars of the movement during its early days, rented a house in their own name to serve the movement and moved into it to conceal the house's true purpose.

A certain degree of tension, which stemmed from their different characters, arose between Enzo and Shmarya. Shmarya had the habits of an underground man: he sought anonymity in crowds, tried not to stand out, to be invisibly gray, to go out of the house only when the work required it. He adapted himself to his assumed identity to such an extent that even people who knew him well failed to recognize him in his guises of wealthy effendi or peasant from the north, whereas Enzo always remained himself — all Baghdad knew him as the "doctor." When he walked down the street he was its center. As in the days of his anti-Fascist activity in Rome, he knew the importance of self-confidence when doing underground work. One day he took with him a member of Kibbutz Na'an, who had come to Iraq to help in the work, on a visit to the British command headquarters where he had some business to attend to, and left him outside confused and frightened for half an hour, dressed in civvies, without proper documents, and without a permit to be in Iraq. When Enzo emerged from the office as if nothing had happened, he was given a dressing down: "How could you do a thing like that to a comrade?" "I want you to know," Enzo answered unperturbed, "that I have a theory contrary to yours regarding underground work. The more dangerous places you go to, the less you will be suspected; the more you seek concealment, the more easily you will be apprehended." Once Enzo had his wallet containing money belonging to the movement stolen while on the street. His anger got the upper hand and he complained to the police, even though this was likely to attract unnecessary attention to him. The complaint made him feel better — the money, however, was not recovered.

In Iraq Enzo found sympathy for the Jewish community in Palestine but no Zionist political awareness. In Germany he sometimes had to convince Jews that they were Jews, while in Iraq Judaism was an integral part of Jewish life. It expressed itself in a life-style based on Sabbath observance, kashruth, and visits to the synagogue on Saturdays and holidays but lacked a deep sense of religiosity. He began to develop systematic activity among numerous and various elements in the Jewish community. He tried to persuade rich Jews to invest in Palestine and solicited contributions to the national fund; he also tried to establish contacts with assimilated intellectuals who had lost their self-confidence as a result of the anti-Jewish riots and with leftist circles.

But there was a great contrast between the tempo that he wished to employ in his work and the means of communication with the Mossad. His letters were transported mainly by Jewish soldiers returning to Palestine on home leave and he often had to wait weeks for replies, for the lucky soldier going home frequently went to his kibbutz first, and only some days later might he remember to pass the letters on to their destination. And in the Mossad itself, the work in Iraq did not have the highest priority. The German victories in North Africa raised the specter of German occupation of the country. The British were considering the possibility of having to evacuate the country, and the Jewish community was planning a desperate last-man stand. From Europe came the first reports of the mass extermination of Jews. Jewish refugees from Russia and Poland began to reach Teheran. To cope with all these emergencies the Mossad had only a small staff and a limited budget. As a matter of fact, there was no definite budget at all: wherever an urgent need arose it was somehow financed by the Histadrut, the kibbutz movement, the Joint Distribution Committee, or by donations from wealthy Jews in England or in Egypt.

Enzo's charisma was more effective in Iraq than anywhere else: the Iraqi Jews loved him, admired him, revered him, and obeyed all his wishes. Their faith in him was unlimited and for his sake they did things that ran against their own wishes and judgment. Sometimes they regarded him as a bit of a madman.

One summer day in 1942 he appeared in the office of Ezra Hadad, the director of a Jewish school and a member of the Iraqi
Academy. He introduced himself as Dr. Sereni and without any
further ado declared: "It is time that you work for the national
cause. Your place is with us." He pulled out of his pocket a story
by the Hebrew writer J. C. Brenner and announced in a tone of
command: "This will interest you very much. It is now Thurs-
day. I will come in Sunday morning and I want you to translate
it into Arabic by then, so that young people could learn from it.
Agreed?" He said good-bye and went out. The entire meeting
lasted less than ten minutes.

Enzo's system was effective. When he came to Hadad's office
on Sunday morning, the story was translated.

He dashed over to Palestine for a few days and reported on
the work in Iraq. When he returned the work expanded. Hundreds were now studying Hebrew. He had an Arabic translation
made of the Zionist classic, *Auto-emancipation*. He established a
library of English and French books on Jewish topics. When his
repeated appeals — "We need more money!" — brought only
partial relief, he obtained loans from whomever he could, and
much later Iraqi Jews appeared in the offices of the executive of
the Histadrut in Tel Aviv bearing handwritten notes "Please
repay the bearer . . ." signed by Enzo.

Enzo's colleagues regarded him as parsimonious. They were
allowed a salary of five pounds a month for their living expenses,
and Enzo confiscated half of it for the needs of the movement.
Ezra used to joke: If the Philharmonic should play in Enzo's
room when he is asleep, he wouldn't wake; but should somebody
whisper in his ear, "Enzo, ten *grush*," he would jump up. As a
matter of principle he seldom appealed to Iraqi Jews for contributions, partly in order not to diminish his status in their eyes.

One of the most vexing problems of work among oriental
Jews was inducing young women to participate in the movement's
activities. When Enzo first expressed his wish to meet with
young women's groups, the spontaneous reaction of the young
men closest to him was: "Be careful. Don't get involved." To
induce a girl to become active in the movement it was necessary
to break down generations of old traditions and to challenge the

authority of the father and older brothers. The girls studied in separate schools and went into the street only when accompanied by a member of the family. Now, after the riots, they would frequently go out veiled like Moslem women, for reasons of security, and if they ever went out by themselves, they had to recount in advance where they were going, how they would get there, when they'd be back. A young woman seen talking in the street with a stranger was regarded as a loose woman. Middle-class girls, and most Iraqi Jews were middle class, led protected and enclosed lives until it was time for them to get married, and then the family chose the prospective husband. Enzo dropped into this situation like a whirlwind.

The first contact with women was established within a family framework. A relative of the family whose home served as center for the movement, an educated and earnest young woman, agreed to arrange a meeting in her home on a Saturday morning when her parents were away at the synagogue. It took a good deal of courage to do this because all meetings were legally prohibited by the government, and also her family's reputation was at stake should news of the meeting leak out. About ten young women turned up and Enzo talked about clothes, fashions, the weather, various countries of the world — entertaining chatter. The young ladies enjoyed this talk and asked to meet again. They had never met such a person before in their lives. The following Saturday some twenty young women appeared and Enzo was delighted to see the room crowded. This time he mentioned Palestine, talked about Jewish holidays and explained their agricultural origins, all the while talking casually in English and French, which the girls had learned in the Alliance school they attended. The girls were entranced.

Daily lessons in Hebrew were now introduced, as well as general lectures, in a number of homes. Enzo joked, asked many questions, talked about the importance of the individual in Palestine and about the independent spirit of the Jewish girls in Palestine who knew how to defend themselves. The Iraqi Jewish girls did not always understand everything he was saying — all the strange words — but that was not too important. He influ-

enced them, redirected their thinking, and provided a goal for all
their vague and concealed rebelliousness.

Three months after his arrival in Baghdad, the first twenty
young women were ready to go to Palestine and Enzo discussed
the problems of their absorption into the country with the appropriate institutions. He stressed that they were not to be brought
directly to a kibbutz — the transition would be too radical —
that they were to be concentrated in women's training farms,
but in any case not in mixed groups.

When the girls first raised the question of immigration to
Palestine with their families, there was general consternation:
"What are you lacking here? Don't you have a family? What
will people say? A girl that works to earn her living is a shame
to her father. Kibbutz? A kibbutz is intended for poor Jews from
Europe who have no families. Palestine? It's a country where
one goes to die. What will you eat there? Sand?"

The first girls who went to Palestine did so legally, with
official passports, claming they were going there to study or to
undergo medical treatment. But when legal departure became
increasingly difficult, the delicate and pampered girls were led,
like the young men, by devious ways through desert and
mountains.

But Enzo's persuasive powers were effective only up to a certain point, and the limit was reached when he tried to convince
them of the dignity of manual labor. To strengthen his argument he would say: "But I too am a workingman." The reaction
was opposite of what he had intended. As a "doctor" his words
carried weight, but as a workingman he lost face with his listeners. Palestine, *aliyah*, even life on a kibbutz sounded reasonable, but choosing the life of a workingman, physical labor, as a
matter of principle was beyond the grasp of the eastern imagination. Some of his listeners even tried to placate him: "Don't
worry. We will do agricultural work until we save up enough
money, then we will turn to trade."

"This is the chief educational problem we face," he wrote.
"They learn Hebrew rapidly, and also Zionist theory, but persuading them to become and to remain laborers is an entirely

THE EMISSARY

different matter." And he did not delude himself: "All indications are that also in Palestine they will become traders."

Indeed, this is how it turned out. The first groups went to kibbutzim, but not many stayed there long. But they did stay permanently in the country, later brought over their families, and thus paved the way for the immigration of more than 100,000 Iraqi Jews after Israel became a state.

The first young immigrants from Iraq went to Givat Brenner, Na'an, Bet Hasheetah, and Maoz Chaim, kibbutzim of which they knew from the talks of their mentors, but they felt isolated there. Their ideological preparation could not compare with that of newcomers from Germany and eastern Europe, and the majority of them had never done physical labor in their lives. At a kibbutz meeting held three months after the arrival of the first group, they declared frankly: "Among the Arabs we felt like Jews, but here we feel like Arabs." Older kibbutz members tried to comfort them: "You must organize. You are still few and that is bad for all of us. When we came here we too were first met with some derision on the part of those who came before us. That's the way things are here." Had Enzo stayed in Givat Brenner, things might have turned out differently. But he put in an appearance only rarely and then his visits were brief. Thus it came about the most of the Iraqis left Givat Brenner. Some went to other kibbutzim; others went to the cities.

As could have been expected, the underground met with a setback. A group of six young immigrants, dressed as Arab peasants, that tried to reach Palestine by illegal ways was captured in the summer of 1942 in the Syrian city of Aleppo, together with their Arab guide. They had been sitting in a café talking loudly among themselves; a secret agent recognized their Baghdad dialect and they were detained. They were incarcerated in a prison for foreigners and were beaten and forced to tell whatever they knew about the illegal route. It was a severe blow to the movement. The hired guides now refused to have anything to do with "laborers." Ezra and Shmarya broke off their contacts for a while and changed their residences. It is true that the six detainees were released quite soon with the aid of bribes, that perennial remedy for all troubles in the Middle East, but the morale of the movement suffered for a short time.

The danger from loose talk, even on the part of the most reliable people, was great. "One must realize," Enzo reported during a visit to Palestine in the summer of 1942, "that we are not dealing with Europeans. My colleagues and I sometimes have occasion to witness inspiring instances of devotion which we never saw anywhere else, and at other times we encounter manifestations more negative than any we have seen elsewhere. Which describes the Iraqi Jew? The first or the latter? I say both."

When the first three emissaries came to Iraq they had assumed that after the riots many Iraqi Jews would be anxious to go to Palestine at once and at all costs. But by the time they got there nine months had been lost since the riots and the opportunities for large-scale emigration passed. In his report to the Jewish Agency on the situation in the country, Enzo wrote: "In recent weeks there has occurred a noticeable change in the mood of the Jewish population in Iraq, which cancels the enthusiasm for Palestine that was brought about by the oppression and the riots of last year. The causes of this change are various. First there is the talent for forgetting and adapting to new circumstances that characterizes Jews everywhere. Then there is the influence of the prevailing prosperity as a result of the war from which all classes, but especially the trading elements, benefit. Many are now confident that the Allies will win the war and that all will end well. There is also the changed attitude toward the Jews of the Iraqi government which now tries to appear 'democratic.' This has taken the form of paying compensation to the victims of the riots."

For the moment life appeared to have returned to normal; Palestine again became merely a theoretical matter. Letters from Iraqi Jews who had gone to Palestine also exerted their influence. "It is becoming ever more certain," these letters maintained, "that in Palestine Jews have no alternative but to engage in manual labor. Opportunities in business are virtually nonexistent, and life is hard."

Late in August there came to Baghdad Moshe Dayan, at that time a young member of the Jewish defense forces, who had recently lost an eye in the fighting with the Vichy French forces in Syria. He came as an assistant bus driver, the customary way to get a free ride to Iraq, and he brought three suitcases full of weapons for the local Jewish self-defense. The British did not permit the buses to enter the city and ordered the drivers to stay in a military camp some thirty kilometers out of town. Dayan concealed the weapons in the camp and himself managed to get out of the camp, taking off his trousers and wading through the sewage canals that led outside. In this way he reached the highway and mingled with the endless procession of Iraqi peasants and their donkeys that moved with their produce to the city. Police checked the documents of all strangers at the bridge at the entrance to the city, but Dayan, half-undressed and covered with mud and dust, was indistinguishable from the natives, especially since he had removed his eye patch, and he entered the city without attracting attention. Once in Baghdad, he put on his trousers and, covered with dirt as he was, he showed up at the fashionable hotel where Enzo stayed to inform him of the weapons shipment. At first he was refused admission to the hotel, but after arguments and a suitable bribe, Enzo was called downstairs. He took Dayan up to his room, ran a bath for him, and lent him some of his clothes, which were a few inches too short for Dayan. When Dayan was about to return, Enzo utilized the opportunity to smuggle two young Jewish refugees from Poland with him to Palestine. The bus driver, it is true, was not overly enthusiastic at first but was finally persuaded to go along with the plan. That night Dayan kept a vigil near the camp fence at an agreed-upon spot nearest the road with the suitcases filled with weapons. A car driven by a member of the movement discharged the two refugees disguised in British military uniforms, picked up the suitcases, and quickly drove away before the guard near the gate noticed what was going on.

Enzo regarded the Communists as "my brother's people," and, as in all other countries he stayed in, he tried to establish contacts with them in Iraq. It is not clear whether he did so out of genuine admiration for their readiness for self-sacrifice (the

Iraqi authorities persecuted the Communists with great brutality) or because he wanted to win the allegiance of their Jewish members or because he retained a spiritual bond with Mimo — who was now somewhere in France fighting for the same cause — and thus to continue at a distance the debate with his brother that he had begun fifteen years earlier. As a consequence of the heroic Soviet resistance to the Nazis, Communist influence among the Jews of Iraq mounted, as they heard that "Jews in Russia enjoy all rights and have attained all sorts of high posts." Ascent on the social ladder — if not success in trade — is the hope of young Jews and therefore, paradoxical as it may sound, many Jews tended to sympathize with socialism because they saw it as a regime providing opportunities for a career. Young Iraqi Jews who had despaired of assimilation now tended to accept the Communist solution which promised peace, well-being, and dignity without, for the moment, demanding a commitment to any serious Socialist program. And Enzo looked for ammunition for the struggle with my "brother's friends who are very active."

As illegal emigration became increasingly difficult, Enzo was convinced that it was not worthwhile to invest such great efforts for the sake of smuggling out individuals here and there concealed in fish tanks, large crates, and as assistant drivers on buses carrying soldiers on leave. The Iraqi authorities systematically restricted Jewish economic activities with the aim of removing them from their economic positions, and Enzo believed that it was possible to exert influence on the authorities by means of diplomatic pressure to permit a part of Iraqi Jewry to leave the country, especially if the United States were to participate in this effort. He suggested drawing up a memorandum on the situation of Iraq's Jews to be submitted to the United States government and to American Jewry through the medium of the Jewish Agency. He was confirmed in this conviction when Nuri Said, the premier of Iraq, complained in the course of an interview with two foreign journalists that "the Zionists with all the hullabaloo they are raising are severely hampering quiet diplomatic efforts which, at the end of the war, could bring about a solution satisfactory to all sides." This convinced Enzo that Nuri

Said feared public pressure and confirmed him in his belief that it was possible to win permission for the departure of Iraqi Jews. (Enzo did not live long enough to see himself vindicated when, upon the establishment of the state of Israel, Nuri Said permitted all 120,000 Iraqi Jews to leave the country.)

The constant stream of visitors to Iraq from Palestine severely interfered with the conspiratorial efforts of the emissaries and attracted the attention of the British. (Many of the best leaders of the Jewish community in Palestine took advantage of the traffic of Solel Boneh personnel to catch a free ride and to visit an unfamiliar country.) "What I feared came to pass," Enzo wrote. "Yesterday I was called in by Major Mason who informed me officially that unless these visits stop, he will recommend that all contracts with Solel Boneh be terminated. His tone was decidedly unfriendly and I fear for the future." But his warning was not heeded and Enzo was furious. "It has come to my attention that more prominent 'stars' are getting ready to visit here and to obtain impressions. In heaven's name I beg you to put an end to these visits for they are destroying our work. It is not visitors we are short of, but additional workers and regular contact with us. Advice we have more than enough."

19

The Well-Known
Underground Agent

In November 1942, under a prisoner exchange agreement, there reached Palestine seventy-eight Jews from ghettos in Poland and from concentration camps in Germany, Belgium, and Holland, and they told of the systematic extermination of European Jewry. The Jewish Agency Executive took down their testimony and made it available to the public in Palestine and to Jewish communities throughout the world. A copy was also passed on to Baghdad where the Zionist movement in Iraq published it in Arabic. A fast day was proclaimed in Baghdad, Jews gathered in the synagogues, read the proclamation, and wept. Enzo's report to the Mossad in connection with this event was highly practical: "News of the extermination of European Jewry made a tremendous impression. The city is agog. We are trying to utilize the situation. Lately many are interested in buying land in Palestine. One group organized to buy ten dunam in North Tel Aviv. Provide detailed offers. Don't neglect this opportunity. Don't neglect it."

But in his letter to his children in December 1942, which, as usual, was written as if addressed to all the children of the kibbutz, or perhaps to all the Jewish children in Palestine, he expressed the great grief that had taken hold of him: "When I read about what is happening there, my heart comes to a halt. But my thinking on the subject is not simple. I cannot simply raise an outcry against the murderers and call the world to our aid. I recall those communities that have now gone up in flames and are totally destroyed. I see before me many in those communities whom I knew and loved, and I ask myself, Why did they remain there? Why aren't they here with us? Why didn't they use every possible opportunity to get to Palestine? Why didn't they come while the roads were still open and the country called to them? Some among them no doubt simply were ignorant. . . . We may perhaps say in their justification that they didn't see the abyss at their feet and didn't know where to go. Our guilt toward them is great and our reckoning with ourselves on this score is complicated. It is true that we went to the Diaspora and tried to talk to the people, to arouse them. But we did not always know how to talk so that all the people should understand us, so that even those remote from us should understand and feel what we said. To the extent that we knew and could have raised the alarm and did not do enough, to the extent that we did not love the Jewish masses enough, we are responsible for those who perished.

"But among those who today still live in that hell there are very many who did hear us, people who knew the Zionist — and even the Socialist Zionist — truth; they knew it but didn't believe it with all their hearts. They studied Zionism, and even used its arguments in debates with opponents, but they were not themselves absolutely serious about the Zionist truth which they advocated. We were all like that. None of us really believed that the misfortune would be so great. The few who did foresee the full extent of the coming tragedy were regarded as madmen or melancholiacs. I recall the summer of 1938 when I appealed to people to greet everything that was liable to postpone the outbreak of war. . . . Did those who welcomed the coming war realize what was likely to happen to the Jews of Poland? Did they understand that as Jews our accounts with the world are more complex than those of other nations? And why wasn't a greater effort made to bring out, by all possible ways, at least those who agreed with us?"

It may have been a coincidence but from the day that news began arriving about the scope of the Holocaust in Europe, Enzo began talking about returning home. "My residence permit," he wrote, "has been renewed after much effort, till the end of January. It will not be renewed again under any circumstances. It is clear that serious thought has to be given to finding a replacement for me while there is time, one who would come here legally, as a commercial agent, or as an officer in some corporation."

Shaul Avigur, who came to Iraq in December 1942 to look over the situation, did not agree. "Enzo must remain in Baghdad as long as possible. His departure will create a void impossible to fill." When he walked with Enzo along Ghazi Street, one of Baghdad's main arteries, they saw buses filled with uniformed Iraqis shouting in unison: "Jews! Jews!" It was upsetting to hear the cries and to see the clenched fists. Shaul fell silent, but Enzo reacted in his own way. He recited entire cantos of Dante's *Divine Comedy*, which in his life filled the same role that the Book of Psalms fills in the life of a God-fearing Jew, and all Shaul could do was to shake his head and think: Sereni will always remain Sereni. Italian. Effervescent. Different.

It was at this time that Enzo's son Daniel asked him to take a stand on an incident among the kibbutz children in the course of which he beat up another boy and was punished for it. Enzo, who was so frequently away from his family, tried to guide his children by means of letters. In this case he answered: "I am not a pacifist who insists that a child must never raise a hand against another. There are times when a few good blows at the right time and in the proper way may have a praiseworthy effect. The danger lies in resorting to physical force as a regular habit of settling disputes. Let Daniel, who knows Italian, ask his mother to read him the poem "Two Brothers" by the famous Italian poet Pascoli, in which the poet tells of two brothers who used to quarrel all day but at night they slept in the same bed, and their mother covered them with a single blanket. We must remember that we are all brothers, and the same night covers us after days of dispute and the few years that are our fate. When I read that Daniel might have injured another boy, I was shocked. How could Daniel have carried the weight of responsibility for inflicting injury, of perhaps a permanent character, on a comrade?

This, as I see it, is the main danger in raising a hand against another. One begins as if in jest and then one is drawn unconsciously into deeds whose meaning and influence are inestimable."

Members of the self-defense units in Iraq were sworn in on a Bible by candlelight to defend Iraqi Jews, to devote themselves to the cause, and to face death for it. Enzo was one of those who conducted the swearing-in ceremonies and his friends in Palestine regarded this as proof that nothing was left of his one-time pacifism. For the first time in the history of Jewish self-defense, weapons were smuggled in a reverse direction — from Palestine to the Diaspora — pistols, grenades, ammunition, and raw materials for the production of Molotov cocktails were transported to Iraq. It was still too risky to smuggle larger weapons, and in any case there was no superabundance of them in the country. The first shipments reached their destination without mishap and were concealed in provisional hiding places in the homes of outstanding Jews. This aroused some argument. Enzo felt that the weapons should be distributed among the members of the defense organization, thus reducing the risk of their being captured. Ezra, who was in charge of defense activities, was in favor of concentrating the weapons in one place for ease of access in case of need.

Searches on the highways were strict. The British military police looked for stolen army goods. Agents of the Free Polish Forces under General Anders, which were stationed in the neighborhood, looked for deserters. Iraqi secret agents looked for Communists, and the Iraqi economic police looked for smugglers. But despite these, the number of shipments increased. In addition to weapons, communications equipment was sent — and eventually a young woman to operate it — as well as used British uniforms, military boots, maps, used books of stubs of the British military forces. All of these came in handy in transferring to Palestine refugees from Russia and Poland who had managed to reach Iraq, and Jewish deserters from Anders's army who had joined his forces in the hope of reaching Palestine.

The refugees who had reached Iraq would be smuggled

across the Shatt-el-Arab and placed in Jewish homes in Basra. There they should be provided with local Arab garb and, two by two, sent by train to Baghdad, accompanied by a member of the movement in Basra. Things were made more difficult by the fact that many of the refugees from Poland and Russia were fair skinned, blue-eyed, and blonde and, naturally, did not know a word of Arabic. To protect them from the curiosity of the Arab passengers, their escort would have to concoct stories about their being deaf-mutes going to Baghdad to seek the blessing of a great saint. At the Baghdad station they would be met by a small chunky man who would take their suitcases as if he were a porter, and order them to follow him. Only after they had reached a secure haven would he be introduced to them as Enzo Sereni.

When some of the refugees became impatient after waiting for weeks in the hideouts, Enzo proposed a new plan: that six of them go with him to the police, admit to being illegally in the country, and the judge, by prearrangement, would sentence them to a fine and expulsion from the country. The young men waited outside while Enzo negotiated with the judge, and when it became obvious that they could not reach an agreement, Enzo went outside and quickly dispersed them and had them returned to their hideouts. In time they were smuggled into Palestine individually in British uniforms.

Zionist officials in Palestine would come to Iraq for visits and learned things about the underground that they were not supposed to know, and many of them talked too much. One American Jew came officially on behalf of PICA Bank and left in his hotel a suitcase full of documents that fell into the hands of the Iraqi Secret Service. The British sent Jewish agents from Palestine to spy on the Zionist underground. A handful of Zionist Revisionists came and worked independently among the Iraqi Jewish youth, creating not only competition but also a security problem. Shmarya was sent home to his kibbutz for recuperation. Ezra, too, who showed signs of weariness and nervousness, was sent on home furlough, and for a time Enzo was the sole emissary. The tension began to show its effects on him. He constantly warned the Mossad: "You mention not a word about additional emissaries. I am afraid that one of these days every-thing will explode, and then, when it is too late, you'll start acting. You must know: the work is becoming more extensive and additional workers are needed, and my situation is not at all secure. I am being watched, and I am too well known to the public." Indeed he was known, and how! At a Purim gathering held in the synagogue, a number of people shouted enthusiasti-cally: "Long live Mordecai! Long live Queen Esther! Long live Dr. Sereni!"

"I don't have the time to do half the things I'd like to do, and you think you can ignore the question of additional emissaries for budgetary reasons. Cancel the work in Iraq altogether and then no budget will be needed. I am here alone. True, I have strong nerves, but don't think that I can continue like this in-definitely."

He found some relief in alcohol. In his requests for liquor he stressed that he needed it for various social activities on behalf of the movement, but it was evident that he needed it also for himself. And in addition to the overall weariness and the feeling that the ground was slipping from under his feet (the British were not so naive as not to have discovered that the representa-tive of Solel Boneh in Iraq was none other than the "Dr. Sim-mons" who had caused them so much trouble in Egypt) there was another decisive reason for his desire to return — he wanted to be at home for the Bar Mitzvah of his son Daniel. "My con-science doesn't permit me to get up and leave," he wrote, "as long as I am not sure that the matter of emissaries will be satisfactorily arranged, but please try to understand: I have one son, and he is deeply troubled when he hears that I will not be home for his holiday. If you are devoted Jews you will at once arrange to permit this Jewish father to fulfill his duty."

Various groups were now interested in Enzo. British Intelli-gence in Palestine questioned the political department of the Jewish Agency about the true activities of Dr. Sereni in Bagh-dad, and British secret agents were asked for information about a number of persons, including Enzo. "I feel," he wrote, "that it were best if I went away for a while before being sent away, but

I can't leave before a replacement arrives. Please understand this and hurry. This is my last SOS."

Enzo did get home in time for his son's Bar Mitzvah which, contrary to kibbutz custom, was celebrated in the old people's synagogue in Givat Brenner in the presence of the entire family. Enzo glowed with excitement. It was a promise of generational continuity and the hoped-for fusion of the traditions of his forefathers with the new life. Here, in the small and pitiful synagogue, the leftist radical sensed ever so keenly the existence of a higher providence in which he had believed all his life.

He returned to Iraq bearing a large package of Palestine matzoth, in time for the Passover, reassured that his stay would be brief. Shortly after his return there was secretly held the founding conference of Hechalutz in Iraq in which eighty delegates representing thirty-five active units participated, a considerable accomplishment for a single year's work. But not only Zionists knew of this conference. In one of the Communist newspapers in Baghdad there appeared an article on the scope of Zionist activity in the country, and Enzo's name figured prominently in it.

The stream of Jewish refugees and deserters from the Polish forces grew, and it was necessary to find additional ways to transport them to Palestine. The bus drivers who transported soldiers between Iraq and Palestine would conceal a few, suitably provided with forged passports, in every party going back. The passport photos in the paybooks of the British soldiers were pinned, instead of glued, to the document, and Enzo would lightly switch photos and stamp them with a homemade stamp. But Shmarya and Ezra, now also back on the job, demanded more than daring action. They wanted to send an entire bus load of illegal emigrants disguised as Solel Boneh employees, with shoulder patches proclaiming them as "Special" which would protect them from too careful scrutiny on the part of the British MPs. At first Enzo was opposed to this project, fearing that it might endanger all of Solel Boneh's activities, but later he consented. An Iraqi Jew who worked for British Intelligence provided the necessary papers and stamps for a suitable fee. Girls in the movement altered the uniforms that had been smuggled into the country, and a special bus was rented to transport the thirty-five members of the "special unit" for home furlough. As the bus was about to leave from busy Raschid Street, two MPs entered it and demanded to see the papers for the group. Shmarya showed them the forged group travel order. The MPs could not talk to any of the others, who invariably responded with "Me no English."

All this time Enzo and Ezra paced about on the other side of the street, ready to alert members of the movement in the event anything went wrong. Finally the bus left and Enzo followed it to the nearest filling station where it stopped for fuel. Enzo dashed in and in great excitement asked what the MPs had wanted. Barely restraining his anger, Sergeant Shmarya hissed at him, "Beat it." The bus finally took to the highway westward and Ezra and Enzo drank to the health of the venture. As it turned out the bus reached Palestine safely, and the "special" unit was dispersed among kibbutzim.

Early in May Enzo was summoned to the office of the Central Intelligence Department and was asked to produce his papers as well as to clarify his peculiar civilian/military status. The documents were retained by the Intelligence officer and Enzo was asked to report the next day. When he did so, he was again questioned as to whether or not he was a Pole, though he had already declared he was a Palestinian. He was informed that the investigation was not concluded and that he would be called for further questioning. Clearly the time had come for him to leave. To camouflage his impending departure, activists in the movement spread the rumor that he was being ordered to North Africa, which by then was under Allied control. And when the British announced, toward the end of May 1943, that Enzo was persona non grata in Iraq, he was already far from Baghdad.

20

Infiltration

In July 1943, Givat Brenner celebrated the twenty-fifth anniversary of its establishment, which provided a suitable opportunity to look backward and to recall the thirty-five young men and women who occupied the wild spot with their handful of possessions. Now Givat Brenner numbered close to one thousand persons, the third largest kibbutz in the country, and despite all the criticism (which flourishes in kibbutzim more than anywhere else) and disillusionments, there was much to be proud of. The tract inhabited by lizards and scorpions which Enzo and Ben-Asher discovered in 1927 presented an entirely different aspect. The eucalyptus trees that had been planted near the first barracks towered high above the kibbutz, which now covered the adjoining hill purchased with money contributed by Italian Jews. The Security House, built after the riots of 1929, occupied the top of the hill and was surrounded by the children's houses — the children now numbered 300 — the school built with the aid of Aunt Ermalinda, members' dwellings, tile-roofed and with small gardens about them, then the two-story Agency Houses built for new immigrants, and in the midst of a pine grove stood the vegetarian sanitarium named after the invalid poet Jessie Sampter. Quite a number of members still lived in wooden huts, and a few even in tents. The chasm that had separated the Lithuanians from the Germans during the early days of Givat Brenner was forgotten as newcomers streamed in from Italy, Iraq, the United States, along with maturing boys and girls from the youth immigration. At the very southern end of the kibbutz stood the barns and other farm structures, and well beyond them, where the orange groves began, a small area approached by way of an avenue of cypresses and pines held the first graves of Givat Brenner.

The Roccas' house — the fortress of the Serenis — stood just outside Givat Brenner, and below it were the large structures of Rimon, the fruit and vegetable cannery that had begun many years earlier as a single vat for cooking jam and a barrel for pickling cucumbers. Now that the world war had brought prosperity, this plant presented the kibbutz with an unexpected problem: a labor shortage and the consequent resort to hired workers, contrary to the Socialist principles of the kibbutz. For the time being the employment of nonkibbutz workers was rationalized with the argument that they were employed only temporarily, to take the place of members of the kibbutz who had volunteered for the British army, Palmach, and the police — altogether some fifty men. As a matter of fact, the general assembly of Givat Brenner, in an attempt to stem the rush to volunteer without taking into consideration the economic needs of the kibbutz, decided that any member who volunteered for the armed forces without the consent of the kibbutz was to be expelled.

It was not hard to understand the urge to volunteer. Who wanted to stay home and pick oranges or tend to the cows at a time when the world was faced with the final attack against Hitler in Europe? The war in North Africa had ended with an Allied victory and now the Allies had also conquered Sicily and were preparing for the invasion of Italy. The loss of its colonies and most of its fleet and the bombardment of its cities convinced the Italians that they were on the verge of total defeat. Mussolini appealed to Hitler for aid, but the latter believed that only barbaric means, such as mass executions, could save the Fascist regime in Italy, and depended on Roberto Farinacci, the secretary of the Fascist party to act. Farinacci convoked the Fascist grand council for the first time in four years.

The council met in the Palazzo Venezia on July 24, and to
Mussolini's surprise adopted a resolution condemning his one-
man rule and demanding a division of governmental functions
among the council, the king, and the parliament, in accordance
with the country's constitution. Only now did the king dare to
oppose the duce, and on July 26, more than twenty years after
appointing him head of the government, did the tired old king
summon courage to dismiss Mussolini and to appoint the seventy-
year-old Marshal Badoglio head of the government. Mussolini
was arrested and the Fascist party dispersed without a struggle.
New times were around the corner.

Enzo followed the events in Italy with mounting disquiet.
After his return from Baghdad he had continued to be active in
the work of the underground in Iraq. He scoured the country for
suitable persons to be sent there as emissaries. He supplied
books, other materials, and advice to the Mossad's agents in
Baghdad, and he followed the acclimatization of the Iraqi immigrants in Palestine, many of whom felt forlorn and isolated in
their new home. When Shaul, the head of Mossad, went to
Constantinople to try to establish new contacts with the Jews in
German-occupied countries, Enzo served as his replacement.
The staff of the Mossad was housed in three small and crowded
rooms on the roof of the old Histadrut building on Allenby
Street in Tel Aviv, and whenever affairs dragged and Enzo's
patience was exhausted, he would flee to one of the restaurants
in the neighborhood. Long-windedness, a trait of many of the
old-timers in the country, annoyed him and very often he openly
showed his irritation. He would ignore the endless discussions
and scribble on small pieces of paper the final chapters of his
book on the history of Italian Fascism, the only book of many he
had planned that he ever completed. For several weeks after his
return from Iraq he dashed about from one British office to
another trying to obtain the release of the manuscript of the first
chapters of this book, which he had mailed from Baghdad and
which the British Secret Service had confiscated at the border
between Iraq and Transjordan, even though nothing in the
manuscript had any direct bearing on the British war effort. But
they were in no hurry to return it to Dr. Sereni. Someone higher

up kept an eye on it. The complete manuscript was found among
Enzo's belongings after his death. It was divided into twenty-two
chapters and was fundamentally intended for Italian youth. It
was never published in Italian, but Enzo's old teacher, Dante
Lattes, translated it into Hebrew and it was finally published by
Hakibbutz Hameuchad in 1951.

It was possible to reach the Jews of Europe only with the aid of
the British, and they were not too eager to help. Ever since the
outbreak of the war there had been some contacts between some
departments of the British Intelligence Service and representatives of the Jewish community in Palestine regarding cooperation in infiltrating agents behind the enemy lines, but few of the
numerous plans discussed in London, Cairo, and Jerusalem were
realized, and these few were on a smaller scale than hoped for.
The Central British Intelligence Department, which was headed
by professionals, mostly followed the British government's pro-
Arab line and considered cooperation with the Zionists only
when the British military situation was in very bad shape and
German invasion of Palestine appeared imminent.

As far back as 1940, an agreement was reached between the
Jewish Agency and the Director of Special Projects (M.O. 4)
regarding sabotage activities in German-occupied areas and anti-
German activities in neutral countries, where the Jewish emissaries would be allowed to act on behalf of Jewish interests.
Plans were worked out for introducing agents to the Balkan
countries, especially Rumania, but little came of it. When the
Germans conquered the Balkan countries, the plans to infiltrate
through neutral Rumania were also abandoned.

This cooperation with British Intelligence nevertheless did
produce some results, such as the interrogation office in Haifa
where thousands of refugees from the occupied countries were
questioned. The information gleaned was passed on to the Intelligence Division of the British Foreign Office, a unit of agents
who operated in Syria and Lebanon, and the German section in
Palmach (the commando unit of Haganah) whose members,
immigrants from Germany, were trained for commando actions
behind enemy lines in the event the Middle East was occupied

by the Nazis. But none of these activities were directly related to the matter most urgent from a Jewish point of view: direct aid to Jews in the occupied areas.

The contacts between British Intelligence and the heads of the political department of the Jewish Agency were carried on in an atmosphere of mutual distrust. The British were accustomed to working with professional spies for a fee and were doubtful about idealists — especially Zionists — whom they suspected of being mainly interested in the Jewish situation, rather than in the overall war effort — as if there were a contradiction between the two. The Palestinian Jews, on the other hand, who had had bad experiences with the British, suspected that British Intelligence was mainly interested in spying on Haganah. In the summer of 1942, Moshe Sharett suggested in London a plan to parachute Jewish forces into Italy, but only by the end of the year was the first practical agreement reached. Early in 1943 four radio instructors were sent to Egypt and one was parachuted to Tito's headquarters in free Yugoslavia. The representatives of the Jewish Agency proposed far-reaching plans to set up Jewish commando units in the Balkan countries. There was no dearth of volunteers in Palestine who were ready to face any danger if only there were the faintest hope of saving Jewish lives. But the British rejected these plans in favor of one much more limited in scope. British officers examined thirty-four volunteers from Palmach and the labor settlements willing to be parachuted behind the enemy lines. Of these only fourteen were chosen and were sent to Egypt for training. The training period was accompanied by much mutual friction, and, when it was completed, the embittered would-be parachutists were returned to Palestine where they cooled their heels for many months waiting for an assignment that did not come.

The morale in Mossad, which handled the recruitment and training of emissaries, hit bottom. But it was decided to carry on, and Enzo too was recruited to work full time on infiltration projects. His job was to advise those members of Mossad who maintained contacts with the British, the Americans, the French, and the Free Poles, to provide political background information on developments in the Balkans and to plan, together with Gideon Rafael, the forged identities and biographies of the emissaries, which were based on the true biographies of a number of living persons. But his main task was to interrogate the candidates for infiltration.

These interrogations sometimes took up entire nights. It was necessary to verify the minutest details of the new identities, and then to prepare the necessary clothing. On the one hand the infiltrators had to be parachuted in military uniforms to provide them with the protection of the Geneva convention in case they were captured (or so it was optimistically hoped); on the other hand they had to be dressed so that they could easily appear as civilians and readily get lost in the crowds.

The British finally agreed to infiltrate parachutists in pairs and slowly progress was made. Contact was established with the British delegation at Tito's headquarters, and the Yugoslav partisans agreed to receive five men and smuggle them into Hungary and Rumania.

Long and tiring discussions with the British concerned the area of the drop. Based on their previous experiences the British objected to blind drops in enemy territory since this involved a high risk of capture; they insisted on drops in territory under partisan control. This was only possible in Yugoslavia, and it lengthened by hundreds of kilometers the distance that the parachutists would have to cover before they reached Hungary, Slovakia, and Rumania. This system also required very precise advance contact work and would slow down the tempo of the drops; the volunteers, mostly twenty-year-olds, were impatient and did not heed the dangers, just so they got going.

Ever since Badoglio became head of the Italian government, secret negotiations were conducted behind the backs of the Germans between Italy and the Allied High Command regarding an Italian surrender, and on September 8, 1943, Eisenhower's headquarters formally announced the cessation of hostilities. Two hours later the first Allied forces landed at Salerno. The Germans quickly occupied the northern parts of the Italian peninsula and liberated Mussolini from his imprisonment.

The events in Italy, the reports of the internment of the Jews of Rome and of northern Italy in concentration camps, were harrowing to Enzo. Italy was the one place in the world where he felt he had to be, and this was the hour, the very last opportunity for him to help Jews and Italians both. Palestinian units were fighting in southern Italy, the Jews of Rome were at the gates of death, yet here he was in Tel Aviv, sending others to risk their lives. He planned his moves well, step by step, without completely confiding in anyone, yet there was no concealing how desperately he wanted to get to the liberated part of Italy, to the Jewish refugees who had found a haven there, or how concerned he was over the fate of his brother Mimo, who had been apprehended as a Communist agent near Nice and was to face a Fascist tribunal. Everybody realized that there was no restraining him.

On the second of February Enzo received a British passport valid for Syria, Lebanon, Egypt, and Transjordan. In it he was listed as a teacher residing in Jerusalem. He exerted pressure on his colleagues in the Mossad and they agreed that he should go to Cairo to look after matters pertaining to the parachutists and, circumstances permitting, to try to get to Italy. On the fifth of the month, at a general meeting of Givat Brenner, he bade farewell to the kibbutz, without going into details about his plans. At a more intimate gathering in his room he mentioned to a handful of his closer friends that his mission might involve more than looking after the interests of refugees in the liberated part of Italy — that he wished also to try to reach northern Italy, which was still occupied by the Germans. But he skirted details. Those present had grave misgivings about his intentions; they knew, however, that there was no point in arguing with him, and they put their trust in his luck and that, as in the past, he would emerge from all dangers. Ada, red-eyed, served coffee — this one time in their eighteen years of married life she energetically opposed his mission and tried to prevent him from going, but he was as if obsessed and driven by a force that no one could overcome.

Years afterward Moshe Sharett declared that Ben-Gurion did not know about Enzo's mission because he was then in London, but Ben-Gurion himself, twenty-five years later when he was eighty-four, revealed that Enzo came to him at the last moment before departing and told him: "I had to conceal my plans because I knew you would not let me go." And there was bitterness in Ben-Gurion's voice as he recalled: "What could I do? Everything was already arranged and ready. They intentionally concealed Enzo's mission from me. I would have done everything to prevent it. I knew the great danger involved and I would not have allowed it. There was no replacement for Enzo. There wasn't another man like him. He was unique. Of course I know how important it was to establish contact with the Jews of Europe, but everything has its price."

Ben-Gurion may be wronging his friends, and especially Moshe Sharett, for they too didn't know all of Enzo's plans. All they knew was that from the day the plan to send parachutists behind the enemy lines became feasible, an inner fire had taken hold of Enzo. And he himself probably did not know how events would unfold in Cairo. For the moment he was to spend only a brief time in Egypt in connection with the handful of candidates to be parachuted. They waited in Cairo for final instructions and for the arrival of four additional parachutists. Not a word had been said about Enzo himself becoming a parachutist. He had never as much as approached a parachute, whereas the others had undergone a parachuting course in Palestine.

Talking to members of his family he tried to belittle the fateful nature of his mission, and in view of circumstances at that time, when so many topics were not discussed, they did not ask him too many questions. Alfonsa sensed that there was something special about his mission, but even though she felt troubled and suspected that this parting might be the last one, she remained true to herself and didn't say a word to dissuade her son who was following his fate and faith. She neither cried nor showed any signs of distress — she remained a true Pontecorvo.

Before he left they took a family picture — an ordinary family snapshot as on a birthday or in the course of a trip. Chana was away on a hike to Massada; Hagar and Daniel weren't in the least depressed, even though Father was perhaps just a touch more excited than usual. Though troubled and apprehensive, Ada suppressed all emotional outbursts.

21

Leap into the Dark

In Cairo things were confused and muddled beyond anything anyone could have imagined in Palestine. How to send the first parachutists was still being discussed and no final date had been set. The parachutists, in turn, were tense and impatient and felt bitter toward the British who, they thought, intentionally placed obstacles in their way, and also against the people of the Mossad who seemed to drag their feet unnecessarily. They did not realize how difficult it was to organize a project of infiltration behind enemy lines. They had come directly from kibbutzim or had fought with the regular forces in Africa and everything seemed simple to them: one knows where one wants to land, one has addresses of contacts, and one knows what to do, so, let's go. What's all this waiting for?

Only here, in Cairo, did Enzo reveal to his colleagues in the infiltration project his true intention to parachute behind the enemy lines. The spontaneous reaction of the representatives of the political department of the Jewish Agency was unanimous: No. Under no circumstances. The arguments to dissuade him were operational — one who knows too much must not endanger himself, for there comes a moment in the life of anyone when he succumbs to torture. What if Enzo were to fall into the hands of the enemy? But Enzo argued: No, nothing like this would happen to him. He is an officer in the Italian army and knows the area perfectly. "But you are too well known there," his colleagues argued. "So what?" Enzo replied. "Randolph Churchill is also well known, nonetheless he parachuted to the partisans in Yugoslavia."

He would not listen to any argument — he had to get to northern Italy. His last card was the argument that one must not send others on a dangerous mission without undertaking it himself. This reasoning annoyed his colleagues in the Mossad, for it placed them in a morally inferior position. Yet what would happen if all the activists were to follow this line of reasoning? Aren't there times when it is more difficult to bear responsibility for others than to act oneself? The argument led nowhere, and it was finally decided to ask the opinions of Berl Katznelson, Itzhak Tabenkin, and David Ben-Gurion. But meantime Moshe Sharett, head of the Jewish Agency's political department, passed through Cairo on his way to London and Enzo produced his arguments: it is essential to infiltrate into the north and to organize the surviving Jews; otherwise they will perish before or during the Nazi withdrawal. His arguments were irresistible and Sharett gave his official consent. Now it was no longer necessary to consult anyone else.

At last matters began to move. On March 8, it was decided that the parachutists would leave for the liberated part of Italy and Enzo would accompany them. During these final two days in Cairo his mood fluctuated between ostentatious gaiety and sentimentality, and moments of depression alternated with practical discussions. But by all accounts he drank much during this time, and the others joined him.

On March 10, the four parachutists destined for Hungary Rumania, and Yugoslavia, accompanied by Enzo, left for southern Italy, which they reached the following afternoon. The first few days they spent in a village near Bari; then Enzo moved to Bari itself where he stayed in the Jewish soldiers' club. Here he looked for Italian Jewish refugees and to his great surprise he discovered an Ascarelli family distantly related both to him and to Ada, which had found refuge from the Germans in the Abruzzi mountains and then reached the liberated area on foot.

Here for the first time he learned what had really happened to the Jews of Rome. "Immediately after the German occupation," he wrote home, "the Germans imposed a fine of fifty kilograms of gold on the Jews of Rome to be delivered within thirty-six hours. It was hard to raise this amount. Those who had no gold gave silver, which friendly Christians exchanged for gold . . . The Germans also took all the lists of Jews in the city from the communal offices. The rabbi escaped, and the community leaders did not stay with their people. There was great demoralization and no guiding hand. Despite the knowledge that the Germans had the lists of Roman Jews, most of them did not leave their homes, trusting that misfortune would pass them by.

"Nothing happened till October 16, and this calm strengthened the conviction of the Roman Jews that all would end well. Then early on October 16, the SS appeared and began a hunt of Jews, taking young and old, men and women, professing Jews and converted 'Aryans' alike. It is estimated that 4,000 people fell into their hands. Since then no Jew openly appears on the streets; all remaining Jews are hiding in the homes of Christian friends, some of whom shelter them out of goodness and others for heavy payment. It is impossible to obtain details about the identity of those deported. (For Ada and Leah only: I was told that the entire Sereni family was deported, though the one who told me this could give me no details or any very concrete information.)"

He tried to comfort his family with the fact that nobody had counted the exact number of those deported, and that people tended to exaggerate in such cases. But there was no doubt about the scope of the misfortune and there was no room for optimism. Though not exact, the figures that Enzo obtained were substantially correct. Twelve hundred fifty-nine Jews were caught in the roundup, including cousins from Milan, but Alfonsa's two sisters managed to find a refuge and survived the war. Most of the Roman Jews captured died in the Auschwitz gas chambers as soon as they were brought there, and the remainder died later as a result of the conditions in the camps to which they were taken. Of the 1259 only fourteen men and women returned at the end of the war.

On April 6, two additional parachutists arrived at Bari and

Enzo met them at the airfield. He gave instructions to the porters in Italian; with the officer who accompanied them he talked in English, and with the parachutists in Hebrew. He was excited and dashed about full of verve. The newcomers wanted to hear about the plans, how long they would have to stay in Bari, and when they could expect to proceed on their mission, but he paid no attention to their questions and excitedly called their attention to the buildings, the people in the streets, the children. Nor did he leave them for a moment. No sooner had they checked into their quarters than he dragged them outside, to the beaches, to the churches, to the narrow alleys, and at the sight of every young woman that passed he exclaimed: Magnificent! An aristocrat! When one of his guests teased him by pointing out that his aristocrats were barefoot, he became serious: Italy has been destroyed by the Fascists, but it will recover its former glory. It is a cultured and artistic nation, with a history almost as ancient as that of the Jewish people.

When speaking, he took cigarettes out of his guests' pockets and distributed them to the people in the alleys, then compelled them to buy sweets and distributed them to the children in the street. "Have a heart! Without compassion you will get nowhere! If you don't sympathize with the suffering of others, you will not feel the suffering of our own people either."

As was his custom, Enzo would go about without documents into military headquarters, airfields, and military installations, and because of his self-assurance no one stopped him. On those occasions when a guard did ask him about his business, he would stare at the poor sentinel with such a look of amazement that the latter would become confused and beg his pardon. His acquaintances among the British officers wondered how, dressed in civilian clothes, he could go everywhere without interference, and even be saluted, whereas they, in officers' uniforms, would have to produce identification.

The Mossad in Palestine entrusted Joel Palgi, one of the parachutists, with the dubious task of influencing Enzo to return, but he brushed off the request with an "Out of the question." Joel tried to persuade him that there was no point in going to northern Italy since no Jews were left there, but Enzo would not listen. The people in Palestine did not know the true situation. He had reliable information that there were still Jews in the north and that was where he had to go. Joel tried to invoke the authority of the movement, the obligation to accept its discipline, but to this Enzo opposed his sense of a greater duty: he must go to the rescue of the few who still remained. Joel hazarded a guess that Enzo did not want to send others on a dangerous mission without going himself, but Enzo only said, "Nonsense," and waved before him a letter from his son Daniel who wrote: "Even if you die, father, the main thing is you should be a hero." He laughed and added: "But I won't die. I will live."

Enzo himself chose his partner for the jump after an accidental encounter in Bari with Roselli Lorenzo del Turco, a native of Florence, twenty-eight years old, stalwart and strong. Lorenzo had served as a communications officer in the Italian army, and when Italy surrendered in the fall of 1943 he was in Sardinia. Since he had an anti-Fascist record, he tried, together with a group of friends, to join the Allied forces to fight against Germany. But neither the British nor the Americans were eager to enlist Italians, partly because of doubts about their political loyalty and partly out of disdain for their military capabilities. Seeing that it was pointless to stay on in Sardinia, Lorenzo stowed away on a motorboat going to the neighborhood of Taranto and then proceeded on foot to Bari. But here too no one wanted his services and all he got from the Italian military headquarters was a voucher for a hotel room. Disconsolately wandering about the streets of Bari, he met some Jewish acquaintances from Florence who took him to a meeting. There a short man was speaking to the audience enthusiastically and with a distinct Roman accent about the political situation and other topics, and Lorenzo decided that this was an unusual man to whom it was possible to appeal when in trouble. After the meeting he was introduced to the speaker, Enzo Sereni, who invited him to meet him the following evening. Enzo took him to the Jewish soldiers' club and later to his room where they talked. "I can't understand the young Italians," Enzo said, "who are anti-Fascist yet refuse to risk their lives." Lorenzo's response was the one Enzo expected: "It is not true. Here am I, ready and willing, if only they'd let me do something."

The first exploratory talks convinced Enzo of Lorenzo's sincerity, and he asked him whether he would join him in a project, without specifying what it was. Lorenzo agreed without hesitation. The following day Enzo introduced him to a British major who interrogated him and finally sent him to a training camp near the city without telling him the assignment he was to be given.

On April 17, Enzo celebrated his thirty-ninth birthday. The following day he commenced his parachutists' course. Though he was an old man among youngsters, he somehow managed to pass the exercises preliminary to the first jump, and hoped that luck would not abandon him, but on the eve of the first jump he became nervous and wrote a farewell letter to his children. "Should anything happen to me and I not see you again, I want you to know that I thought of you at this moment, of you and of Mother and Grandma, as the most precious possessions I have in life. I wish that you grow up to be what we have not succeeded in being — natural, Jewish working people, and also that you preserve the zeal and the consistency that brought your mother and me to the country and to the pioneering movement. . . . Should I not return, then remember me. Take care of Mother and of Grandma. Study well and remain true to yourselves and to me. . . . . Shalom to all of you. Shalom to Givat Brenner, for I am here also for its sake. Shalom to the land of Israel. When one is away from it one feels more than ever that one belongs to it wholly and that all the rest is just so much froth upon the waters."

The first jump on April 19 was taken without incident. It was a highly accelerated course — six daylight jumps in four days — and Enzo was entitled to call himself a trained parachutist. In his letters one could detect his sense of relief: "My experience in the parachutists' course was revealing. Despite my age I was not among the worst. My height and weight stood me in good stead, and I remained in the air longer than any of the others each time. It's true that every time you have to jump you worry

and feel scared all over again, but the sensation when you are in
the air is wonderful, and when you reach the ground you feel
like a king. Now I feel confident. Now I know for sure that I will
make my way."

Moshe Sharett stopped in Italy on his way from London to
Palestine and Enzo boasted to him of his accomplishments as a
parachutist. When Sharett was about to leave Bari, Enzo
escorted him to the airport and said to him: "Tell Ben-Gurion
and the others not to try to prevent my mission. In a few days I
will parachute behind enemy lines. In addition to my former
mission, I was assigned to contact two Italian generals who may
come over to the Allies if suitably influenced. This could hasten
the end of hostilities on this front. I am confident that I can
perform this mission." He gave Moshe letters to Ada and the
children and told him of the Italian communications officer
whom he had himself picked as his jumping mate, and added:
"Just wait. I will yet make my way all the way to Switzerland."

Lorenzo did not know about the two Italian generals. He too
had undergone an accelerated course that consisted of four day-
time jumps. A few days before the completion of the course, he
was taken to Bari by the British and asked whether he was ready
to jump behind enemy lines without delay, while the moon was
still new. It was now explained to him that Enzo and he would
have to try to reach Florence and help escaped British POWs to
cross to the Allied lines, as well as to obtain detailed maps of the
environs of Florence in anticipation of the fighting that was to
take place there, and to establish contacts with local residents.

The location of the drop was determined on the basis of an
ordinary tourist's map. Enzo found on the map a spot near Florence named Campo di Hanibale, and logically concluded that if
Hannibal could have set up a camp there, the spot must be flat.
The British photographed the place from the air and found it
suitable. Lorenzo was given a Corsican identity so that he could
jump in the uniform of a French officer, and also to account for
his faulty French. Enzo was asked to jump in American or
British uniform, but he chose the identity of a Palestinian officer
named Shmuel Barda who had retired from the service. (It was
important to hold the identity of a real person in case the para-

chutists were taken prisoner and the Germans checked with the Red Cross.)

The first attempt to get behind the enemy lines took place on May 7, but the drop area was covered with dense fog. Enzo wanted to jump there and then, but the pilot responsible for the operation refused his permission. On the way back the plane encountered strong antiaircraft fire and everyone breathed more easily when they landed safely. Nor was this the only mishap, for they now discovered that the battery in Lorenzo's communication equipment leaked and the acid ate through the civilian clothes they had taken with them; as if this were not enough to show the sloppiness of the British, they discovered that the clips of bullets given them did not fit their pistols. The failure of this first attempt to land behind the enemy lines depressed both Enzo and Lorenzo and gave them a clear idea of the dangers facing them.

The second attempt was made on May 15. Their plane took off at 11 P.M. Some other pairs of parachutists destined for other missions were also with them. There was complete silence in the plane. Everything had already been said. They jumped in pairs, and when the light went on for Enzo and Lorenzo, Enzo jumped first, as agreed. During their training period their instructor would order, "Ready. Go." But now no such instructions were given. Only the red light signified the order to jump. Lorenzo followed Enzo too soon, and being heavier he descended more rapidly, so that Enzo's feet almost became entangled in the ropes of Lorenzo's chute. Lorenzo tugged at the ropes without knowing how far above the ground he was. It was dark and a strong wind was blowing. He landed on a slope, rolled a few yeards, hit his head, and lost consciousness. When he partly came to, he heard Enzo whistling as agreed and replied. Enzo responded.

When Lorenzo finally fully regained consciousness it was two o'clock in the morning and there was no further response to his whistling. He walked in the direction from which he had heard Enzo whistling before, and some two hundred meters away he found his parachute open, contrary to all instructions, but Enzo himself was nowhere around. The transmitter and other equipment were also missing. When it began to dawn he heard, at a distance of about one thousand meters, the familiar sounds of a military camp waking up — reveille, whistling, the banging of metal utensils, and realized that he had to get away quickly, without Enzo, without equipment, and without civilian clothes. He buried the two pistols and his iron ration under a tree and went in the direction of a small village on the horizon. When he entered a house at the edge of the village, the frightened peasant informed him that a few days earlier the Germans had executed a number of partisans, but when Lorenzo flashed some gold coins before him, he became more amenable, provided him with some peasant clothing, and went with him to retrieve the pistols and iron rations from their place of concealment. Then he went to a neighboring village which had a hotel and rented a room where he slept a couple of hours. Recalling that he had an acquaintance in this village, he solicited his assistance, but in vain, and finally took a taxi to Florence. Here he contacted the man whose address had been given him by the British, but an unwelcome surprise awaited him. A man who was supposed to be a Yugoslav partisan had been exposed some days earlier as a German agent, and, for greater security, the local National Liberation Committee also condemned Lorenzo to death. He was saved at the last moment through the intervention of the commander of the underground in the region.

Lorenzo tried to contact the British by means of the underground to inform them that Chaim (Enzo's code name on this mission) was missing and the equipment lost, but that the maps they wanted were available and contact with the underground had been established. However, before he succeeded in doing so, the Germans uncovered the transmitter and nine men of the underground were executed. (After Tuscany was liberated by the Allies, Lorenzo was to be thoroughly interrogated by the British who suspected that he might have killed Enzo, but accepted his version of events and found him innocent.)

Enzo's disappearance remained a mystery for Lorenzo as well as for the British. Had he been apprehended by the Germans the moment he landed, then Lorenzo, before losing consciousness, would have heard a commotion, shots, and he would have seen lights. And Lorenzo, too, would have been sought since the

Germans knew that parachute drops were usually made in pairs. But the night had been quiet and no sounds had been heard. Had Enzo been wounded during the landing, he would have remained on the spot, and if he were not wounded, how could the open parachute be accounted for? Lorenzo concluded that Enzo, who like himself had had no practice jumps at night, must have lost consciousness upon landing. But what really happened nobody knew.

From British reports it is clear only that Chaim and Julius (the code names of Enzo and Lorenzo) landed far from the designated spot because of the strong wind that blew that night, and that Enzo fell into the hands of a Todt unit that worked nearby constructing fortifications for the Germans, of which the British had not previously known.

The mission on behalf of the Allies thus ended before it began.

22

The Final Test

When and under what circumstances Enzo was captured by the Germans, whether immediately upon his landing or the following day, nobody knows. What is known definitely is that he was at first held as a British officer for several weeks in an ordinary POW camp in Germany and was there interrogated. It is likewise unknown whether he identified himself as a Jew, the Germans themselves discovered his Jewishness, or they took it for granted because of his rank of captain in a Palestinian unit. But suddenly he was sent back to Verona in northern Italy where he was incarcerated in the ancient city prison. The news about a British captain from a Palestinian unit was relayed to the political prisoners in the prison by the anti-Fascist underground — an indication that he had succeeded in getting in touch with the underground either while in Germany or on the way to Verona.

Professor Giovanni Dean, a political prisoner who had been condemned by a special tribunal for his anti-Fascist activity, saw the "British captain" when all the prisoners were concentrated in one place during the frequent air bombardments, but did not succeed in talking to him. Some days after the "captain's" arrival, Professor Dean was permitted to see his wife, and she informed him, on behalf of the National Liberation Committee of the Veneto district, that the "British captain" was really an Italian named Dr. Sereni, but that his true identity must be kept a deep secret, and the Committee requested all political prisoners to extend to him all possible assistance.

Despite all his efforts, Professor Dean did not succeed in establishing contact with the "captain," but was informed that he had been severely tortured during the interrogations and was kept chained for a while, but that he had succeeded in establishing friendly relations with a number of the prisoners, one of them a notorious criminal who had been sentenced to a term of twenty-five years, and who was of great assistance to Enzo because of his extensive experience in various prisons. When the order came to transfer Enzo, the two embraced in parting.

On August 25, Professor Dean saw Enzo being taken out of the prison, together with members of the National Liberation Committee who were held there. Professor Dean had permission to keep books in his cell, and he noted down the names of a thirteen of those being transferred who were known to him, including Captain Shmuel Barda. He wrote down their names between the lines of a book on Italian classics.

The group was taken for a short trip, from Verona to Bolzano in the foothills of the Alps, in the South Tyrol, an area that had been annexed to the Third Reich. The camp was in the Bolzano suburb called Gries and was named after it. It was the largest concentration camp in Italy and held 3,000 prisoners. The camp occupied a number of buildings with arched roofs which from the air looked like hangars. Inside they were partitioned by concrete walls that created large halls known as blocks.

In its organization this camp resembled other German transit camps. Security was in the hands of the SS, but internal administrative functions were assigned to the prisoners who were divided into different categories: politicals, forced labor, hostages, and Jews — the latter constituting a minority throughout the existence of the camps. Enzo was included among the dangerous political offenders, each of whom wore a red triangle, were kept apart in a fenced-in area, and were not sent outside to work for security reasons. In the same room with him were an American officer and twenty-three Italians. Most of the prisoners in camp wore blue overalls and wooden clogs, but Enzo continued to wear his British uniform, and, in addition to the red triangular patch, a yellow triangle that identified the Jews. The diet consisted of thin noodle soup twice a day and a ration of 150 grams of bread, but some of the Italian prisoners, especially skilled workers, were allowed to get packages from outside or to buy additional food with their own money.

Being in a special category, Captain Barda was not officially permitted to have any contact with the other inmates of the camp, but discipline within the camp was not severe at that time and it was possible to talk to him. Luigi Tardini, an Italian of Egyptian descent, later related that among the special prisoners there was also an officer from de Gaulle's forces, an Italian admiral, and an agent of American Intelligence, Renato Bianci. It appears that Enzo revealed his true identity only to a very few trusted persons. With Tardini Enzo spoke in English or Arabic and discussed only matters pertaining to their homes overseas.

Enzo's relations with the Catholic priest Mauro Bonci were more frank. They discussed the progress of the war, which held out hopes that because of the Allies' rapid advance northward the Germans might not manage to transfer the prisoners from Gries, where it was possible to hold out. The priest later related that he was "at once impressed by his inner peace and I felt encouraged in his company. He gave me books to read and we frequently quoted verses from the Bible to encourage one another. . . . He often surprised me by his extensive knowledge of the Holy Scriptures which he could quote in Hebrew, Greek, and French."

The priest Bonci, Enzo, and some other prisoners shared the supplementary food — bread and potatoes — which they obtained in various ways, and it was told in camp that once, when Enzo was severely beaten by a German guard, his courageous bearing so much impressed the SS guard that he gave him some money to buy bread.

On October 8, six weeks after Enzo had been taken to Gries, the Germans emptied the camp, as they often did, and sent two large transports of prisoners to Germany. Such orders always came suddenly, to discourage any attempt to escape. About three hundred men were jammed into cattle cars, eighty men to a car. In the same car with Enzo were the priest Bonci, Luigi Tardini, the de Gaulle officer, Colonel Paolo Rossi, Captain Armano Bertolini, a long-time member of the Italian Socialist party, two other priests, and some young Italians. When they passed the Brenner Pass a deep depression seized them, for as long as they were in Italy they could hope that the battle lines would overtake them, but now it was doubtful that they would survive to return home. Enzo tried to encourage them and they felt that a certain contagious cheerfulness emanated from him.

When the train finally reached its destination and they left the cars, they knew where they were — in Dachau. But the name said little to the Italians. It was a gray and drizzly day. After a short walk they entered the camp through a gate bearing the inscription *Arbeit Macht Frei* and were assembled in a broad area for roll call. They looked about themselves curiously and saw the electrified fence, the high wall and the guard towers, and shuddered. "Suddenly a name was called," Tardini later related. " 'Barda!' Enzo faced the SS man with a smile, as he always did, and the latter struck him in the face with his fist. Enzo remained standing at attention. The Italians were horrified. It was their first encounter with brutality in the new place."

Everyone was assigned a number. Captain Barda's number was 113,160, and in the camp office the clerk noted the other data. First name, Shmuel. Birthdate, June 22, 1895. Jew. Followed by the letters E and Sch, indicating that he was English and arrived by prison transport. The date of arrival — 9/10/44 — was stamped in red. The new arrivals were divided into groups and those in the front line deprived of everything they had — cigarettes, medicines, mementos. Those in the rear lines tried to hide whatever they had as fast as they could, but it was useless. They all were ordered to undress and were marched, naked, to the shower rooms near the entrance to the camps, where, as they shivered with cold, all the hair on their bodies was shaved with dull razors, their skin was painted with a burning greenish fluid, and after showering each one was issued a torn shirt, a pair of underwear, old trousers, and a torn jacket, without regard to size. Within a couple of hours a shocking transformation occurred in the appearance of the prisoners from

Gries — from being human beings they were transformed into *lagermenschen*.

While they were still standing in the roll-call area, another shipment of French hostages and underground fighters arrived, who had not eaten for four days. The Italians tossed to them whatever little bread they had left, as they would have done in Italy — spiritually they were only on the threshold of a world in which there is no mercy.

Shivering from the cold, weariness, and tension, they stood a long time near the entrance to barrack number 25, and whoever, seeking a little warmth, tried to lean against the barrack wall was doused with cold water. Then they were given their first Dachau meal — a grayish, cold liquid, smelly and foul tasting, which many could not swallow — though later they learned to dream of it. Here in Block 25, which served as a kind of quarantine station, the Italians made their first acquaintance with the assistants of the camp police, mostly Russians and Poles, whose cruelty to the prisoners was the measure of their value to the SS. The Italians were assigned to bunks arranged in three tiers, three men to a bunk wide enough for one. The first days they spent locked in the barrack, learning the ways of the camp, and in interminable roll calls morning and evening. All illusions vanished. There would be no letters from home nor food packages nor any contact with the outside world. Bolzano seemed like a remote paradise.

At night they would often hear the Allied bombs falling on Munich, and whenever the sirens sounded the Germans would black out the camp area and light up an empty field some distance from the camp to confuse the bombers. One night the Italians were wakened, issued striped clothes, and after a roll call were loaded on cattle cars and taken a distance of some fifteen kilometers to the approaches to Munich where they were made to work repairing the railroad station that had been hit. They had to march through the center of the city to reach their destination, but most of the passersby pretended not to see them; some spat at them and cursed them and threatened them with their fists.

One evening when the Italians returned from Munich they were taken to the shower room instead of to their barrack. They were subjected to a superficial medical examination, and the stronger ones, including Captain Barda, were chosen to be transferred to one of the numerous labor camps associated with the main camp at Dachau.

On October 20, a Sunday, less than two weeks after they had been brought to Dachau, they were loaded on a truck and taken to the camp at Muehldorf, some eighty kilometers away. Here the officials were more thorough, because there was a smaller turnover of prisoners, and additional information was added to Captain Shmuel Barda's records: Born in Jerusalem on June 22, 1905 (instead of 1895, as the Dachau records stated, but still incorrect). Professor of philosophy, married, father of three children. Last residence, Tel Aviv.

New transports of prisoners were a rarity in Muehldorf, and since this was a Sunday when the inmates did not work, the old-timers crowded about the fence surrounding the roll-call area, hoping to hear something of what was going on in the world. They watched as the camp commander and his assistant walked among the newcomers. The camp commander, Aberle, of whom it was said that he was of a German Templar family that lived in Palestine and could speak Hebrew, stopped and asked: "Who is the Jew who came to drop bombs on us?" The old-timers, mostly Jews, could not believe their ears. A swarthy, bespectacled man stepped out and declared: "That's me." The camp commander wanted to know details, where he was from, what army he served in, what was his rank.

A few minutes later, when the Germans left the area and the old-timers approached the newcomers, David Srulovitz, a man of thirty who had been brought to Muehldorf from Vilna after the ghetto in that city had been liquidated, approached and started a conversation with Enzo in German. Soon they passed to Hebrew. "Where did you learn Hebrew?" Enzo asked him. "I attended a Hebrew school in Lithuania."

Enzo told him that he was a parachutist. But the Hebrew schools in Lithuania had not been taught that term, and Srulo-

vitz marveled at the word. What root was it derived from? he
wanted to know.

"Do they know in Palestine what is being done to the Jews of
Europe?" he asked.

"We know everything," Enzo assured him.

Srulovitz ran back to his friends to tell them of the miracle of
a Jewish parachutist, from Palestine, a British officer. There
were many Zionists among the prisoners, most of whom were
from Lithuania, and the news struck them as if an angel had
come from a long forgotten world. It sounded unbelievable.

The following day the Italians were divided up into groups. A
number of skilled ones remained in Muehldorf; the others were
taken to a tent camp in the forest, a *Waldlager*.

Captain Barda was appointed interpreter since he was the
only one who knew German well. Most of the others brought
from Italy were assigned to construction work. They carried
heavy stacks of cement to the mixer for twelve hours at a stretch,
in day and night shifts, with a break of half an hour for lunch,
which consisted of a lukewarm liquid designated as soup.

Haimowitz, a Lithuanian Jew who was assigned to work with
the Italians, once heard the German guard ask the interpreter
what his nationality was, and was told, "A Jew." On the first
occasion that presented itself he engaged him in conversation.
Haimowitz later related that the Italians invariably obeyed the
"capitano," as they called Enzo, and in the numerous quarrels
that constantly erupted under the camp conditions he would
mediate between the antagonists and urge them not to shirk
their work at the expense of others. Once the guard punished
one of the Italians by ordering him to keep lifting a heavy piece
of iron for three hours, and when it was obvious that the man
was laboring with his last ounces of strength, Enzo pleaded with
the SS man to lighten the punishment, even though such an
intervention usually led to an equally brutal punishment for the
supplicant. The Italians were mostly like bewildered children in
the conditions prevailing in the camps, compared to the Jews who
had been hardened by ages of oppression. The transition from
the protected environment of their homes to the brutalities of the

camp was too sudden, and they clung to the "capitano" as to a father, or a helping brother.

Early in November, three men from the Italian group escaped, and, as usual, the Germans imposed a severe penalty on the entire group — to stand an entire day at attention, and Enzo passed between the ranks and encouraged the men to hold fast and not to give in. A few days later the fugitives were captured and brought back to Muehldorf, broken by torture. They were led to the Italian group, which was then at work, so they could be seen swollen from the beatings they received; on their necks hung signs: "We are back." Then the three were taken away and were seen no more.

Captain Barda was now the spokesman of all the Italians at Muehldorf, at their request. As interpreter he had a bit more freedom than the other prisoners, and he utilized his knowledge of languages to organize dissemination of news about what was going on in the world. One of the causes of the low morale of the prisoners was their total severance from the outside world, the feeling that what went on outside no longer concerned them, that this was the end for them. He also tried to improve relations between the Italians and the French and Greek prisoners and to bridge the gulf of hostility between them.

The work of carrying the sacks of cement exhausted the prisoners, but what they dreaded most was some breakdown in the machinery, for then the Germans compelled them to load and unload the trucks to no purpose, simply to keep them working; or they would hold searches on their bodies or in other ways torment them simply to pass the time. "Captain Barda acted as intermediary between us and the Germans," wrote one of the surviving prisoners in his memoirs, "and in this capacity he revealed not only his moral stature but also his tact and intelligence. He helped us in uncounted ways . . . and whenever the tempo of the work allowed it, he would manage to keep us away from the attention of the Germans."

On the night of November 17, four weeks after the Italians were brought to Muehldorf, two SS men came into the barrack and called for Captain Barda. When, taught by experience as a prisoner, he wanted to take his blanket and personal effects with

him, the SS man ordered: "No blanket." The meaning of those
two words was clear: he would no longer need a blanket. The
next day the Italians looked more depressed than usual. When
Haimovitz asked them what happened, one answered: "Caputo il
capitano."

Enzo's return to Dachau was noted in the camp files as "administrative arrest." Who issued the order to return him to
Dachau, and whether it was in any way connected with the
attempted escape of the three Italians, or whether the authorities
discovered that he had never been a captain, is unknown. No
document has been discovered that provided an answer to these
questions. Nor is there anyone to testify whether he died under
torture or was hanged on one of the three gallows that stood at
the southern end of the camp or was shot, whether alone or with
others. The day after Enzo was returned to Dachau the clerk in
the office took out the card of Shmuel Barda from the file and
stamped it: *Verstorben 18. Nov. 44.*

Postscript: 1976

More than thirty years have passed since the death of Enzo
Sereni. Givat Brenner, now numbering a population of two
thousand, has become the largest kibbutz in the country, as
Enzo had once dreamed, and its life-style is much different from
what he had visualized in his imagination. Givat Brenner is no
longer at the southern edge of Jewish settlement but in the heart
of the country, and the town of Rehovot is constantly reaching
closer to it. Most of the Italians have left Givat Brenner and
have joined another kibbutz nearby, which they named Netzer
Sereni — an offshoot of Sereni.

When World War II ended, Ada Sereni went to Europe to
learn the fate of her husband, and when she had no choice but to
accept the fact of his death, she followed in his footsteps. For
three years she was active in the organization of the illegal emigration of Jews from Europe to Palestine by way of Italy. Al-

fonsa Sereni, Enzo's mother, bore the death of her second son
with the same inner fortitude that she bore the other misfortunes
that befell her family. She died in 1961 in Givat Brenner.
Enzo's sister, Leah, and her family went to live in Tel Aviv. And
when Ada returned from Italy, she felt she could no longer stay
in Givat Brenner and moved to Jerusalem. Her two daughters,
Chana and Hagar, also live in the city. Of the entire Sereni
family there remain in Givat Brenner only two granddaughters
of Enzo and Ada, and two little great-granddaughters. Ada
Sereni Feinberg, the daughter of Enzo's older brother Enrico,
lives in a kibbutz near the Lebanese border.

Daniel, Enzo and Ada's only son, who was to continue the
Sereni "dynasty" — his *kaddish* as Enzo used to refer to him —
passed his adolescence without father and with a mother far
away. He was a handsome boy, turbulent and restless. During
Israel's war of independence, he volunteered for the commando
force Palmach, contrary to the wishes of the kibbutz. He participated in some battles, was wounded, and returned to Givat
Brenner where he worked as a mechanic and agriculturist. He
found a center and an anchor for his life in his love for Ofrah
Kitron, whom he married in 1953 — the first couple of the
children born in Givat Brenner.

On July 29, 1954, Daniel and Ofrah participated in a meeting commemorating parachutists from Palestine who died in the
fulfillment of their mission, of whom Enzo was one. The ceremony took place near the Sea of Galilee, late in the afternoon, on
the grounds of kibbutz Ma'agan. A large crowd gathered for the
occasion. Before the unveiling of the memorial monument, a
small Piper cub plane flew over the audience and tried to drop by
parachute a scroll on behalf of the Flier's Club. The letter became entangled in the wheels of the small plane and the pilot
tried his luck a second time. This time he flew too low and
crashed into the crowd. Fifteen people died in the crash, including Daniel Sereni, twenty-four years old, and Ofrah, twenty
years old. No sons were left to the Sereni family. No one to carry
on the name.

THE END

Afterword
by
Golda Meir

Based on remarks by Golda Meir delivered on the 25th anniversary (November 1969) of the death of Enzo Sereni

I would like to speak about Enzo as I knew him in the days when we used to meet in our work and in debates. When I think about Enzo there is one thought on my mind: he was unique. Of course, he lived in our midst, in the kibbutz, in political life; he had many friends who were near to him; he loved people — and yet, I always felt that he was one of a kind. You cannot say about Enzo: he was one of those who . . . There was nobody like him. He was different. There was a feeling that he did not tell everything, that there were things on his mind which he could not reveal yet, that he wanted first of all to struggle with them alone, by himself.

I met Enzo not only in Eretz Israel. I had the chance to see him after his arrival in the United States, where he had come to work for the "Hechalutz" movement. He came without knowing the language, and the young people with whom he worked used to say they never before heard such bad English spoken in such a torrent. And yet, there were few *shlichim* — emissaries — sent from Eretz Israel who charmed the young as he did. When he spoke about the need for deeds, without preaching, there was such a strength in his personality that it was difficult to stand up against his will.

He wanted to persuade American Jewish youth to go and settle in Eretz Israel. It seems to me that he was the first one who dared to speak about the Arab problem in Palestine. He had his doubts that we, the Jews, did everything that could have been done. I have to confess, when I heard him speak in this way for the first time, I was alarmed. I was afraid: maybe they will get confused, maybe their doubts will overshadow their belief. But I came to the conclusion that Enzo was right and I was wrong.

He talked frankly about any subject, never trying to "beautify" or gloss over anything. And there were things on his mind, doubts, criticism. Everything he laid out before his young listeners, and so made them share his work and his thoughts, rejecting the idea that there were things which should not be discussed. His directness did not repel anybody; on the contrary, maybe this was what attracted them, maybe this is what convinced them more than anything else: his frankness, his complete identification with the Zionist cause, the country, the kibbutz, the settlement.

I do not know what was in his heart when he went on his diverse missions. It seemed to me that he went full of confidence, first of all full of certainty that it had to be done. Maybe he had some misgivings; if so, he never showed them. I shall never forget the day when — late in the afternoon — he came to my office in the main building of the labor unions, after we had said good-bye to our friends, Hanna Senesh one of them, who went on their mission to parachute behind the German lines — and Enzo with them. He came into my room, in high spirits as usual: "Golda, I came to say good-bye!" There were some rumors that Enzo wanted to join those young people he himself had sent to their dangerous mission. And yet, I did not want to believe that he too would be going. I was stunned and I said to him (there was no sense in arguing with him): "Enzo, are you really going?" And he answered with such an air of ease: "Why not? Why are you so sad? I shall return!" I am not sure if he really believed it. I had my misgivings, and to my sorrow, my doubts and misgivings proved to be right.

We used to discuss a lot, and in many things we worked

together. He was the image of an educator. Maybe not so much in words, but in his deeds. There was truth in him, and when people heard him speaking and saw him at his work, they could not resist the charm of his personality, his way of doing things. I do not think there can have been many who came to us as he had done. In those days we were not used to seeing in our midst pioneers from Italy, we were not used to people who came from a Jewish community as assimilated as the Italian Jews. Even with those Jews who came to Palestine not directly from eastern Europe, but from other countries, one could always feel that their roots were here. But Enzo was different. He loved Italy with all his heart. I remember that we met in the States at the time when Mussolini had invaded Abyssinia. Sereni suffered and objected to the invasion as fiercely as anybody, but his pain was twofold: "his" Italy had committed a crime such as this. I remember that I failed to understand him. I had never and I do not now have any such strong emotions for Russia, which I left when I was a child, and not even for America, where I grew up and went to school.

Enzo was like a miracle in my eyes: a man living in Eretz Israel, identifying himself with everything in our life, and yet with such great love for the country where he was born.

It was a pleasure to discuss things with him. He was a marvelous conversationalist. I cannot remember one discussion with him that was mere small talk. There was always content and a touch of humor in it, always some stimulation, thoughts that demanded thinking, unusual ideas. There were always questions unanswered, waiting to be resolved, and he did not let us evade them, especially as far as the Arab problem was concerned. He did not tire of the search for a solution: maybe there were other ways of living together in Israel.

His words on the day he went out for his last mission in German-occupied Italy were characteristic of all he did. He said to me: "Golda, I have sent friends to this dangerous mission. I cannot remain behind, I have to join them."

It seems to me that no one who ever knew Enzo could remember a single case when he put demands on somebody to act in a situation that he was not willing to participate in himself.

Many times a thought comes to my mind: If only Enzo would have lived in the years of our independence. There are friends, gone from us, whom I cannot let go from my mind. Destiny has been cruel not only to them, but to us as well, because they are not with us anymore, they do not live with us through these years. Enzo was one of them. There were so many who loved him, admired him, who still, after all these years, feel the void he left, because he meant something to anyone who had the privilege to be with him.

Sources

CHAPTER ONE (1905–1914)

Historical and Political Background
Abraham Berliner, *Divrei Yehudim B'roma* (History of the Jews in Rome). Vilna: Biblioteka Press, 1913 (Heb.).
Cecil Roth, *The History of the Jews of Italy*. Philadelphia: The Jewish Publication Society, 1956.
Benedetto Croce. *The History of Europe in the Nineteenth Century*. Jerusalem: Mossad Bialik, 1953.
Enzo Sereni, *Sources of Italian Fascism*. Tel Aviv: Hakibbutz Hameuchad Press, 1953.
Elizabeth Wiskeman. *Fascism in Italy*. Tel Aviv: Massada, 1969.

Personal Interviews Touching on Family Background and Childhood
Emilio Sereni, Rome.
Elena Ascarelli-Pontecorvo, Rome.
Silvana Ascarelli-Castelnuovo, Ramat Gan.
Ada Sereni-Ascarelli, Jerusalem.
Leah Roccas-Sereni, Tel Aviv.
Dvora Elon-Sereni, Tel Aviv.
Alberto Milano, Rome.
Anda Amir-Pinkerfeld, Tel Aviv.

Background of Sereni and Pontecorvo Families
Xenia Panfilova-Silberberg. "Beth Sereni." *Mibifnim*. Ein Harod. vol. 11, no. 3. January 1946. Also her remarks at the memorial to Enzo Sereni on the anniversary of his death, November 18, 1945.
Attilio Milano. "Angelo Sereni," *La Rassegna Mensile di Israel*. November 1936.
Quotations from Enzo are from his diaries, translated by Caleb Kastel. The complete translation is in the Central Archive of the History of the Jewish People, Jerusalem, Box 34. Minutes, brochures, speeches, some of Enzo Sereni's handwriting. Givat Brenner Archives, file 12/2–28.

CHAPTER TWO (1914–1918)

Caleb Castelbolognese. Introduction to *HeAviv Hakadosh*. Tel Aviv: Am Oved, 1969.

Dai diari e dalle letteri di Enrico Sereni. Alberto Stock, Roma, 1931.

Itzhak Minervi. "Angelo Levi Biancini and his Work in the East," *Hatzionut. An Anthology.* Published by the University of Tel Aviv and Hakibbutz Hameuchad.

Shir Hagola (Song of the Diaspora). Rome, 1917. Archives of Givat Brenner. File 12/2–2.

"Judaism and Clericalism." *HeAviv Hakadosh* (August 20, 1917).

"Semitism and Anti-Semitism." *HeAviv Hakadosh* (December 3, 1917).

"Remarks on a Bar Mitzvah." *HeAviv Hakadosh* (March 29, 1918).

Tom Antognioni. *D'Annunzio.* London: W. Heinemann, 1938.

"The Campanellist Manifesto." *HeAviv Hakadosh* (October 12, 1919).

CHAPTER THREE (1918–1921)

Most of this chapter is based on Enzo Sereni's diaries translated by Caleb Kastel, in the Central Archives of the Jewish People, Jerusalem, Box 34.

"Self-Portrait." *HeAviv Hakadosh* (December 4, 1919).

Interviews with the Following on Enzo's High School Years
Professor Guido Calogero, Rome.
Enricetta Valenziani, Rome.
Paolo Milano, Rome.
Ada Sereni.

Memoirs of Maria Azulani transcribed in 1959 by Dvora Elon-Sereni.
Guido Calogero. "Memoirs of Youth." *Niv Hakevutzah*, vol. 4, no. 1.

CHAPTER FOUR (1921–1922)

Enzo Sereni. "Ritorno al Congresso." *La Rassegna Mensile di Israel*, vol. 6, nos. 3–4 (1931).

Israel Reichert. *The Zionist Revolution in the Life of Enzo Sereni.* Hapoel Hatzair (December 2–9, 1947).

Background for Avoda Group
Program of Avoda group, from *The Way of Enzo Sereni*, by Caleb Castelbolognese. *HeAviv Hakadosh*, 34.

Enzo Sereni's report as secretary of Avoda group in Rome. Israel (July 20, 1922).

Regular Avoda column published in *Israel* the first half of 1922.

Interview with Dr. G. N. Cividali, Ramat Chen.

Chaim Weizmann, *Vision and Fulfillment*. Jerusalem and Tel Aviv: Schocken Publishing House.

Background for the Zionist Movement in Italy
Dante Lattes. "The Youth of Enzo Sereni." *Mibifnim*, vol. 11, no. 3 (January 1946).
Address at the cornerstone laying of Sereni House in Givat Brenner. *Davar* (April 2, 1946).
Tamar Eckert. *Pioneering Zionism in Italy*. Tel Aviv: Youth Division of the Religious Kibbutz Movement, 1962.

Personal Interviews
Alfonso Yehuda Menachem Pacifici, Kfar Haroeh.
Albert Viterbo, Rome.

Per non Morire. *Israel* (September 7, 1922).

CHAPTER FIVE (1922–1923)

Background for the Fascist Attitudes toward Jews
Renzo de Felice, *Gli ebrei Italiani sotto il fascismo*. Torino, 1961.

Background for Mussolini's Attitude toward Zionism
Daniel Carpi. "Weizmann's Political Activity in Italy 1923–1934." *Zionism*. Published by Tel Aviv University — Hakibbutz Hameuchad, 1971.

Excerpts from Enzo Sereni's diary that appeared in *HeAviv Hakadosh*.
Enzo's letter to Enrico Sereni, January 1, 1923. Givat Brenner Archives.
N. Trafaglia, Carlo Rosselli, Laterza, Bari, 1968.
Max Ascoli. Letter. New York, November 30, 1970.
Chaim Weizmann. *Vision and Fulfillment*.
Minutes of the Thirteenth Zionist Congress. Zionist Archives.
Enzo's letters to Enrico Sereni, April 21–24, 1923.
Xenia Panfilova-Silberberg. *Mibifnim* (January 1946).
Enrico Sereni's diaries.

Background for Relations between Palestinian Students in Italy and the Sereni Family
Yaakov Tzur. *Yesterday's Dawn*. Tel Aviv: Am Hasefer, 1965.
Rivka Ashbel. "Strange Was My Fate." *Bamaaleh* (November 29, 1946).

Interviews
Dr. Rivka Ashbel, Jerusalem
Raphael Ben-David, Jerusalem

252   A LIST OF SOURCES

Dvora Elon-Sereni, Tel Aviv
Yaakov Tzur, recorded memoir, Jerusalem, May 4, 1970, and recorded
    broadcast on Kol Israel, November 1964.

CHAPTER SIX (1923–1927)

"Discussions on Jewish Schools." *Israel* (December 24, 1923–February
    21, 1924).
Enzo's attitude to Croce and Gentile: Max Ascoli. Letter, January 30,
    1970.
Relations between Enzo and Prof. Buonaiuti: "Un Testimon dell'ideale,
    G. Buonaiuti." *Israel* (February 15, 1945).
Enzo Sereni. "The Matteoti Case." *Ahdut Ha'Avoda* (1943).
Enzo Sereni and Nello Roselli. "The Leghorn Conference." *Israel* (No-
    vember–December 1924).
Marina Sereni. *I giorni della nostra vita* (Edizioni di Cultura Sociale,
    1955).
"Vera Sacrum." *Israel* (October 7, 1926).
E. S.: "Il Libro di Tobia, Riserche religiose." 1928.
Enrico Sereni's diary.
"Saluto." *Israel* (February 18, 1927).

Personal Interviews about Sereni's University Years
Professor Francesco Gabrielle, Rome.
Professor Enzo Taliacocco, Rome.

CHAPTER SEVEN (1927–1928)

Personal Interviews
Mary Yatziv, Tel Aviv.
Yonah Kesseh (Kossoi), Tel Aviv.
Chaim Ben-Asher, Eilat.
Itzhak Yaakobi, Rehovot.
Moshe Tzemach, Givat Brenner.

Correspondence between Enzo Sereni and his brother Emilio between
    October 1927 and February 1928.
Early days of the kibbutz in Rehovot—Recollections of members of Givat
    Brenner: Avraham Katz, Sara Zverina, Atara Sichuk, recorded in 1966.
Letters from Palestine by Enzo Sereni published in *Israel* (March 17,
    1927; March 31, 1927; April 28, 1927; October 27, 1927; October 5,
    1928).
Letter from Secretariat of Hakibbutz Hameuchad to Merkaz Haklai
    (March 28, 1928). Givat Brenner Archives.

Letter from J.N.F. to the Labor Council in Rehovot (January 26, 1928). Zionist Archives.

Exchange of letters between the Agricultural Workers' Organization and the Settlement Department of the Jewish Agency (March 3–April 19, 1928).

"Letter from Israel." *Israel* (May 4, 1928).

Minutes of the Executive of the kibbutz in Rehovot (April 24, 1928). Givat Brenner Archives.

Mary Yatziv. *One Man and One Woman.* Tel Aviv: Massada Press.

Avraham Katz. "Givat Brenner" — Essay in the Anthology of the Hakibbutz Hameuchad. 1930.

CHAPTERS 8, 9, AND 10 (1928–1931)

Most of the information is based on the minutes of the general meetings of the kibbutz in Rehovot. Givat Brenner Archives.

Interviews with: Eliezer Regev, Shlomo Rogoler, Binyamin Zakai, Batya Zakai, Uri Rosenblatt, and Esther Heiman, conducted by Malkiel Savaldi and Dvora Elon-Sereni in 1959.

"Enzo Sereni, On the Tenth Aniversary of his Death." Memorial volume published by Givat Brenner, 1954.

Interviews
Menahem Dorman, Tel Aviv.
Melvin Israel, Givat Brenner.
Joseph Kitron, Givat Brenner.
Dov Shiren, Givat Brenner.

H. Ben Asher. "In the Steps of a Sacrifice," *Niv Hakvutzah*, volume 41.

H. Ben Asher. "The Pure Parachutist," *Hahayal* (November 15, 1945).

Chaim Enzo Sereni. "Letters from Eretz Israel" (Zhabotinsky and the Yishuv). *Israel* (November 11, 1928).

Chaim Enzo Sereni. "Letter from Eretz Israel" (on Brith Shalom). *Israel* (December 12, 1929).

Chaim Enzo Sereni. "Our Work Plan in the Villages." *Davar* (March 17, 1930).

Growing Pains. The Large Kibbutz and Freedom of the Individual. Notes by Enzo Sereni. Givat Brenner Archives.

Mimo's Arrest. Marina Sereni. *I giorni della nostra vita.*

CHAPTERS 11 AND 12 (1931–1934)

Based mainly on letters from Enzo and other members of Hechalutz in Berlin to the headquarters in Tel Aviv, protocols and pamphlets of Hechalutz published in Germany (Archives of the Histadruth Executive).

Interviews
Baruch Azaniah, Givat Chaim.
Nehemiah Ginzburg, Givat Chaim — Ichud.
Emi Horwitz, Givat Chaim — Ichud.
Ate Merom, Givat Chaim — Ichud.
Eliezer Livneh, Jerusalem.
Dr. Aryeh Harel, Tel Aviv.
Recha Freier, Jerusalem.
L. Karlinski, Ramat Chen.
Dr. Wellbach, Tel Aviv.
Dr. Chaim Shatzker, Haifa.
Gideon Rafael, Jerusalem.

Richard Merkel. "Brith Haolim" (JJWB), *Bulletin des Leo Baeck In-stitutes*, no. 34 (Tel Aviv, 1966).
Herman Meyer-Cronemayer. "Judische Jugendbewegung." *Germania Judaica*, Hefte 1–4 (1969).
Uri Rosenblatt, Baruch Eisenstadt, and Emi Horwitz. "In Memory of Enzo Sereni." *Hapoel Hatzair*, no. 7 (October 30, 1945).

CHAPTER 13 (1934–1935)

Most of the chapter is based on correspondence between Zeev Ohrbach, emissary of the Habonim movement in Germany and Enzo Sereni, secretary of Givat Brenner.

CHAPTER 14 (1936–1937)

Based mainly on correspondence between Enzo Sereni and the Hechalutz Department of the Executive of the Histadrut, chiefly with I. Mereminski. Also minutes of the sessions of the Executive of Hechalutz in the United States and circular letters to individual members. Archives of the Histadrut Executive Committee.

Personal Interviews
Shlomo Grodzenski, Tel Aviv.
Professor Ben Halpern, New York.
Saadia Gelb, Kfar Blum.
Joe Criden, Kfar Blum.

Background Information about America
Enzo Sereni. Letter to members of Givat Brenner. Spring 1937.
Report to Mapai Executive, February 9, 1937. Beth Berl Archives.
"America Ebraica 1937," *La Rassegna Mensile di Israel* (July–August 1937).

Zalman Shazar. Memorial address, November 18, 1945. Also tape record-
ing in the president's house in November 1969.
Golda Meir. Memorial address on the twenty-fifth anniversary of Sereni's
death, November 18, 1969.
Shlomo Grodzenski. "Sereni in New York." *Davar* (December 4, 1969).
Ben Halpern, Niv Hakevutzah, February 1965.
Saadia Gelb, Niv Hakevutzah, February 1965.
Letter from Max Ascoli, November 30, 1970.
Enzo Sereni. *Towards a New Orientation on Zionist Policy* (*Jews and
Arabs in Palestine*). New York: Hechalutz Press, 1936.

CHAPTER 15 (1937–1940)

Minutes of Givat Brenner meetings.
Two letters from Enzo Sereni (September 10, 1937; June 19, 1939) to
Aunt Ermalinda Sereni in Rome.
"Letter from Italy" under Enzo's pen name of Tiberius which appeared
in three installments in *Hapoel Hatzair* (September 9, 16, and 23,
1938).

On the Italian Immigration to Palestine
Malkiel Savaldi.
Livia and Caleb Kastel.
Sylvia and Moshe Hartum.
Nino Hirsch-Ben Zvi.
All members of kibbutz Netzer Sereni.

On His Trip to Europe in the Spring of 1940
"Wandering in Turbulent Europe." *Mibifnim*, vol. 6 (August 1940).
Enzo's letters to the kibbutz, March 25, 1940; to his parents, March 31,
1940; to Chaim Ben-Asher, April 19, 1940; to his daughter Hagar,
May 4, 1940.

Background for the Problems of Mobilization
Yehuda Bauer. *Diplomacy and Underground*. Merchavia: Sifriat Poalim
Press, 1966.

Sereni's Enlistment with the British
Introduction to *HeAviv Hakadosh*, by Moshe Sharett, and letter from
Sharett to the British Military Command in Cairo, September 20, 1940.
Zionist Archives.
"On the Way to Egypt," by Enzo Sereni. An Autobiographical Fragment.
Published on the tenth anniversary of Sereni's death. Givat Brenner.
1954.

CHAPTER 16 (1940–1942)

Correspondence, reports, and memoranda by Enzo Sereni, as well as more than eighty newspaper articles published in Egypt (Givat Brenner Archives).
Interview with Emil Najar, Tel Aviv.

The Greek Interlude
Interviews with Itzhak Ben-Aharon and Yoseph Bankover.
J. Bankover. *Five Years*. Hakibbutz Hameuchad Press.
Letter from Sereni to Moshe Sharett, June 11, 1941. Zionist Archives.
Correspondence between Sereni and Max Ascoli, New York, August 13, September 13, October 22, 1941.

Sereni's Arrest
"Enzo Sereni," by Moshe Sharett. Introduction to *HeAviv Hakadosh*.
Notes from the Diary of Moshe Sharett, December 1941 (Zionist Archives).

CHAPTERS 17 AND 18 (1942–1943)

Largely based on correspondence between the Mossad Center in Tel Aviv and Enzo Sereni and other emissaries of the Mossad in Iraq. File 14/19, Haganah Archives, Tel Aviv.

Interviews
Shaul Avigur, Tel Aviv.
Moshe Carmel, Tel Aviv.
David Hacohen, Haifa.
Ezra Kaduri, Tel Aviv.
Yonah Kaduri, Tel Aviv.
Tikvah Sofer, Holon.
Mordecai Nahumi, Tel Aviv.
Zvi Netser, Tel Aviv.
Dr. Henry Rosenfeld, Ramat Gan.
Moshe Dayan.

Reports on the situation in Iraq to the Jewish Agency by Enzo Sereni (Zionist Archives — 25/5289–90).
Report on Iraq to the Executive of the Histadruth (March 31, 1943).
Hayim Cohen. *The Zionist Activities in Iraq*. Jerusalem: The Zionist Library, 1969.
Jehuda Atlas. *To the Gallows*. Tel Aviv: Maarchot publishing, 1969.
Meir Mardor. *A Secret Mission*. Tel Aviv: Maarchot publishing, 1965.
Bracha Habbas. *Brethren Near and Far*. Tel Aviv: Am Oved, 1963.
Shabtai Teveth. *Moshe Dayan*. Tel Aviv: Schocken Publishing House, 1971.

Letters of Enzo Sereni to his children (December 7, 1942; February 4, 1943).

Shmaryahu Guttmann, radio interview, April 1960.

CHAPTERS 20 AND 21 (1943–1944)

Most of these two chapters is based on documents of the Mossad and copies of Enzo's letters preserved in the Haganah Archives (File 8 14–488) and on Enzo's letters to his wife and children that are available to the public.

Personal Interviews
David Ben-Gurion, Tel Aviv.
Gideon Rafael, Jerusalem.
Hagar Sereni-Confino, Jerusalem.
Tzvi Yechieli, Givat Chaim.
Joel Palgi, Tel Aviv.

A LIST OF SOURCES

Joseph Bankover, Tel Aviv.
Gershon Blumenfeld, Tel Aviv.
Aryeh Eliav, Tel Aviv.
Irma Shealtiel, Jerusalem.
Ruth Aliav, Tel Aviv.
Dr. Daniel Carpi, Tel Aviv.
Ada Ascarelli, Rome.
Lorenzo Rosselli del Turco, Florence.

Shaul Avigur (Meirov). *Our Parachutists*, Jerusalem: Secret Shield, Jewish Agency Publishing, 1949.
Yoel Palgi. *A Great Wind Is Coming*. Tel Aviv: Hakibutz Hameuchad Publishing, 1946.
Daniel Carpi. The last exchange of letters between L. Carpi and Enzo Sereni. Leone Carpi Memorial volume. Jerusalem: Sally Mayer Foundation, 1967.
Efraim Urbach. From a diary. Enzo Sereni Memorial volume. Jerusalem: Sally Mayer Foundation, 1970.
Protocols from the meetings of the MAPAJ party executive (September 24, 1943; January 5–10, 1944). Beth Berl Archives.

Testimonies in writing
Tony Simmonds, Cyprus.
Akiva Eiger.
Bruno Sevaldi.
Eliezer Regev.

Radio interviews: Reuben Gaphni, Hayim Hermesh (April 1965).

CHAPTER 22 (MAY–NOVEMBER 1944)

Testimony about Enzo Sereni's fate as prisoner of the Germans leaves
many questions unanswered. So far all the searching after German
documents in Germany and the United States has been in vain.
The only man I talked to who saw Enzo as a prisoner was Dr. David
Israel of the Bar Ilan University.
There exists testimony in writing by Father Mauro Bonci of the Como dis-
trict in Italy and of Luigi Tardini of Milan in the possession of Anda
Amir-Pinkerfeld, the sworn testimony of Professor Giovanni Dean of
Verona, written testimony of Father Corbinian Roth, Italo Vecio, and
Mme. Toto Kopman in the Sereni file of the Haganah Archives.
Also testimony of soldiers of the Jewish Brigade, especially of Sergeant
Ben-Zion Applebaum and Chaim Dan, who searched for traces of Enzo
as soon as the war ended.

Enrico Piccaluga. *Una Fuga da Dachau, Il Movimento di Liberazione in
Italia.* Milano, 1955. 38–39.

Index

Tardini, Luigi, 235, 236
Tel Aviv, 46, 60–61
Terni-Chialente, Miss, 183
Thompson, Dorothy, 140
Thornhill, Colonel, 178, 180, 182–183

United States: ES's mission to, ix, 135–151; Zionism in, 135–137, 149; Jews in, 148–150; Italian anti-Fascists in, 186

Valenziani, Enriquetta, 37
Verona, 233
Victor Emmanuel II, King, 3, 10
Victor Emmanuel III, King, 5, 36, 43, 133, 155, 217
Visconti Gymnasium, 12, 23

Wailing Wall, 63, 83
Wauchope, Sir Arthur, 128
Weizmann, Chaim, 16, 36–37, 45–46, 130, 166, 167
Weizmann, Vera, 130–131
Wertheim, David, 147
Wingate, Gen. Orde, 180–181
Wise, Stephen, 138

World War I, 12–13, 15, 19
World War II, 161–163, 165–169; Jewish sabotage activities, 218–220
World Zionist Organization, 45, 73, 74, 77–78

Yaffe, Leib, 155
Yiddish language, 46
youth movement, Jewish. See Germany
Youth Rescue Organization, 196
Yugoslavia, 219, 220

Zemach, Shlomo, 62
Zionism: Socialist, viii, 39, 136; in Italy, 16, 34–40, 45, 48–49, 52–55; congresses, 33, 46, 118–119, 131; Labor, 34, 36, 61, 66, 131, 135–136, 144–145, 149–150; in Germany, 106, 115–119, 121–123, 131; in U.S., 135–137, 149; World War II and, 165, 211, 213, 218–219. See also Revisionism; Sereni, Enzo; World Zionist Organization